100 MILES
of
Baseball

FIFTY GAMES, ONE SUMMER

**Dale Jacobs &
Heidi LM Jacobs**

BIBLIOASIS

WINDSOR, ONTARIO

FIRST EDITION

Library and Archives Canada Cataloguing in Publication

Title: 100 miles of baseball : fifty games, one summer / Dale Jacobs & Heidi L.M. Jacobs.

Other titles: One hundred miles of baseball

Names: Jacobs, Dale, 1966- author. | Jacobs, Heidi L. M., author.

Identifiers: Canadiana (print) 20200371754 | Canadiana (ebook) 20200372483 | ISBN 9781771963909 (softcover) | ISBN 9781771963916 (ebook)

Subjects: LCSH: Jacobs, Dale, 1966- —Travel. | LCSH: Jacobs, Heidi L. M—Travel. | LCSH: Baseball fans—Travel. | LCSH: Baseball fans—Ontario—Windsor—Anecdotes. | LCSH: Baseball—Anecdotes. | LCSH: Baseball fields—Anecdotes. | LCGFT: Anecdotes.

Classification: LCC GV873 .J33 2021 | DDC 796.357—dc23

Edited by Sharon Hanna
Copyedited by Emily Donaldson
Text and cover designed by Gordon Robertson
Map designed by Tiffany Munro

 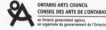

Published with the generous assistance of the Canada Council for the Arts, which last year invested $153 million to bring the arts to Canadians throughout the country, and the financial support of the Government of Canada. Biblioasis also acknowledges the support of the Ontario Arts Council (OAC), an agency of the Government of Ontario, which last year funded 1,709 individual artists and 1,078 organizations in 204 communities across Ontario, for a total of $52.1 million, and the contribution of the Government of Ontario through the Ontario Book Publishing Tax Credit and Ontario Creates.

PRINTED AND BOUND IN CANADA

For our fathers, Elmer Jacobs and Jerome Martin

CONTENTS

100 Miles of Baseball: LOCATION LEGEND

1	Nicolay Field, Adrian MI
2	Champions Stadium at Frank Joranko Field, Albion MI
3	Ray Fisher Stadium, Ann Arbor MI
4	Sprenger Stadium, Avon OH
5	Progressive Field, Cleveland OH
6	Harwell Baseball Field, Detroit MI
7	Comerica Park, Detroit MI
8	Police Athletic League Field, Detroit MI
9	Classic Park, Eastlake OH
10	Cooley Law School Stadium, Lansing MI
11	Labatt Park, London ON
12	The Pipe Yard, Lorain OH
13	MacDonald Park, Port Lambton ON
14	Cardinal Field, Saginaw MI

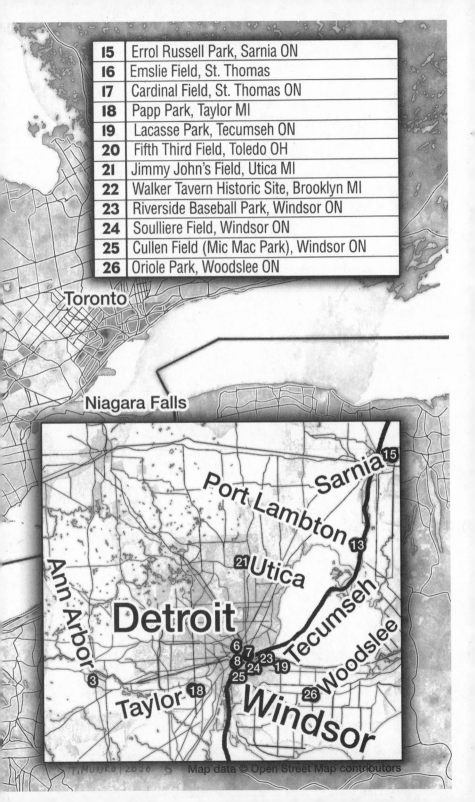

15	Errol Russell Park, Sarnia ON
16	Emslie Field, St. Thomas
17	Cardinal Field, St. Thomas ON
18	Papp Park, Taylor MI
19	Lacasse Park, Tecumseh ON
20	Fifth Third Field, Toledo OH
21	Jimmy John's Field, Utica MI
22	Walker Tavern Historic Site, Brooklyn MI
23	Riverside Baseball Park, Windsor ON
24	Soulliere Field, Windsor ON
25	Cullen Field (Mic Mac Park), Windsor ON
26	Oriole Park, Woodslee ON

Toronto

Niagara Falls

Port Lambton

Sarnia 15

13

Ann Arbor

21 Utica

Detroit

Tecumseh

Woodslee

6 7
8 23
24 19
25

3

Taylor 18

26

Windsor

T. MOORE 2020

Map data © Open Street Map contributors

PROLOGUE
Friday, March 30, 2018
Detroit MI

Dale: It's Opening Day for the Tigers, and we're at Motor City Brewing on Canfield, sitting at the top of the oval-shaped bar, across from the television mounted over the taps and a bumper sticker that reads "Cass Corridor: The Heart of Detroit." We had not planned to be in Detroit for Opening Day, but yesterday's scheduled home opener was washed out, the casualty of trying to play baseball in Michigan in March.

Like every other bar in Detroit today, the place is packed and noisy. It doesn't matter that the Tigers traded away Justin Verlander, JD Martinez, Justin Upton, and Ian Kinsler. It doesn't matter that the Tigers are at the beginning of a massive rebuild. It doesn't even matter that the Tigers are likely to lose many more games this season than they win. It's the Home Opener for the Tigers and that means, despite all meteorological signs of the past few days, that spring is coming to Detroit. What matters on this day is not the quality of the team, but the fact of baseball itself.

Heidi: This year Opening Day snuck up on me and I find the sudden appearance of baseball in this still-cold weather jarring. Even those filling this Cass Corridor bar, donning Detroit Tigers caps, t-shirts, and jerseys in celebration of Opening Day, seem indifferent to the actual game on TVs scattered around the room. I see Jordan Zimmerman on the mound, blowing on his hands to keep them warm between pitches.

While I recognize Zimmerman, there are many Detroit players whose names I've never written in my scorecard. In years past, the players have been my main connection to the game. Not knowing most of their names feels indicative of my current relationship with baseball.

Early in our season ticket days, the Tigers had a "Who's Your Tiger?" theme, and I unabashedly answered Curtis Granderson. I know it sounds both trite and hyperbolic, but I cried real tears of grief in December 2009 when the Tigers traded Curtis to, of all teams, the Yankees. It wasn't just that I lost my favourite player, I lost something bigger: Curtis was my connection to baseball. It was from watching Curtis that I learned what the game could mean to me and the space baseball could and would occupy in my life. I wondered then if my love for baseball could survive not having Curtis step up to the plate for the Tigers 162 games a year.

I take a drink of my beer, glance up at the TV. The Tigers just loaded the bases with no outs in the first. Maybe this team won't be as bad as everyone predicts. But Ivan Nova, the Pirates pitcher, settles down, getting three quick outs, including strikeouts of both Nick Castellanos and James McCann on weak swings on sliders away. It might be a long year for the Tigers after all.

And here I am watching it all unfold on a TV screen, at a bar less than two miles from Comerica—a ballpark where Heidi and I watched so much baseball since coming to work at the University of Windsor in 2000, the same year the Tigers moved from Tiger Stadium to Comerica Park. In those years, the Tigers were woven thoroughly into the fabric of our lives, from days of having whole sections to ourselves in the 119-loss 2003 season to Magglio Ordóñez's walk-off home run that sent the Tigers to the World Series in 2006 to the next ten years of partial season tickets that saw us at the park for every Sunday home game. Though we had skipped quite a few Home Openers over the years, preferring to forego the rowdiness for the calm of the first Sunday, we'd never been in Detroit on that day and not been at the game. It's our second year without season tickets, but it still feels very strange to be drinking a beer in Detroit on this particular day, getting ready to go to a baseball game that isn't the Tigers.

Until recently, I used to look forward to two things arriving in my mailbox in late January. One, the Veseys Seeds spring bulb catalogue, which miraculously comes every year on the day when I have the least faith it will ever get warm again. And two, the Tigers season-ticket renewal package. Both reminded me that the grey-dark days of winter were finite, and, while I could see no outward signs, spring, sunshine, and green were on their way.

This year, I clung to the Veseys catalogue but quickly recycled the envelope of promotional materials the Tigers sent to tempt us back into season tickets. I distinctly remember the dark January night when, hauling our recycling to the curb, I saw the Tigers envelope in the bin and placed my box of cans and bottles on top so it wouldn't blow away in the snowy gusts. Shuffling back to my warm house, I mourned both the absence of summer but also the self who sent the Tigers season ticket renewal back the day it arrived.

I recall sitting on the corner of my bed in January 2013, looking out my window at a grey day, phone on my ear, patiently waiting to talk with a Tigers ticket representative about switching our twenty-seven games to a smaller package because we'd be travelling a lot that spring. While I was on hold, they replayed Dan Dickerson's play-by-play highlights of seasons past. After hearing the replay of Ordóñez's 2006 walk-off home run, the Tigers answered. "How can I help you?" and without missing a beat I said, "I'd like to renew our regular package if I could please." After reliving that home run, I knew we'd make that twenty-seven-game package work. I couldn't imagine a spring without baseball and spending every Sunday home game with my Tigers.

In 2015, I became part of a historical research team documenting the 1934 Chatham Coloured All-Stars—the first Black team to play in the Ontario Baseball Amateur Association (OBAA) league and the first Black team to win the OBAA Championship. In 2016, I spent most of my summer days scrolling through microfilmed newspapers to recreate the All-Stars 1934 season through box scores and game recaps and my weekends and evenings watching the Tigers.

By July of that year, Dale and I started dragging on Sunday mornings, reluctantly assembling our ball caps, water bottles, and sunscreen. By August, as we waited in line for the border agent to let us into the US, one of us said something neither of us had ever said before: "I sort of wish we weren't going to a game today," and the other agreed. What had happened to us and baseball? Maybe we'd feel differently in the spring. But we didn't. In February 2017, we didn't renew our tickets. I thought I was through with baseball.

Though we occasionally attended a local men's league game in Woodslee, Ontario or a Mud Hens game in Toledo, Ohio, since moving to Windsor baseball had, for us, really become Major League Baseball. More specifically, baseball had become synonymous with the Tigers. Without tickets in the 2017 season, I found myself at a loss, wondering where baseball fit into my life.

We saw a few Tigers games that summer, making the drive across the Detroit River when we found ourselves free and the weather conducive to baseball. But those nights at Comerica were infrequent and I still wanted to see as much baseball as we had in previous years. I started to seek out other forms of the game across different levels of baseball. Minor league and NCAA games in parks close to us in Michigan. Amateur men's league games in Essex County. Everything within easy driving distance of our house in Windsor as I tried to maintain a connection to baseball that seemed to be slipping away.

One beautiful spring night we saw the University of Windsor Lancers club team at the Libro Centre in Amherstburg, the sun a perfect orange as it set beyond left field. The hill beyond the outfield was covered in dandelions and seemed to shine in the twilight. There were only about thirty people there that night and we were close enough that I could hear the talk on the field, see the way a pitch would break out of the pitcher's hand. Kids chased foul balls. Players acted as coaches at first and third base. It was sloppy at times, but there were also beautiful defensive plays. I felt like I was back in Alberta, in Amisk or at Czar Lake, sitting with Dad behind home plate or chasing foul balls with my friends. It wasn't the same—I wasn't the same—but it felt familiar, like coming home to a place I didn't know I had left and didn't realize how much I had missed.

On one of the first warm days of May of 2017, I took a break from a research day at the Chatham Public Library and walked east to Scane

Street, near where Boomer Harding grew up. If you know what you're looking for, you'll find Stirling Park, the field where the neighbourhood gathered on evenings and weekends to cheer on the Chatham Coloured All-Stars. I was alone in the park but conjured the crowds and placed the players whose faces I knew from team photos at their positions. Earl "Flat" Chase was pitching his legendary smoke balls. Left-handed King Terrell making brilliant plays at third base. Boomer Harding smiling back at the boisterous crowd after a somersaulting catch at first base that saved the game. Boomer, Flat Chase, and all the other Chatham Coloured All-Stars were showing me a different side of baseball. When, a few days later, Dale suggested we go see other kinds of baseball in the region instead of watching the Tigers, I eagerly agreed.

As we travelled around Southwestern Ontario and eastern Michigan in the summer of 2017, I started to understand that baseball could still have a place in my life and in the life I shared with Heidi. As we talked, sometimes driving, sometimes sitting on our porch in Windsor, we both realized that we live in an incredibly rich area for baseball. If we drew a radius of one hundred miles with our house at the center, what kinds of baseball experiences could we have? What if we took a summer and devoted ourselves to such a journey? What if we wrote about that summer and what we learned about baseball, ourselves, and our relationship with the game? And just like that, the idea for this book was born. One question that lingered was whether this story was bigger than the two of us. Would anyone else care?

We sent a synopsis of what we wanted to do to Sharon Hanna and Dan Wells at Biblioasis—fifty games within a hundred miles of our house in Windsor between the end of March and Labour Day, when classes at the university would resume. A summer of baseball that would take us from London, Ontario in the east to Albion, Michigan in the west to Cleveland, Ohio in the south and to Sarnia, Ontario and Saginaw, Michigan in the north. A summer of baseball that would encompass high school, college, amateur, historic, and professional games.

At Anchor Coffee in Walkerville, Dan and Sharon listened as we explained what we hoped to explore about baseball, about the region, about ourselves. When the conversation finally hit a lull, Dan looked up, asked, "When would you start?"

"Tomorrow. Wayne State plays tomorrow."

"OK. We're in. We'll publish the book."

In under an hour, we had gone from proposing a book to Biblioasis to having a book contract. Walking through the cold rain to our car after our meeting with Sharon and Dan, Dale and I were excited to have the go-ahead for our new project. When we got home, Dale went online and found games we could go to on Friday, Saturday, and Sunday and I started to understand the full scope of what we had just committed to do: amongst all our other commitments, we would travel a 100-mile radius to watch fifty baseball games in five months. I hoped my panic wasn't visible to Dale. I comforted myself by saying to him, "At the end of this weekend, we'll only have forty-seven more games to go."

Instead of heading south to Comerica when we finish lunch, we drive north to Harwell Field for the Wayne State-Ashland game. We are going to a National Collegiate Athletic Association (NCAA) Division II on Opening Day in Detroit. I don't know what to expect from this project, from this movement through different kinds and levels of baseball. I just know that baseball has somehow become diminished for me. The Tigers alone are not enough to sustain my interest in this game that I've always loved, this game that my father loved, this game that Heidi and I have shared for so long. Right now I just want to see where these fifty games take us. No preconceptions, just a summer of baseball.

Putting on my coat and mittens to get ready to go to Wayne State, I look at the TVs over the bar. The bases are loaded and there's one out. The Tigers hit into a double play to end the inning. No one in the bar seems to notice or care. It's the end of the fifth, the Tigers are down 3-2, and I'm about to go to my first of fifty games.

One

OPENING INNINGS

March 30 – April 1, 2018

Wayne State University
vs
Ashland University

Henry Ford Community College
vs
Macomb Community College

Detroit Tigers
vs
Pittsburgh Pirates

Friday, March 30, 2018

Wayne State University Warriors
vs
Ashland University Eagles

Harwell Baseball Field, Detroit MI
Game Time Temperature: 42°F

We park on the service road behind the park and walk around the right field wall towards Harwell Field, dedicated just last year to honour Ernie Harwell, longtime radio voice of the Tigers. Above us looms the enormous "Wayne State University Athletics" sign, tall enough to be visible to the cars that speed by on I-94 and the Lodge Freeway, in the near distance beyond the outfield walls.

We round the corner, expecting the players to be warming up for the second game of the doubleheader. Instead, the end of game one is arrayed before us. 3-2 Ashland in the bottom of the seventh; since it's a doubleheader today, they'll play seven rather than nine innings. Wayne State with a runner on first and one out. We stop to watch along the fence just past first base as the runner advances to second on a passed ball, putting the tying run in scoring position. A groundout to second base moves the runner to third, but with two outs. There's no time to settle in, no infield practice to ease me into the game. No slow build-up to this moment.

I'm wearing thermal hiking pants, two thermal shirts, a pink down vest and black puffy down coat. I have a hat, gloves, and mittens and still, compared to many other people here, I am woefully unprepared for the weather. One man has a propane heater beside his elaborate chair and umbrella set-up. I know there will be a time during the summer when I will be incredulous I ever wore this many layers.

There's a concession stand, a long table with fruit, Costco cookies, chips, and coolers with drinks. The long, forest-green scoreboard on the left field wall hearkens back to a pre-digital era and remains one of my favourite things in all the baseball parks I've visited. "Detroit" and "Visitors" are painted in white, as are the lines and squares for scorekeeping. It is timeless and classic, representing all that is baseball—hope and infinite possibility.

As I try to think about something other than how cold I am, I focus on the word "Detroit" on the scoreboard across the field. As befits the Motor City, there is a constant hum of traffic and I watch as cars arch along the freeway, disappearing into the skyline of downtown Detroit. My favourite part of my daily commute is looking across the Detroit River to the art deco Guardian Building, the neo-Gothic spires of the Ally Detroit Center, and the imposing dark glass towers of the optimistically—and ironically—named Renaissance Center. When I was growing up in Edmonton, Alberta, Detroit was a place I knew from song lyrics and from watching the Red Wings play the Oilers. I've lived here long enough that it no longer seems strange that Detroit lies to the north of my Canadian city. I also understand that Journey did not employ a fact checker when they wrote the lyrics to "Don't Stop Believin'." If they had, they would have known that South Detroit does not exist, except in the hearts and minds of Windsorites who like to embrace the idea that South Detroit is Windsor.

An intentional walk puts men on the corners with two out and Ryan Mergener up to bat. As Mergener steps into the batter's box, I can see why Ashland would rather pitch to the much smaller outfielder than to Brad Baldwin who now stands at first. The move changes the calculus, opening up a different set of possibilities, changing the board so that it now tilts slightly more in Ashland's favour. A home run or even an extra base hit is now more unlikely, but a single still scores the run. Or a wild pitch. Or passed ball. A couple of walks. A strikeout would cleanly end the game, but any contact puts the onus back on Ashland to make a play on defense. So much can happen and each event alters the next set of possibilities like an ever-branching and almost infinitely intricate decision tree.

The short version of what happens, what you'll read in the game summary, is this: "Ryan Mergener grounded out to shortstop to end the game." What that sentence doesn't tell you is what I see as I gather myself into my coat and watch Mergener make contact with the ball. The scoop at short isn't clean, and as the ball is bobbled, the shortstop has to rush his throw to first base. Mergener is called out, but the play is extremely close, with the first baseman's foot pulled off the bag because of the hurried throw. There is no real argument, though, and no chance of appeal. In every level but Major League Baseball, the call by the umpire forestalls any other possible outcomes, turning a bobbled ball, a hurried throw, and a questionable call into "Ryan Mergener grounded out to shortstop to end the game."

As the players regroup at their respective dugouts, we retreat to the car for the half hour break between games. It's a relief to be out of the cold and the wind, listening to Dan Dickerson call the Tigers game. In the bottom of the seventh, the Tigers score four runs and take a 6-4 lead. Dickerson's excitement is contagious, and I wonder again if this team might not be so bad after all.

On the way back to the ballpark, I do up buttons I've never used on my hood before. I try to think about things other than how cold I am. Thoughts like "What have I just agreed to do?" and "I will do this forty-nine more times this summer" come at me like pitches. I foul them off, wait for more positive thoughts.

The biting wind hasn't let up, but at least it's sunny as we take our seats in the tiny grandstand behind home plate. There are groups of players tossing the ball around in the outfield while the infielders take some final ground balls before the game begins. Thin clouds ribbon the air above Wayne State's version of the Green Monster, a thirty-foot wall that stretches from the foul pole in left field to dead center where it juts straight back towards home for ten feet before dropping back to six feet and continuing to the left field pole. Above and to the right of the 310 marker down the right field line is a depiction of a classic radio microphone superimposed on two crossed bats. Between an insignia that includes a microphone and a baseball that fits over the bottom tip of the home plate sits a banner with the inscription, "Harwell Field." A scoreboard that features Detroit and Visitors abuts the warning track farther into left field, while the Wayne State logo and "1918" predominate over left center. I can't imagine we'll see a home run over that wall.

The field in front of me shows all the wear of a Michigan winter, the grass a pale shadow of the green of late summer. As I watch the game I'm always half aware of the steady line of cars on the Lodge beyond the park in right field. The rhythm of all those people going about their days settles me, gives a backdrop to the action on the field.

Behind the grandstand is the centerpiece of the new Harwell Field complex, a replica of the exterior of the Ebbets Field Rotunda, while inside is a recreation of the Ebbets Field scoreboard, all of it a tribute to the beginning of Ernie Harwell's career with the Brooklyn Dodgers in 1948. Photos and quotations from Harwell's forty years as a broadcaster in Detroit overwhelm the small interior space with nostalgia. Tiger Stadium. "Welcome to the corner of Michigan & Trumbull." A young Al Kaline. "That ball is looooong gone." Lou Whitaker turning a double play. "It's two for the price of one." Sparky Anderson. The 1968 Tigers. Mark Fidrych. "He stood there like the house by the side of the road." The 1984 Tigers. Pure Tigers. Pure Harwell. And another reminder of the game that's happening right now, just a few miles south.

In the bottom of the first, Wayne State's catcher, John Blaszczak, hits the pitcher on a throw to second on a steal attempt. In the third, the new Wayne State pitcher, Brennan Cox, walks two and then hits the next batter to load the bases. After a strikeout, he allows a walk to score a run and a single to score two more. It's a lonely walk off the field for Cox, but his teammates in the dugout try to pick him up, telling him, "It's okay. There's a lot of game left." By the time Wayne State bats in the third, it's already 7-0 Ashland.

Still trying to distract myself from how cold I am, I think about how, when we first started going to Tigers games at Comerica Park, I loved sitting way up in Section 325 because the game seemed to unfold like a silent chess match on a vibrant and vast green field. Here, sitting a few feet away from the catcher, I'm keenly aware of all the sounds of the game. I can hear on-field banter, coaches talking to players, and players talking to each other. I can hear an Ashland player taunting a player named McCaw by cawing his name like a crow. "McCAAAW, McCAAAAAW." They call a player named Vinnie 'V.' They say "Go V!" "Hit it hard, Vinny. Nice and relaxed." Used to the sonorous crack of a wooden bat, I find the metallic "twank" of Vinny's aluminum bat jarring. I hear players call each other by their numbers. #23 isn't twenty-three, he's "two-three" and #22 is "twos."

Behind the grandstand is a small, newish brick building with restrooms, Wi-Fi, exhibits, and, I am happy to discover, heat. I scan the tribute exhibit to Ernie Harwell as I try to warm up. I copy something Ernie said about his wife, Lulu, into my notebook—"She planted perennials in places we rented"—and I feel warm thinking about the kind of person she must have been. My core body temperature restored, I return to my bleacher seat and try to settle my mind on the game. It's the bottom of the fourth and it's 7-1 for Ashland. The Wayne State Warriors are bantering amongst themselves like it's 1-1 in the final inning of a World Series game and anything is possible.

Watching Wayne State struggle makes me appreciate all over again that baseball is hard. It's hard to hit a baseball. Hard to snag a sharply hit grounder. Hard to pitch with consistency. Watching the major leagues sometimes makes me forget this basic truth about the game.

As Wayne State come to bat in the bottom of the fifth, the game has officially settled into blowout territory. With little doubt about the outcome of the game, my mind begins to wander, drifting to the cars on the Lodge and to wondering about the score in the Tigers game. The sound of aluminum striking the ball brings me back to the game. It's hard-hit to the left side of the infield. The shortstop ranges far to his right, makes a beautiful pick up on a tough hop, then executes a tremendous throw to first from deep in the hole. The next batter hits the ball to the right of the infield, but the second baseman is able to move quickly to his left, go down on one knee, and flip to first for the third out. Even in a blowout there are moments of transcendence, reasons to keep watching, to be in the moment of the game.

It's 4 degrees Celsius and the wind has picked up. Dale seems not to notice or care how cold it is. In fact, I see he has a small smile that no one else would notice. "You're going to win this one yet," yells a Wayne State fan behind me. I admire their optimism. The two teams stand in their dugouts, shifting their weight, looking a little like cattle in a shed trying to stay warm on a chilly night.

Wayne State are down 10-2 in the bottom of the sixth, but there's no quit in their bench. All the players have been intensely upbeat for the whole game and they remain positive—it's one of the most raucous benches I've ever heard, even when they're down eight runs. Though it's not yet April, these players have been together since early mid-February, working out and playing exhibition games in Florida before starting conference play a week ago. They feel like a team rather than a bunch of guys who happen to play together.

Chance Hitchcock is still pitching for Ashland, but seems to be tiring. Sitting this close allows me to concentrate on his mechanics and the movement of his pitches, a luxury I'm not used to having. I ask the Ashland pitchers in front of us, recording speed and charting pitches, how fast he is throwing. He's still topping 93 so he's been sitting low 90s with his fastball most of the game. With movement, it's been too much for the Wayne State batters, though they do manage to score two more runs.

I check the Tigers score on my phone. It's 10-10 in the top of the twelfth.

It's 10-4 for Ashland. Moms around me are keeping scorecards. I've decided not to keep one for this project so I can focus on other things at the game, but I acknowledge the irony of how much my mind wanders without one. I realize, too, that I've missed a whole half-inning because I've been listening to the redwing blackbirds in the outfield and thinking about how their song sounds like summer to me. Dale wakes me from my reverie by pointing out that we can see the movement of the pitches from where we're sitting. I watch the pitches, not noticing that my mind has again drifted away to the birds' song until a foul ball comes screaming toward us, stopped by the chain link fence a few feet in front of me. I gasp and am reminded that I used to keep a scorecard so I would keep an eye on the ball when we had our season tickets just past first base at Comerica Park.

The game isn't close at all and my mind goes down the rabbit hole of fearing I don't have what it takes to do this baseball project. Dale's attention is keenly attuned to the game's nuances while I am watching birds in the outfield. Behind me, a man says, "You're doing great, honey," and for a moment I think he's talking to me about my writing. More likely he's the Wayne State pitcher's dad, but I love what he says, even though it's 12-4 at bottom of the seventh for Ashland. I force myself to concentrate. A ball goes over the fence into foul territory and a fan picks it up and passes it to a player in the Ashland dugout. Then a ball fouls off the building behind us and a Wayne State player trots over to retrieve it from the parking lot. It's the final inning.

A man near me, pacing behind the back stop to keep warm, spots a Tim Horton's Roll-Up-the-Rim-to-Win cup in the trash bin, retrieves it, reads the already-rolled-up rim. I assume it says "Please Try Again," because he tosses it back into the bin. It's the final inning. Still 12-4. Three balls, two strikes, and two out. There's a hit and a man on base now. I can't feel my toes. #42 comes up to bat and hits a long fly ball into center to end the game. "Can of corn," I say contentedly, and look over to Dale. I smile to see that he's still smiling. It's a smile that lingers.

As I watch the players and the people in the stands after the game, I realize that Heidi and I are perhaps the only people in the crowd of fifty who don't personally know some of the players. The Ashland players talk to the parents who have made the trip up from Ohio, working their way slowly towards the team bus after a quick talk with family and friends. Instead of a team bus for the Wayne State players, it's rakes and rollers and hoses as they spread out to work on the field. Life as a Division II college baseball player.

I check my phone again: 10-10 in the top of the thirteenth in the Tigers game.

Walking back to the car, we take a selfie of ourselves all bundled up beside the Detroit/Visitors scoreboard I love.

"Happy we're doing this?" he asks.

"Yeah," I say with hesitation, thinking about my cold toes and frozen cheeks. "You?"

"Absolutely."

Final Score: 12-4 Ashland

Saturday, March 31, 2018

Henry Ford Community College Hawks
vs
Macomb Community College Monarchs

Papp Park, Taylor MI
Game Time Temperature: 48°F

As the players go through pre-game routines, I notice how often they look up to the sky for some kind of sign about the coming weather. They began play in early March with a series of games in South Carolina, but have only been back in Michigan for a little over a week. Two games have already been cancelled due to weather. A few of the Hawks players make a final pass with rakes over an infield that is more dirt than grass. Coaches from both teams meet the umpires at the plate to exchange lineup cards while checking watches against an unknown weather deadline. They have two seven-inning Michigan Community College Athletic Association games scheduled today, but everyone is worried about the prospect of rain.

Watching the umps gear up in the parking lot, I count five fans here. Me, Dale, and two very prepared people, parents I assume, and a chocolate lab named Bella. The parents have brought their own chairs, blankets, coolers, and umbrellas, and the woman has a scorecard. Waiting for the game to start, I watch fallen leaves gamboling around the chain-link fences in gusting winds. Bella rustles in the nearby underbrush looking for her ball. It starts to rain, gently but persistently. The third base coach says to us, "We should have played at 9 am. It was warmer." There's not a sprig of green grass or hint of a leaf bud to be found, no signs of spring birds. If you'd plunked me into this day at random and made me guess what time of year it was, I'd say early November.

We're sitting so close to the field that I can hear the left fielder singing to himself with his ball glove resting on his head. I watch the players attempting to replicate the gum chewing and swagger of MLB pros. Some do it with aplomb.

The game begins without preamble. No anthem, nothing more than a signal from the umpire to the Henry Ford pitcher to deliver the first pitch of the game. There aren't many places to sit—a couple of benches along the baselines on either side of home plate and two small stands even with first and third base. We are, like the narrator of W P Kinsella's "The Thrill of the Grass," first-base-side fans, but against our usual practice, we settle in at third. The woman near us sits huddled in a lawn chair, the hood of her raincoat pulled tight over her ball cap, umbrella up against the rain that has just started to fall. She's keeping score while her husband walks around the park, presumably trying to keep warm.

Macomb is retired in order in the top of the first. I don't know what to expect from this level of baseball or these field conditions, but a couple of nice fielding plays at short and second remind me of what these players are capable. Most are playing Junior College baseball in order to get noticed or to qualify academically so they can play in one of the NCAA's three divisions. All but one of the Henry Ford players are from Michigan—and that player is from Windsor—and all were among the best of their high school teams. Even in these conditions, it's clear they all love to play baseball and aren't yet ready to give it up.

The Hawks' pitcher hits a two-run home run in the bottom of the first. The home run ball bounces off a red car in the parking lot and a player runs across the dirt to get it, his cleats clicking on the small rocks that litter the ground. I watch him scouring the parking lot in search of the ball. I get up to retrieve our umbrellas from the car and realize we're parked next to that red car. I move ours down the lot.

Between innings I take my cue from Bella's man and begin to walk around the park, stopping for a few minutes at first base, then behind home, where I'm so close I can hear the catcher asking the ump where exactly a ball was out of the strike zone. Another homer in the bottom of the second, a monster shot to right field by Macomb's first baseman in the top of the third, and a misplayed fly ball in center field in the bottom of the third make it 7-1 after three. The rain has turned from a light mist to a steady downpour.

I try to write while holding an umbrella. I think I finally understand what they mean by "fair-weather fan." I totally get those people who took one look at the forecast and stayed home today. I wonder what the left fielder is thinking as he stands in the cold rain, without the benefit of an umbrella or gloves or puffy coat. As dry, winter leaves gather around his feet, does he also wonder why he's here?

Incrementally, my soggy puffy coat becomes stuck to my body and I'm trying not to think about how unpleasant this feeling is. I also realize a fountain pen was a bad choice for a rainy day, as there are blotches of running ink all over my page. I look up from my notes and see a ball hit far into right field. The right fielder misses the ball and tumbles, somersaulting across the mud and dead grass. The third base coach yells, "Run, run, run!" In the time it takes me to watch how this double scores two runs, I forget how wet and cold I am.

A couple more people show up and sit on the stands. Friends maybe? No one looks like a hopeful girlfriend. If a girl shows up to watch you play in this weather, you know she loves you. There's no working scoreboard and I am not paying sufficient attention to know the score. I ask Scorecard Mom and she tells me it's 7-1 for the Hawks. I don't ask what inning we're in—it would reveal my lack of attention right now. Dale is standing by the other team's dugout, which is more cage than dugout. I can tell he's paying attention to the game, watching the plays, remembering how many balls and strikes. My notebook's pages are flapping in the wind and my umbrella is struggling to liberate itself from my non-writing hand.

It occurs to me that it's easy to pay attention to a ball game when it's 70 degrees and a nice summer day. My wet puffy coat feels like an increasingly cold, soggy sponge. In contrast, Scorecard Mom seems perfectly content. I look over at Dale, who must be equally cold and rain-soaked, but even at this distance I can tell he's very happy. I write a note to myself: "How *does* a Jane Austen fan from Edmonton find herself soaked and shivering at a junior college baseball game in Metro Detroit?"

I wander back to where Heidi and Bella and the scorecard lady are sitting. None of them look very happy. The players are as soaked as we are, but they're clearly having fun, kids frolicking in the rain and the mud as their parents stoically look on. Every few minutes I hear "Caw! Caw!" but I don't immediately recognize that it's the Henry Ford players calling out to each other by mimicking hawk sounds. Their constant chatter reminds me of the Wayne State bench yesterday. They're taking it seriously, but at the same time they realize it's a game and that they won't be able to play it forever.

We're very close to the airport, and planes arc upward or downward overhead. The park is surrounded by those wide six-lane Michigan suburban streets with paperclip left-hand turns and miles of box stores and fast-food chain restaurants. Papp Park has a few more small ballparks like this one, plus a brightly coloured playground. The scoreboard isn't functioning, and the coaches and players are trying to fix a gate to the field that keeps swinging open. One coach fiddles with it, and, believing it fixed, returns to the dugout. Two seconds after he turns his back, the gate pops open again, but I don't have the heart to tell him.

As the game proceeds, I realize that the couple sitting next to us are likely the parents of the Henry Ford third baseman, Steven Milke, less because of his interactions with them than because of the way he talks to Bella. He looks like a ballplayer—tall and lean with muscular legs. As the infield become progressively muddier, Milke spends a lot of time grooming the dirt in front of him with his foot, running his toe back and forth to break up the slick surface. In his crouch at third before each pitch, he starts on the balls of his feet, ready to react to a ball down the line or in the hole between third and short. When he comes to bat in the bottom of the fifth, Milke hits a three-run home run to make the score 12-3. His mother, father, and, I suspect, even Bella, are hoping for one more run so that the 10-run mercy rule can be invoked and we can all go home.

I can hear the left fielder chattering to himself and making a strange "AA-oooo!" sound. His height and build remind me a little bit of Curtis Granderson and that makes me happy. I look at Dale and Scorecard Mom, convinced they're both captivated by every pitch and every play. I imagine their appreciation of the beauty of this game is blocking out every raindrop and cold gust of wind, while I'm the only one distracted. The left fielder makes his "AA-oooh!" sound again and a teammate answers back. I realize this is the Hawks' rally call and I am amused.

Dale walks back to where I'm sitting and says, "If they score a run, they'll have a ten-run lead and call the game." My attention is piqued: a mercy rule? For the first time in the entire game, I now have something to focus on. I notice that Dale, Scorecard Mom, and the left fielder are all stoically engaged in observing the finer points of the game and I chastise myself for merely cheering for the mercy rule. Yesterday's doubts about having what it takes to do this baseball project haven't gone away.

Henry Ford fail to score another run in their half of the fifth and in the top of the sixth, Macomb hit two more home runs to make the score 12-6. The home run total for the game stands at six. There is no bullpen at Papp Park so Jacob Hanoian warms up among the trees behind the backstop before coming in to get the final out of the top half of the sixth. There is little chance of the mercy rule now.

By the time Macomb take the field for the bottom of the sixth, it's raining so hard that the Henry Ford players have to scramble to put Quick Dry down on the mound. The game should be called, but everyone involved seems determined to play all seven innings and no one in the small crowd is leaving. I'm more than ready to be out of the rain, but unwilling to leave before the end of the game.

Dale walks over to me and says, "It's funny to see you here, soggy and watching baseball." I concur though "funny" might not be the word I would pick. I keep thinking about how we have forty-eight more games to watch. I write "Forty-eight," in my notebook and retrace the words with my pen until the raindrops blur my letters together. What have I got myself into? I begin to imagine a conversation that starts, "I need to back out of this project," but stop myself.

Scorecard Mom pulls me out of my downward-spiraling thoughts by yelling, "C'mon! Let's finish this up so we can get out of the rain." My ears, like Bella's, perk up. I'm not the only one cold and miserable and wanting to go home? I look at the field anew. The leftfielder, I notice, is calling everything. "Two more, two more, two more. Let's wrap this up." I look at the other six people in the stands and realize everyone, including, I think, Dale, is cheering not for a victory or a comeback but for a finished game. If I were the sort of person who yells in public, I'd be standing on the top of this rain-soaked, three-level bleacher yelling, "Git 'er done! Git 'er DONE!" like the guy behind me a few seasons ago at a Cincinnati Reds game. But I don't yell in public. Instead I say, "Strike out strike out strike out" in my head, willing the game to be over. Dale stands beside me and says, "One more out and we can go. Maybe get some beer and some soup?" Now I can't stop thinking about soup.

There are no real scoring threats in the last at-bat for either team and the game ends 12-6. As we're walking to our car, two different men in trucks stop to ask the final score, and if they're playing the second game. I tell them the score and try not to show what I think of their second question.

Nobody lingers after the final out. We walk to the car in silence and find a restaurant with a good beer list and big bowls of soup. As our core body temperatures return and my puffy coat gets a little puffier, I realize that this book is making me do things I wouldn't normally do. If I'd left this game because I was too wet and cold, that would have been the end of this project for me. It's unlikely we'll be this wet or this cold again. I'll stick it out. If you're going to learn about baseball, you can't just go on the sunny days.

Final Score: 12-8 Henry Ford

Sunday, April 1, 2018

Detroit Tigers
vs
Pittsburgh Pirates

Comerica Park, Detroit MI
Game Time Temperature: 37°F

Today feels a little like a homecoming, returning to our Sunday Detroit routine. For ten years, we spent the first Sunday of the baseball season doing exactly this: leaving our house a bit before 10 am to avoid the Windsor-Detroit tunnel traffic, parking at the Milner Hotel, and then walking to our ritual coffee place, 1515 Broadway, with its mismatched tables and chairs and fans instead of air conditioning. On hot days, they'd keep their doors wide open and the large, burly dogs, who lolled in the sun while their owners had a coffee and a cigarette on the patio, would sometimes peer in.

The back of 1515 was a community space where you could see performances of all kinds, listen to poetry readings, and attend political gatherings—today's consciousness-raising groups. The coffee at 1515 Broadway was decent, there were always good bagels, but the people who worked there were the reason we kept coming back. Over the course of each baseball season, we got to know the staff. We talked about the Tigers' ups and downs with Danny. Once, two games in a row, I bought Junior Mints before each game and both times the Tigers won. After that, we'd stop in before each game and, if Danny was working, we'd discuss which candy purchase might bring the Tigers the most luck. We talked about books and Detroit history with Crystal. We'd talk about Detroit restaurants and bars with other staff members. One of the women painted a lovely "Free Coffee with Purchase of Wurlitzer Building" just outside the doors of 1515 on the shaky plywood that surrounded and supported the equally dodgy looking scaffolding that surrounded the Wurlitzer Building when the façade started to crumble and pieces of concrete fell to the sidewalk below.

We enter the park through the gates beyond left field, not because the gate is close to our seats, but because it is the nearest to the statues to the right of the video scoreboard. It's almost an hour before the game so I still have time to stop and pay my respects to men I never saw play. Willie Horton. Ty Cobb. Hank Greenberg. Hal Newhouser. Al Kaline. But most of all Charlie Gehringer. The larger-than-life bronze statues depict the players in action, freezing them for all time in the midst of a kinetic energy that is almost palpable. Horton at the end of his swing, eyes tracking a ball that has just left his bat. Cobb sliding into second, spikes up and dirt flying. Greenberg in the midst of a towering swing, his power traced by the three connected balls that extend off the end of his bat. Newhouser in the middle of his windup, right leg extended to head height in front of him, ball dangling from his left hand behind his back. Al Kaline in full extension as he leaps to catch a fly ball. Gehringer in the air, the ball just leaving his hand as he turns yet another double play.

I stop at the statues partly because these men are a big part of the history of my adopted team, but mostly because they feel like a connection to my father, especially the stoic Gehringer—The Mechanical Man—who never had much to say. He just got on with it and did his job, never flashy, but always positioned exactly where he needed to be. Like Dad. And since it's 1,800 miles to Dad's grave and only five to Gehringer's statue, on days like today I stop and visit for a minute with Charlie and with Dad, my fingers tracing the words under Charlie's statue, which read "A quiet man who played with remarkable grace and efficiency."

From our seats behind the visitors' dugout, I can see the Milner Hotel. For years, we parked on the street outside the Milner for free on

Sundays and weekday evenings. Now it's impossible to park for free on weekdays, but Sundays are still free. There are few other cities in North America with free street parking a few short blocks from an MLB park. This morning, as Dale parked the car, I looked at the recently added parking payment boxes and a lady stopped and told me I didn't need to pay. I thanked her and said, "So much has changed here in the past few years, I just wanted to make sure." The Milner Hotel had been a hotel that seemed easy not to notice, but now it has an upscale wine bar on the main floor. We'd been there once, and the waiter became considerably less friendly and helpful once we selected a bottle of wine below $60. On the corner was a place that used to have paper signs with "Fresh Squeezed Kool-Aid" written in large, coloured letters. It's now Dilla's Delights, a doughnut shop.

As game time approaches, the players retreat from their warmups and the grounds crew leave the field. The lineups are announced and the video board gives way to this season's hype video. It starts with highlights from Tigers history—with special emphasis on the '68 and '84 seasons—interspersed with shots of baseball cards from the period. Some of the cards are stacked while others flip, and the quick cuts between cards and game action create both excitement and nostalgia. The video then transitions to the current team, both in action and on baseball cards, so that we see them in the context of those previous players and that long Tigers history. Nostalgia. Tradition. Baseball cards. It's what you sell when you are in the midst of a rebuild year.

Heidi and I first started coming to games in the early 2000s, sometimes alone, sometimes with our friend Dave Burke. At first, we went to the park a few times a year, buying tickets on the day of the game. We'd buy cheap seats and sit wherever we wanted, moving around the park to check out different angles on the game. In those years the Tigers were a bad team, so bad, in fact, that in 2003 they went 43-119—the most losses ever for an American League team and one loss shy of the most losses ever by a major league team. For me, though, having a team so close and being able to go to games any time was magical. Just being at the park was more than enough.

Top of the first and the Tigers make a nice play to throw out the Pirates' Gregory Polanco at third as he tries to stretch a double into a triple. Nick Castellanos fields the ball cleanly in the right field corner and throws home to try to prevent Adam Frazier from scoring from first. The throw is up the line, but John Hicks catches it and immediately fires to third where Jeimer Candelario applies the tag on the sliding Polanco. It's a well-executed, heads-up play, but not one we'd likely have seen at the Henry Ford or Wayne State games—what's routine here would be highlight reel at other levels. It's the kind of baseball I once thought I would only see on television.

As a kid growing up on the Canadian prairies, I never had a natural allegiance to any ball team, never got to see a major league game live until I was in university. But I grew up the son of a baseball man who, though he was also raised on the prairies, cultivated a love of the game throughout his life. In the 1930s and 1940s, it was the Cardinals, their broadcasts cutting through the summer nights all the way from St. Louis on KMOX, and the Yankees, the narratives of all their World Series floating to him on syndicated radio. Late in his life it was television broadcasts of the Cubs in the afternoon and the Blue Jays in the evening. In between, when I was growing up in a small town in Alberta in the 1970s, it was the Expos, the team that made me love baseball as I sat beside my father listening to Dave Van Horne's gentle voice call the games on the CBC.

Sitting in the living room, me slouched on the couch and Dad in his easy chair, I began to learn the nuances of the game. How the catcher transfers his weight to his front foot as he rises from his crouch and throws to second. How a runner on first can read when a pitcher is throwing over. How a changeup looks just like a fastball out of the pitcher's hand. What it means to go the other way, taking only what the pitcher is offering. Dad spoke little, saying only "nice play" or "good pitch," leaving me to puzzle out what was important about what had happened. As I grew to know the game better, he would ask me what I thought about the Expos/Cubs/Blue Jays bullpen or if they had a shot this year. Like many fathers and sons, baseball was our lingua franca until the very end.

Through most of my adult life, baseball was an occasional pleasure, not part of the tapestry of my everyday, the background hum that it later became. Until we moved to Windsor and started to follow the Tigers, I never appreciated the rhythm of the season, never really understood how one game formed part of a larger whole. Like today's tough loss, in which Fulmer gave up only four hits and two runs over eight innings. One game in long season and, ultimately, a long rebuild.

1515 Broadway is closed now. The space it used to occupy is currently under construction. I'm uncertain what will open in its place but a valet from the hotel next door stands outside, where the burly mutts used to loaf.[1] When 1515 closed, we settled for a place down the street with pour-over coffees, an unreliable supply of bagels, rotating staff, and an aspiring hipster vibe. This morning we walked past that café to explore other options. Fifteen years ago, these streets were empty, your breakfast and coffee options nearly non-existent. On Woodward, we passed a couple walking two well-groomed Airedale terriers dressed in matching doggie tracksuits. John Varvatos has opened a shop and there are Lululemon, Nike, and Under Armour stores in what used to be abandoned or nearly empty buildings. The beautiful Whitney building has been retrofitted to house an Aloft hotel where guests wait for valets to deliver their shiny SUVs. Shinola is opening a hotel, too. I ask Dale, as I often do, "Do you think we'll talk about missing Detroit the way it used to be?" Maybe we do already. Someone has purchased the Wurlitzer. I wonder if they got their free coffee.

When my father died in 2008, Tigers baseball and those Sunday afternoons in Detroit were a constant I needed to help me through my grief. I know it's a cliché, but baseball is what my father and I had, what we always had. Not hockey, not really. It was always baseball. Yes, I'm guilty of being the kind of man who can't really talk about his emotions, especially with other men. So was my father. Where we come from, you just don't. We dealt with each other and I dealt with his death the only way we knew how: through baseball. I felt the tears streaming down my cheeks as I read about Tom Stanton and his father attending the final games at Tiger Stadium in *The Final Season*. I found myself with a lump in my throat when I saw something new at the ballpark because I wanted my Dad to see it.

Even now, I want to sit next to him at a baseball game, talk to him about pitch sequence. Or the pick the shortstop just made deep in the hole. Or the importance of hitting the cut-off man.

I felt him with me yesterday, in the rain at Papp Park when Milke snagged a hot grounder just inside the third base line that looked like a sure double. I felt him at the game on Friday when Hitchcock threw fastball after fastball that overmatched the Wayne State hitters. Wherever there is a ballpark, I know I will find my father.

Final Score: 1-0 Pittsburgh

Two
RAIN DELAY

April 14 – 22, 2018

Albion College
vs
Adrian College

Saturday, April 14, 2018

Jackson MI

It's been raining since before we left Windsor a couple of hours ago, the drive on the interstate past the Detroit airport familiar in its dullness. The only change is the incessant rain and the only interesting thing to cut through the curtain of gray was the billboard for the Michigan Whitetail Hall of Fame Museum in Grass Lake. As I drive, I think back to this morning's tweet from Lancer Baseball: "Our Series at home vs Bowling Green on April 7th & 8th has been postponed due to field conditions. Our next games are April 14th & 15th at home in Amherstburg against Central Michigan." The accompanying image was a closeup of a baseball sitting in slush.

I just tweeted a video I took on the highway with all the rain and captioned it, "Road trip to Albion College and Michigan is a case study in baseball optimism." Getting fifty games in this summer is going to be an exercise in meticulous planning, patience, flexibility, and, when necessary, letting go of those plans. Maybe that's baseball, too.

The weather has meant we've been struggling to find games to attend. The plan for this weekend is to meet our friends Tim Ackerson and Suzanne McMurphy at the Albion College-Kalamazoo College doubleheader today, stay overnight in Marshall, and then stop in Ann Arbor for the Michigan-Maryland game on the way home on Sunday. Suzanne is an alumna of Albion College and I'm really interested to hear her talk about the school and about the town.

The rain shows no sign of letting up any time soon, and I hold little hope that they'll play at all today, especially when I read that Detroit City FC have cancelled their home opener and the Tigers-Yankees game scheduled for today in Detroit has already been postponed. Split doubleheader tomorrow. If we hadn't already paid for our rooms at the bed and breakfast in Marshall, I doubt we'd have left Windsor.

The weather never really lets up all day, at least not enough for any baseball to be played. We do, however, take advantage of a brief break in the otherwise steady rain to walk from our B&B to Dark Horse Brewing. Ceramic beer steins cover the walls and the ceiling, making the bar feel like a small cave where the four of us can shelter from the storm. It's a cave with very particular rules about what music cannot be played, all detailed on a ripped, well-worn signed affixed to the front of the jukebox with scotch tape.

DO NOT play AC/DC on this juke box.

Your song will be skipped.

NO REFUNDS!

"I hate AC/DC." – Aaron Morse, Owner

DO NOT PLAY AC/DC

PLEASE, DO NOT PLAY AC/DC.

Also, you can't play: Nickelback, Hoobastank,
Matchbox 20, Hinder, Buck Cherry, Def
Leppard, the song Wagon Wheel or any other
shitty, overplayed music.

Thank you for your patronage and no AC/DC.

Sunday, April 15, 2018

Marshall MI

We wake to ice on the trees, ice encasing our cars. By the time we finish breakfast, the Tigers have already cancelled both ends of their split doubleheader. No word yet from the University of Michigan.

We'd stopped briefly at the Albion College ballpark on the way to Marshall, Suzanne noting how much more impressive the athletic facilities were compared to when she was there in the early '80s. Immaculate in its upkeep, the campus was, from all outward appearances, prospering. The same couldn't be said for downtown Albion, with its many boarded-up storefronts, like gaps in a fading smile, providing a backdrop for the few people who walked its streets. The city's best days looked to be behind it.

After breakfast, our host, himself originally from Albion, tells us that there's no longer a high school or a hospital in Albion and that those absences have accelerated a decline that had been coming for years. We were not imagining the contrast we saw between Albion, the elite liberal arts college, and Albion, the declining Midwestern town.

As we drive home in even harder rain than the day before, Heidi keeps checking to see if Michigan have cancelled their games with Maryland yet, but the team's Twitter account maintains that they're going to play. At five o'clock, long after we're back in Windsor, they finally begin play, a game that Michigan wins 6-3 in eight innings. It had to have been the most miserable game, one that would have made the Henry Ford game feel like baseball on a sunny afternoon in July. We haven't watched any baseball since April 1 and I'm anxious to see a game, but not even this project could have coaxed me out today.

Tuesday, April 17, 2018

Detroit MI

I check the weather forecast obsessively, worrying that all these delays will put our goal of fifty games in jeopardy. I search Twitter to see what information I can glean about who might be playing, only to see that the Tigers have cancelled yet more games.

Split doubleheader tomorrow—1:10 p.m. and 7:10 p.m. And, if you're wondering, yes, tomorrow's forecast looks equally as miserable.

Baseball in April in Detroit. Fun, right? @jamesschmel (Tigers beat writer)

It's not encouraging. When I open up the *Detroit Free Press* to see if they have any more information, I'm confronted with the headline, "Detroit Tigers (and MLB) have a weather problem. Blame climate change?" I pour another cup of coffee and read Shawn Windsor's depressingly accurate lines: "[B]aseball, like many aspects of our past society, got some things wrong. What it got right was that it's a game best played in warm, or at least relatively warm, weather."

Sunday, April 22, 2018

Albion College Britons
vs
Adrian College Bulldogs

Champions Stadium at Frank Joranko Field, Albion MI
Game Time Temperature: 61°F

The game begins with a horn-heavy recorded version of the American national anthem. The fans, caps removed, silently stand, turning away from the field at an awkward angle to face the flag flying over the broadcast booth. This is a classically picturesque baseball park, accented with Albion's purple and yellow colours. There are plaques throughout, documenting who donated what. Everything in the park seems to have a sponsor: the dugout, the stands, the concourse. It is a well-kept field and signs tell us that sunflower seeds aren't allowed in the ballpark, which adds to its pristine feel. The crowd is about a hundred people, a mix of students, community members, parents, and grandparents. They're quiet but attentive, most are wearing alumni sweatshirts or collegiate attire and seem to know the players by name.

The weather is the best we've had so far but it's still far from what you'd call hot. Or even warm. It's not quite the kind of day that says, "Let's go to a baseball game!" Some people are wearing shorts, others are under blankets. Some seem to be dressing for the weather they want, not the weather we have. Two girls in front of me are wearing shorts and crop tops. They're covered in goosebumps, trying to pretend they're not cold.

The sun warms my arms and my face as I sit behind home plate. It's the top of the second and already 3-1 for the Adrian College Bulldogs. For the first time this year, I am at a baseball game, I am not cold, and there's no threat of rain in the forecast.

Runner on second with Sean O'Keefe, the Adrian shortstop, at the plate, desperately trying to lay down a sacrifice bunt. Everything from Mitch Shedlowsky is inside, though, a couple of pitches almost brushing O'Keefe's arm before he is finally walked. Zack Zschering, up with the bunt still on, is hit in the back. Bases loaded, no one out, despite the Bulldogs' willingness to trade an out for runners at second and third. Single, double, and it's suddenly 6-1 with no outs in the second. End of the day for Shedlowsky as David Kauff trots in from the bullpen that sits just beyond the foul pole in left field. By the time he records the third out, one more run has scored on a sacrifice fly. 7-1 Adrian in the middle of the second inning.

Dale asks me if I saw that ball curve. I did not. He points out that Adrian's pitcher keeps throwing to the outside corner and his pitch count is low. I'd been watching a pair of geese fly over the field. I remind myself to watch the pitches. I see two strikes before I notice turkey vultures circling over a stand of trees beyond right field. There are still no visible leaves or even buds on the trees. "Did you see that?" Dale asks again. I say "No, sorry." Before I can ask what I missed, something else on the field has happened and people are clapping. I am missing more than I am seeing. My anxiety about this project grows steadily with every pitch I fail to see. I worry that I don't know how to watch baseball that isn't a Tigers game.

Top of the third and the Albion shortstop makes a good play on a hard ground ball. You could see him gather himself, arms out, maneuvering his body behind the incoming ball, scooping and then setting himself for the throw to first base. Good, but not fluid, almost as if you could see him thinking about each step in the process. It wasn't part of his muscle memory, wasn't yet effortless. It's the difference between watching Jose Iglesias or Francisco Lindor field a ball at short and the play that was just made by the shortstop for the Britons or the infield plays at the Wayne State or Henry Ford games. It's the difference in talent, yes, but also in the act of repetition until it's second nature. Muscle memory. No thinking necessary.

The starter for the Bulldogs, a freshman from Westland, Michigan named Jordan Williams, has been impressive, especially from our seats directly behind home plate. A big right-hander, Williams has a classic delivery. Feet shoulder-width apart, glove raised to his face, Williams begins his motion facing halfway between third base and home before a slight pivot of his right foot brings his left shoulder in line with the plate. Left leg comes up parallel with his hip in an easy motion. The right leg then bends at the knee, left leg striding towards home, while the glove hand comes straight up, as if counterbalancing his throwing arm, which dips below and behind his hip. In his motion, Williams is smooth and deceptive.

Before each pitch, the Adrian coach calls out a set of three-digit numbers to indicate both pitch selection and location. The catcher, Frank Resto, checks the cheat sheet on his wrist guard before translating the digits into a set of signs for the pitcher, mainly the firm fastball with an occasional changeup mixed in. Set the glove and Williams hits it, his fastball painting the outside corner to right-handers, while it sets up his changeups to left-handed hitters. Through four innings Williams has still only given up two hits.

It's the top of the fifth. Instead of watching the game, I watch people watching the game. Am I the only one whose attention isn't fully on the field?

There's one out and the bases are loaded. I concentrate on pitches but a flock of geese flies overhead and I miss a run being walked in. I refocus. A pile of napkins escapes from someone's picnic beside first base and the wind scatters them. The napkins collect in the netting of the infield. Ten people scramble to extricate them.

Time to get my mind back in the game. I study the scoreboard and the distribution of hits, runs, and errors. Runs accumulate quickly and it's now 12-1, then 13-1. I look at the scoreboard again. For a moment, the 1 in the home team's slot appears to be burnt out. I imagine the Albion bench looking up and thinking some sort of miracle has happened and the score is only 3-1. Imagine the hope they might feel, realizing they could come back and win this game. But then, as quickly as it vanished, the 1 lights up again and a run is scored. The score is now 14-1 but I don't know how the run happened. Suddenly, and inexplicably, I find myself missing Curtis Granderson.

As anyone who knows me well can testify, I've never really gotten over the Granderson trade. The summer I became a Granderson fan was the year that I, like Curtis, was at a make-it-or-break-it time in my career. He, like me, often swung and missed. But, inning after inning, he kept stepping up to the plate as if this at-bat could be the one to seal the deal. Every time my professional self-doubts crept in, I'd summon the look on Curtis' face when he stepped up to the plate and stared down the pitcher.

For the first few seasons after he was traded, I'd run my own "Who's Your Tiger?" promotion, hoping to find someone to replace him. At first, I thought Austin Jackson might fit the bill, but then when he was traded—stunningly—in the middle of a game, I couldn't handle the heartbreak of losing another player. Without having a single player to watch, I had to watch a team. I began focusing more on the Tigers' ups and downs throughout the season, rather than on the narrative of a single player.

The Albion pitchers have had no command as the walk totals have mounted throughout the game. By the end of the fifth inning, I've lost count of how many Adrian batters have been hit by pitches. More walks, more hit batsmen in the seventh. Yet another pitching change for Albion as Chris Janson's "Buy Me a Boat" plays over the PA system. Rural Michigan. Another hit batter and the Adrian bench cheers.

The cheering crowd pulls me back into the game. Watching the crowd watch the game, I feel like an outsider not cheering for either team or rooting for a particular player. I *am* a complete outsider. I'm not an alumna of either school, nor do I have a loved one or favourite player on the field. I have no stake in this game, no reason to cheer for a particular outcome. Without Curtis, I had to change how I watched the Tigers. Without the Tigers, I might have to change how I watch baseball. Comforted by this new reality, I find myself settling into the game.

The bases are loaded again. A man in the front calls out to the Albion pitcher, "It's okay. You got it." A grandma says, "Focus. Let's finish this." Silence drops on the crowd as the pitcher winds up: there's a collective drawing of breath. Just as an Adrian player yells, "Come on, baby!" his teammate gets plunked and the Adrian dugout erupts in cheers and laughter. It's 15-1 now. A walk makes it 16-1 and the bases are still loaded. Another walk makes it 17-1. A steadfast man in an Albion sweatshirt claps a few times and shouts, "Come on, you got him!" to the Albion pitcher. Another pitcher is brought in.

They're down seventeen runs but the fans are still here, clapping and saying "Good eye, good eye." A player gets caught between bases and is chased down. I'm glad I'm not trying to record this play in a scorecard. "Go Drew!" shouts a lady, perhaps someone's mom. She then adds, "Come on, someone's got to cheer for these kids." An easy fielding play gets flubbed; there are two Britons on base and two outs. A can of corn finishes it all off.

Despite the score, the crowd remains supportive throughout, encouraging both the pitchers and the hitters, always looking beyond the score. Anything close to this kind of home loss at a Tigers game and the park would be empty. I doubt we would have left, but if I were watching it on television, I guarantee I would have turned it off by this point. Either way, if it were the Tigers I certainly wouldn't be enjoying myself. At this game, though, I *am* enjoying myself. Some of it is the weather—just sitting in the sun watching baseball after all the bad weather we endured over the past month. But that's not all of it.

Watching Williams pitch brings me joy. Trying to figure out what the Adrian coach was doing with his numerical signals fascinates me. Seeing the approach of the Adrian players, taking every at-bat seriously, fielding all their chances, no matter the score. The whole game—and the score in it—is no longer the unit that matters, but instead the inning and the individual encounters on each pitch. Those are, of course, the moments that make up any game. But there is a difference when you're forced to pay close attention to the smaller moments, to the adjustments each player makes, to how the pitcher (and coach) approach each hitter, to the way the fielders set themselves, to the *game* instead of the score of the game.

Final Score: 18-1 Adrian

Three

THREE GAMES IN
TWENTY-FOUR HOURS

May 1–2

University of Michigan
vs
Eastern Michigan University

Toledo Mud Hens
vs
Indianapolis Indians

University of Michigan-Dearborn
vs
Concordia University

Tuesday, May 1, 2018

University of Michigan Wolverines
vs
Eastern Michigan University Eagles

Ray Fisher Stadium, Ann Arbor MI
Game Time Temperature: 82°F

Tonight is the first night of the year I'm thinking in Fahrenheit, a switch from Celsius that many Windsorites make when the spring begins to yield to summer and the temperatures begin to soar. It's a beautiful cloudless evening as we watch players from Michigan and Eastern Michigan go through their warmups. Just a few days ago I was still very much entrenched in Celsius, despite the fact that we were in Chicago, huddled together under Cubs promotional fleece blankets, fighting both the unwanted shade of our seats on the third base side and the cutting wind off the lake as we watched Yu Darvish pitch a gem in a 3-2 Cubs win over the Brewers.

We had planned the Chicago trip months ago, a weekend of baseball, ballet, and beer to celebrate the end of the academic year. Despite the weather, I was happy to be back at Wrigley with all its history and tradition. Whenever I'm there, I think about my father and all the years he watched the Cubs on WGN in his living room in Wainwright, Alberta. He never saw them live, never set foot in Chicago at all. Never saw them when they were any good, like they are now. But those games were part of his itinerant baseball fandom, part of the thread that connected us across the miles from Windsor to Wainwright. "Is it the Cubs' year?" he'd ask when we talked on the phone in the spring, launching us into a conversation about their prospects. By the time it finally was the Cubs' year in 2016, he was gone. But when I'm in The Friendly Confines, he's there with me. Pointing out a "good pitch" from Darvish. Praising a "nice play" by Javier Baez. But he's here, too, in Ann Arbor, on a night that was made for baseball.

The Wilpon Baseball and Softball Complex on the University of Michigan campus is state of the art for college baseball. We're in Ray Fisher Stadium, a beautiful park that was completed in 2008 with a capacity of 4,000. Our seats, for which we paid one dollar each, are behind home plate, the brilliant green of the artificial turf contrasted against the dark brown of the similarly artificial basepaths. The traditionalist in me balks at this, but that's the reality of trying to run a major collegiate baseball program in Michigan, where grass won't reliably grow until May.

Nothing could be farther from that cold, rainy Henry Ford Community College game we saw a month ago. Tonight is the kind of night you'd decide to go to a baseball game even if you weren't a fan. I'm sitting in full sun and it's easy to believe that I've never been cold watching a baseball game in my life. I'm wearing my City Cyclery t-shirt, jeans, and ballet flats, but the vast majority of people are wearing maize and blue Michigan gear—"the blue of a summer sky" and "the yellow of ripe corn." The fact that they sell "popped maize" instead of popped corn adds to the atmosphere of collegiate partisanship. The rest of the crowd is wearing EMU colours, which are described in considerably less poetic detail on the school website as "green and white."

The outfield walls tell us that University of Michigan has eight regional titles, seven College World Series appearances, thirty-five Big Ten Titles, and National Championship Titles in 1953 and 1962. We're clearly in the realm of collegiate sports royalty here.[1] Walking across campus, we passed the field hockey and lacrosse fields. From our seats we can see the softball field. I went to the University of Nebraska for graduate work so I understand the scale of college athletics. My first alma mater, the University of Alberta, had 30,000 students when I attended, but I had only the vaguest inkling of the existence of Golden

Bears/Pandas sports. A dissertation could probably be written about the difference between Canadian and American collegiate sports.

Kenny Chesney's "No Shirt, No Shoes, No Problem" echoes through the park as these student-athletes get ready for the game. Having gone to graduate school at Nebraska, I experienced the impressive athletic amenities available to regular students, but also saw on occasion the hidden facilities available to student athletes. So I know that the rest of the Wilpon Complex is actually the most impressive aspect of baseball at a large Division I school like Michigan. Imagine being a high school baseball player and reading this description on the University of Michigan Athletic Department's website:

> Adjacent to the stadium is a 1,600-square foot locker room that features 30-inch lockers, five television screens, a lounge area, a training room and a nutrition lounge. The locker room connects directly to the 5,750-square-foot indoor hitting facility that includes retractable doors for ventilation during the summer months and is heated for year-round use. The hitting facility includes two dirt mounds, pitching machines, three indoor batting cages and a state-of-the-art video hitting system. Along the left field line are three outdoor hitting cages, in addition to four down the right field line.

Ray Fisher Stadium and the Wilpon Complex might be a world apart from a city field in Taylor, Michigan, and there might be a thousand people here instead of a dozen, but when Michigan takes the field and the first batter for Eastern Michigan strides to the plate, all of that ceases to matter and it's only the game in front of me.

My friend and fellow Tigers fan, John Wing, believes you'll see something you've never seen before at every baseball game you go to. As I try to re-learn how to watch baseball, John's approach seems like a good way of structuring my baseball watching.

I'm sure Eastern Michigan would like nothing better than to beat Michigan, the bigger, more prestigious school just up the road from the EMU campus in Ypsilanti. Eastern is, like Michigan, an NCAA Division I school, but the Mid-American (MAC) conference to which it belongs is not the Big 10, even in baseball. And even though some EMU players are from other parts of the country, most of the roster are from Michigan and Ohio. These players likely not recruited by any of the major programs, just as the Wayne State players were very likely not recruited by any Division I schools. Michigan, on the other hand, features players from all around the country. While its geographical location might make it harder to compete for the top recruits, the players who choose to attend Michigan are among the best in the country. To a high school player wanting to play collegiate baseball, who recruits you matters, and slots you into a set of expectations. The Eastern Michigan players would like to transcend those expectations tonight.

Between innings, there are fan contests. For one, spectators had thirty seconds to name as many Disney films as they could. Lori named six but Austin named considerably more and was rewarded for his pop-culture prowess with an unnamed prize and fleeting admiration from tonight's crowd. Young Caleb has just triumphed in the frozen t-shirt contest. He and another kid struggled to unwrap a frozen shirt while Vanilla Ice serenaded the crowd with "Ice Ice Baby." It's unclear what Caleb has won, aside from bragging rights at school tomorrow.

As Max Schuemann steps into the batter's box for the top of the third inning, a middle-aged man in an EMU shirt a couple of rows ahead of us tells his companions that he expects Schuemann to be drafted this year.[2] From what I've seen so far tonight, there's no doubt he has the arm to play shortstop at the next level, and a glance at the program confirms that he's currently hitting .340. And, according to the amateur scout in the next row, he's got a good glove too, though his full assessment is interrupted by the distinctive sound of ball hitting metal. It's hit to the left of the second baseman, fielded cleanly, but Schuemann is able to beat it out for an infield single. Schuemann then proceeds to go from first all the way to third on an infield single from Zachary Owings, before finally scoring on a Kolton Schenker single. Turns out he's fast, too, basically manufacturing a run with his speed on the basepaths. By the time EMU has finished batting, they're up 3-0 in the middle of the third inning.

There's a man near us who's showing his Michigan loyalty by wearing a royal-blue button-down shirt and maize pants. I spend a lot of time thinking about the maize pants and what would compel someone to wear such a colour. Just as I'm thinking how glad I am that Dale never takes his University of Nebraska allegiance as far as wearing red pants, Maize Pants Man walks down the stairs and right in front of us.

Dale says, "Whoa. Did you see that?"

"Yeah! I know. Wow, huh?"

"You saw the movement on that pitch?"

"Sorry. What? I thought we were talking about the guy wearing maize pants?"

"What are you talking about?"

"He walked right in front of us. He was wearing maize pants! How could you miss him?"

"Well, I was watching the game."

"Ah. Right." It occurs to me that Dale and I aren't even watching the same game, which, I also realize, happens quite often. No matter who I'm with, they always seem incredulous at what I do or do not notice at the ballpark.

With runners on second and third for Michigan in the bottom of the third inning, Ako Thomas hits a ground ball to second that yields an out at first, but scores the run and moves the other runner to third. Luke McGuire, the starter for EMU, comes back to strike out the next batter, but Alex Wolanski, the catcher, drops the ball. On the throw to first, Jack Blomgren tries to score from third. Wolanski is a bit up the first base line and has to run back to cover home, where he catches the ball just in front of the plate. Blomgren hits him at full speed, the collision causing Wolanski to roll violently backwards, ball in his raised fist so the ump can see he's held on. Out at the plate, Wolanski appears to be fine, but it takes Blomgren several minutes to get up. After three innings it's 3-1 EMU.

In front of us is an older man with weathered skin and no chin, dressed in a yellow Michigan hat, a blue U of M baseball shirt, khaki shorts, and sunglasses. His companion is slightly younger and favours a blue Michigan hat, a white U of M golf shirt, shorts, and GO BLUE sunglasses. They seem to know all the players and it's clear from their talk that this isn't the first baseball game they've watched together. "McGuire's pitching well." "Good offspeed stuff." I listen to their commentary as I watch McGuire strike out both Jesse Franklin and Dominic Clementi on straight changeups. Friends sitting in the sun, watching the game they love. For me, it was watching East Carolina games with Rick Taylor, our shared love of baseball making us more friends than colleagues. Or all those days watching games at Nebraska before the Huskers were any good, listening to my grad-school friend Kurt Haas yell at the outfielders to hit the cut-off man. We were always on them to do the small things right.

I continue to think about the maize pants while the game proceeds apace. I text John, "I saw something I've never seen before in a baseball game. I saw a man wearing maize pants." He texts back "LOL" and I respond, "And Dale didn't even see it!" "No kidding?" he writes back, and I hear his bemused sarcasm. "Kind of like Curtis and the bug?" he adds. "Yeah, I guess so." And then I imagine John's signature laugh.

In the bottom of the sixth, Jordan Nwogu, Michigan's freshman left fielder, singles in the second run to make it 4-2 EMU. After all these years of watching mostly MLB, it's still odd for me to see a player wearing #42, a number that has been retired throughout the majors since 1997, in honour of Jackie Robinson. As Nwogu rounds first base, I wonder if that's why he chose that number, but my thoughts are interrupted by the Michigan Fight Song, which begins to play when Engleman crosses the plate to score the run. It's almost like a football mindset brought to a baseball game, a different set of rituals than I'm used to seeing.

Behind me a young woman sits with a couple of friends, one eye on the game and one on her book as she studies for the LSAT, highlighting great swatches of text in green. To my left, a father tells his sons to watch the shortstop and second baseman with a runner on second, to look at how they try work with the pitcher to control the running game. Behind home plate, a Michigan player aims a radar gun at the pitcher, while beside him an intern charts pitches. Between innings kids chase the beach balls that have been released into the stands for one of the many in-game promotions. On the field, the score remains 4-2 EMU after seven innings.

Over the past decade, John and I have been to a lot of baseball games together. It's probably impossible for me to write honestly about the sport without sharing John's tale about himself, me, Curtis, and the bug. It's a story he loves to tell. More than once I've met friends of his who say, "Oh! You're the Curtis and the bug person!" As John tells it:

> Attending a game with you was always fun, since you kept score, but you'd also occasionally have to ask me what the last play was because you were concentrating on some fringe aspect of the contest. Your favourite player was Curtis Granderson and when he was in center field, you liked to watch him, even when he wasn't doing anything. So, late in one game—a tense battle—the Tigers had been ahead and the tying and go-ahead runs were threatening as the bases were loaded with two out. Joel Zumaya, a pitcher who could throw faster than a speeding bullet but had inevitable control problems, was 3-2 on the batter. There were two out. Joel threw the pitch high. Ball four, walking in the tying run. The entire stadium groaned except you. At that moment, you tapped me on the shoulder and I turned to see you looking intently out to center field. You pointed and said, "I think Curtis just got bitten by a bug!"

Man on first for EMU in their half of the eighth. On what is supposed to be a sacrifice bunt, the ball takes a big hop off the artificial turf. The Michigan third baseman barehands it and tries to get the lead runner at second, but the throw is too late. Safe. I can hear Kurt saying, "You have to take the safe out there." Another bunt moves the runners up and, on the play, the second baseman, Thomas, is hurt covering first base and has to come out of the game. With one out, Jack Weisenburger comes in to pitch, trying to keep it close enough for a Michigan comeback. After striking out the first batter he faces,

Weisenburger gets the pinch hitter, Mike Monahan, into an 0-2 count, but Monahan stays patient, taking several pitches out of the zone and fouling off pitches that are close. After an eight-pitch at bat, Monahan draws a walk to load the bases, giving EMU a chance to break the game open, to transcend expectations.

Nate Jones comes to the plate with two outs and the bases loaded. So many ways that EMU can score—hit, walk, wild pitch, error, balk—but so many ways the score can remain the same. In the end, it's Weisenburger's fastball that Jones can't catch, a strikeout that keeps the score 4-2 EMU heading into the bottom of the eighth.

Tonight, I can't hear the players' banter and chatter from the dugout, only the blended murmurs of the crowd and the multiple conversations happening around me. There are so many things to see and watch at a baseball game, both on and off the field, and all of it is worth noticing. Perhaps this is why I see bugs biting outfielders, men in maize pants, and all the other "aspects on the fringe of the contest," as John called them, instead of the dipping movement of a single curveball or the seemingly effortless but magically precise way an outfielder positions himself for an inning-ending fly ball.

Clementi leads off the eighth inning for Michigan with a walk, bringing Nwogu to the plate. Just as the video board in center field flashes that he's hitting .352, Nwogu singles, putting runners at the corners. Blake Nelson then draws a walk to load the bases.

A woman is bellowing encouragement. She has a smoker's voice and is waving a U of M flag. I'm not sure what she's yelling at the players but she's louder than both dugouts combined. At times, she sounds a little like a harbour seal. "It's a great day for baseball," she broadcasts to no one in particular. Michigan is rallying and the lady with the flag is going wild. She's right. It is a great day for baseball.

Brock Keener comes to the plate with no outs and the bases loaded. Thomas House, a freshman right-hander, is on the mound for EMU so Keener, the switch-hitter, settles in to the left-hand batter's box. House clearly doesn't have Weisenburger's fastball, so it's going to take some serious sleight of hand with location and a mix of his secondary pitches for him to wiggle out of this jam. But it doesn't take long for Keener to rip a bases-clearing triple to the right field corner to make the score 5-4 Michigan. Another run scores on a sacrifice fly before the inning ends. Weisenburger returns to shut down EMU in the ninth.

Two bases-loaded at bats. Two moments when everyone in the ballpark hung on every pitch. Two moments when a well-played game teetered on the edge of possibility.

Final Score: 6-4 Michigan

Wednesday, May 2, 2018

Toledo Mud Hens
vs
Indianapolis Indians

Fifth Third Field, Toledo OH
Game Time Temperature: 79°F

Today's game started at 10 am so we left early this morning. The drive to Toledo was an hour and a half, which offered lots of time to think about the differences between the games we've seen. As Dale and I chatted, I said I need to learn to watch baseball without a scorecard, without a team, without a favourite player. I have no idea how to watch baseball other than just to watch and see what I see.

Instead of having all-stars' names or retired numbers painted on the walls like most ballparks, Fifth Third Field has cartoons of two fictional characters: Crankshaft, the curmudgeonly school bus driver from the comic strip who allegedly played for the Mud Hens, and Corporal Max Klinger from M*A*S*H*, who was a loyal Mud Hens fan. Having grown up with M*A*S*H*-loving parents in Canada, much of my knowledge of the US comes from watching TV. I text a smiling selfie beside the portraits to my parents, and my dad writes back, "Klinger!"

as I knew he would. I know when we stop for lunch at Tony Packo's after the game that I will text, "I'm at Klinger's favourite lunch place!" and that my parents will be excited again. Dale nods, knowing exactly why I am gleeful. Undoubtedly, he remembers the road trip detours I made him take so I could go to Ottumwa, Iowa, where M*A*S*H*'s Radar is from, and to Needles, Arizona, where Snoopy's brother Spike lives. It still seems strange to wake up, drive an hour and a half, and find myself in Toledo, Klinger's hometown.

In my wanderings around the park, I notice there aren't veggie dogs nor anything remotely healthy at the concessions. I ask two ushers about vegetarian options and they shrug. "There's always popcorn," they suggest. I've added "veggie dogs" to the tallies I'm keeping at the back of my notebook and so far there's only one tick: Comerica Park.

The early start is to accommodate school field trips and the park is filled with kids, undoubtedly grateful for the opportunity to flee their classrooms and enjoy this gorgeous day in a baseball park. The kids' chatter sounds like Sandhill cranes landing for the night.

We've barely taken our seats behind home plate when Christopher Bostick doubles off Ryan Carpenter. In fact, it seems like I've barely had my first cup of coffee. We were on the road again before 8:30 this morning. It's only fifty miles from Detroit to Toledo, but you always have to factor in an hour for the border, just in case. We usually end up with time to kill.

Today that extra time meant that we could be leisurely as we walked from the car to the ballpark, taking in the new development since we were last here almost ten years ago. It's a gorgeous park, everything a minor league field should be, built in a way that feels organic to this neighbourhood of former warehouses. In the right field corner, the architect even incorporated one of the old buildings, complete with seating that juts into the park from the second and third floors. Outside the main entrance is a square named for Moses Fleetwood Walker, who played for the Toledo Blue Stockings in 1884. Walker was one of the first African Americans to play major league baseball, and the last to do so before Jackie Robinson started for the Brooklyn Dodgers in 1947.

As we approached the park, we weaved our way between bus-loads of students, ranging all the way from elementary to high school. They streamed past both the sign and the plaque erected in Walker's honour, beneath the warehouses that mark the history of Toledo as a manufacturing and transportation hub. The Mud Hens know that baseball fans are an aging lot and that early games like this one, which cater to school field trips, are a way to get younger people into the park. Will that mean they come back on their own or ask their parents to take them to another game? That, of course, is the hope.

Bostick on second and Kevin Kramer squares to bunt. The ball is completely deadened, rolling along the fringe of the grass, just inside the third base line. Carpenter can only watch, hoping it will roll foul. It doesn't. It's a textbook bunt down the third base line, the kind of fundamentally sound play that both Kurt and my father would love. Runners at first and third with no one out.

I'm wondering how bad the ballpark coffee will be and whether that outweighs my need for it when Jordan Luplow homers to left center. Carpenter seems unfazed, however, just takes a new ball from the umpire and walks behind the mound, rubbing it until he's satisfied. The next three batters all strike out swinging. 3-0 Indianapolis after a half inning.

A woman a few rows ahead of us is having the game explained to her by her two male companions. I'm having trouble believing she doesn't know you're out after three strikes, but it's possible. A promotion for Toft's Ice Cream just encouraged kids to scream—it was a sound only dogs could hear. I start to wonder if it's easier for the woman in front to just nod and let the mansplaining blend into the roar of screaming children.

The ballpark is clearly trying to make this event "educational" by highlighting science activities happening at the Imagination Station in the concourse. Last inning, they broadcast an experiment on the scoreboard that involved liquid nitrogen, a garbage can, and a hundred brightly coloured balls. Currently, I'm watching an experiment involving methane bubbles and open flames that, I have to admit, makes me wonder if it's really suitable for children—especially since someone lit the methane on fire as it was sitting on the hand of a segment host.

Because the Mud Hens are the Tigers' AAA affiliate—the highest level in the minor leagues—I can't help but think about the rebuild, about the prospects that might play in Detroit over the next few years. Dawel Lugo at second base. Christin Stewart in left field. Ronny Rodriguez at third base. Jim Adduci at designated hitter. Grayson Greiner behind the plate. And players like Mikie Mahtook, who was with the Tigers for almost all the 2017 season, but unexpectedly demoted to Toledo on April 11. He's currently hitting .194, still struggling to find his form as a hitter, but in the leadoff spot today he gets hold of a 1-0 pitch, homering to left center to make the game 3-1 Indianapolis. Jim Adduci adds a two-run home run in the bottom of the second to tie the game at 3. Good signs.[3]

Two outs follow before Pete Kozma walks, bringing Mahtook to the plate once more. He stands in, as always starting in the center of the right batter's box before striding towards the plate to take his swing. This time, though, he's hit on the hand, an inside fastball—maybe a message pitch because of the home run in the first—that gets away from Austin Coley. Watching Mahtook flex his hand as he makes his way to first base, I think about fear and hitting and how the two are always intertwined. Leonard Koppett, in his book *The Thinking Fan's Guide to Baseball*, sums up this relationship when he writes, "Fear is the fundamental factor in hitting, and hitting the ball with the bat is the fundamental act of baseball." Fear. At the center of the game, another piece of the daily routine, a detail that can never be far from a player's mind. The key, of course, is what the player does with that fear when he steps in the batter's box. Will the next batter be wary of Coley, think he doesn't know where the ball is going? Will he be able to stay in the box on an inside pitch? Get close enough to the batter's box to hit a pitch on the outside corner? Conscious or not, fear lurks behind the confrontation between pitcher and hitter, and every at bat happens in the context of the events of particular games and earlier encounters between pitchers and hitters. But for the next at bat at least, Jason Krizan tamps down the fear. He does his job, and singles in Kozma, who is able to score on a good slide, just under the tag, on a throw the pitcher looked to be cutting off. 4-3 Mud Hens.

In front of us, a high school student tells his friends he's on the waitlist at Michigan for the fall, with a full-ride scholarship if he gets in, community college if he doesn't. Heidi points out that none of the kids are actually watching the game. Few of the adults are either. Getting young people in the park is important, but how do you get them to pay attention and appreciate the game? How do you get them to see what Dad saw, what those two guys at the Michigan game see, what I'm coming to appreciate more with every game we attend this summer?

Another experiment is on the scoreboard. This one also uses nitro and a trashcan, but welding masks and rain slickers are involved. The sound isn't working so I'm not sure what exactly is happening but huge white puffy clouds just emerged from behind right field, so I'm assuming something blew up. The players meander around the field as if this happens every day. Maybe it does. It's times like these when I wonder if the inter-inning activities supplement the baseball experience or distract from it.

Carpenter strikes out nine in six innings of work, but two home runs to Luplow mean he will not get a decision today. By the time Paul Voelker comes in to pitch in the top of the seventh, the game is tied at 5. His 0-1 pitch is a fastball straight at the head of Pablo Reyes. As he hits the dirt, the bat flies out of his hand. It's an inside pitch with a purpose: to exploit that element of fear, to make Reyes wary of what might come next, to move him back in the box and away from the plate. He watches strike three go by, unable to swing, set up by the inside pitch on the 0-1 count. The radar gun puts Voelker's fastball in the mid-90s, more than enough velocity to make the hitter think about what it would feel like to be hit by that pitch. More than enough to strike out Kramer and Luplow as well.

Scanning the crowd around me, I see it's only Dale and two other guys who are actually watching the game. Ten percent are looking in the general direction of the field. At this particular moment, I cannot see a single child watching the field, but they're still having a grand old time being at the ballpark. And that's okay. My mind is wandering too. I've watched fourteen innings of baseball in under eighteen hours and there will be quite a few more before I sleep tonight. Dale's focus, on the other hand, has never strayed from the play on the field.

When Rodriguez comes up to bat for Toledo in the bottom of the eighth, the score is 7-5 for the Mud Hens and Damien Magnifico is on to pitch for Indianapolis. The first pitch bends Rodriguez backwards. Fear. The catcher walks to the mound as Grover Washington Jr's "Just the Two of Us" plays over the PA system. The count goes to 2-2. Rodriguez sets himself in the batter's box. Foul. Sets again. Foul. And again. Foul. Again. Soft line single to left field. Overcoming the fear. The kind of at-bat you want to see.

Erich Weiss singles to lead off the ninth for Indianapolis. Reyes then bunts, but Greiner makes a diving catch in foul territory, full extension to get the out. After Bostick singles, Stewart is able to track down Kramer's liner in left field. Two on, two out, but Luplow, who had already hit two home runs, is only able to manage a fly ball to right field to end the game. The prospects looked good today.

Final Score: 7-5 Toledo

Wednesday, May 2, 2018, afternoon

University of Michigan-Dearborn Wolverines
vs
Concordia University Cardinals

Police Athletic League Field, Detroit MI
Game Time Temperature: 84°F

As we drive to Detroit from Toledo, Heidi and I talk about how different our notes are on games, about what completely different things we notice. And we talk about what compels us to finish this project. What are we trying to learn? Before we began, I had a vague notion that the answers to those questions, at least for me, involved something about how baseball both changes and remains constant as you move between different levels of the game. But that's not quite it any more, at least not completely. It's more about the universe of baseball that's contained in this one-hundred-mile radius, about the soul of the game that inhabits these parks, about trying to understand why embarking on this project felt so important to me. It's about what I can learn about baseball and my relationship to it by seeing games in parks like Ray Fisher Stadium, or Fifth Third Field. Or Police Athletic League (PAL) Field, the small park that now sits at the corner of Michigan and Trumbull Avenues, the former site of Tiger Stadium, the long-hallowed center of the baseball universe in Detroit.

The layout of the field is just as it was in Tiger Stadium, though there is no longer an upper deck looming over the diamond, enclosing the park and insulating it from whatever was happening in the city beyond. Now, in the distance beyond center field, I can see the Masonic Temple. The old water tower a block to the east serves as a backdrop to right field, while Motor City Casino dominates the view beyond left. Across Trumbull, beyond the outfield walls, stands the Ace Hardware/Brooks Lumber store, at this location since 1896. Look towards foul territory down the right field line and you'll see the Detroit skyline, a mix of familiar buildings and new construction.[4] The grass and infield are artificial, out of step with what traditionalists wanted to see on this site. But then again, the real purists never wanted Tiger Stadium torn down in favour of Comerica Park, a mile and a half to the east. With PAL Field, at least there is baseball at the corner of Michigan and Trumbull again, a site that hosted Tiger baseball from 1895 to 1999. Bennett Park. Navin Field. Briggs Stadium. Tiger Stadium. And now PAL Field.

A few weeks ago, I caught myself telling someone I hadn't given much thought to baseball over the past two or three years. Hearing those words out loud, I had to correct myself. For the past three years, I've thought constantly about baseball—just not MLB or the Tigers. My work on the Chatham Coloured All-Stars with my historian colleague Miriam Wright has occupied my thoughts since 2015. More recently,

Miriam and I have been researching a book about the All-Stars' 1934 season. And so, when I find myself saying that I haven't been thinking about baseball, I need to remind myself that I've thinking about baseball for most of every day for several years.[5]

By the time we moved to Windsor in the summer of 2000, I had twice been to Tiger Stadium. The first time, in early September 1989, my friend Peter and I rolled into Detroit for a game against the Royals. Living in Edmonton, it seemed to me that the two-hour drive from Peter's home in London, Ontario was more than reasonable. I remember emerging into downtown Detroit. The manhole covers steaming. The people slouched into their coats in the early September chill. The wonder and fear of being in Detroit, its reputation extending all the way to the prairies. But as we drove down Michigan Avenue, I began to see the bustle of the neighbour- hood around the stadium. Hear the men outside hawking extra tickets. Feel the pull of the stadium on a cool September evening. We parked as close as we could and followed the crowd into the park. Today, we wandered around the neighbourhood before the game, walking the few blocks over to Batch Brewing for a bite to eat. Tiger Stadium is gone and Corktown has gentrified.

The only concrete image of that game that I can summon is Bo Jackson hitting a home run into the upper deck off Frank Tanana, a baseball memory as acute as any I have. In my mind, the park was packed to see Bo slam that ball into the night sky, but the box score tells me that there were less than 13,000 people there that night. For me, though, that crowd was electric and I knew I wanted to be part of it, again and again.

Ten years later, I was back at Tiger Stadium with Heidi and our friend Steve Shively. As always, I felt the familiar draw of the crowd and the excitement of being in a Major League park, but I also felt strangely at home. We were visiting from North Carolina and as Steve drove us along Jefferson Avenue, he pointed across the river and told us that was Canada. Less than a year later, we would move to our new home in Windsor, while the Tigers would move to their new home at Comerica Park.

The years the Tigers won the World Series at this corner: 1935. 1945. 1968. 1984. The players who took the field here. Ty Cobb. "Wahoo Sam" Crawford. Henry Heilmann. Mickey Cochrane. Charlie Gehringer. Hal Newhouser. Hank Greenberg. Al Kaline. Alan Trammell. Lou Whitaker. Kirk Gibson. The baseball legacy of Michigan and Trumbull, still alive in the memories of everyone who ever saw a game here. As history and memory wash over me, part of me wonders how much these college players, most of whom are from Michigan, recognize what this site has meant to baseball fans and to the city of Detroit. But another part of me doesn't want the past to intrude on the present, on the game being played in front of me.

A day doesn't go by when I don't think about the Chatham Coloured All-Stars. In 2017, I spent most of the year reading eight months of the *Chatham Daily News* from 1934 on microfilm, reading every article I could find about the Chatham Coloured All-Stars. Over the months, I got to know the players through the game coverage, box scores, and editorials in the same way fans today might follow a team. As a result, I feel a certain kinship with them, especially having had the opportunity to meet the siblings, children, and friends they left behind. The more I read, the more I saw how the colour barrier, while not formalized in Canada, still existed, and robbed Canadian athletes like Boomer Harding, King Terrell, and especially Earl "Flat" Chase[6], of opportunities to excel because of the colour of their skin. Everyone who saw Flat Chase play, all say the same thing: he could have made the big leagues.

Sitting at this storied corner, it's not hard to rattle off the names of those who called this corner their home field. It's much more difficult but no less important to think about the names of players who were never able to play here. Detroit was the second-last team in MLB to integrate. It wasn't until 1958, when Ozzie Virgil broke the colour barrier with the Detroit Tigers.

In 2017, when I heard about PAL's "Buy a Brick" campaign to help build this new ballpark and saw that I could get a brick on the storied corner of Michigan and Trumbull, I knew instantly what I wanted to do.

Today, I was anxious as I walked along Michigan Avenue to the gates of PAL Field. It took me a few minutes to find it, but there was my side-walk brick: "In honour of Boomer Harding, Earl 'Flat' Chase and the 1934 Chatham Coloured All-Stars." The mezzanine was empty and I took the opportunity to kneel down and brush away the fallen leaves around my brick. "Hey guys," I whispered. I spend so much time writing and thinking about this team that sometimes I forget I never met them or saw them play. But here they are. At Michigan and Trumbull. At last.

It's 3-1 for Concordia in the top of the second inning and the pitcher for UM-D has walked the first two batters. The UM-D coach ambles to the mound, has a brief talk with his starter. "Settle Down. Throw strikes." The first pitch is a strike that results in a fly ball to center field for the first out. A deeper flyout to center then allows the lead runner to advance. First and third with two out. As the next batter waits for the pitch, the runner at first seems to stray too far off the bag. On the throw to first, the lead runner breaks from third. The runner on first attempts to get himself caught in a rundown so that the lead runner can score before the tag is applied for the third out. Maybe a mistake, maybe a set play. Either way, the UM-D first base-man has to come home with the throw to try to prevent the fourth run from scoring. Out on a close play at the plate. Score it 1-3-4-2 for the third out. 3-1 Concordia in the middle of the second.

I notice an African-American man, maybe mid-thirties, in business attire, suit jacket over his arm. I watch him watch the game through the fence as he walks west on Michigan Avenue, slowing down until he stops twenty feet from the gates to witness an at-bat. I see him notice the open gate and come in. He sits down at a table and loosens his tie. I imagine him marvelling at being able to watch a few moments of live baseball while walking from point A to point B on a sunny, late-spring work day in Detroit. I marvel at all of this too.

On the same day that John Hicks bunts to score JaCoby Jones with the winning run for the Tigers against Tampa, the bunt fea-tures prominently in Concordia's eventual 11-6 win. For the rest of the game, Concordia lays down bunt after perfect bunt. It's not an easy thing to do, especially with an aluminum bat, but they are consistently able to deaden the ball in the perfect spot, moving runners over, sometimes managing infield singles.

As we walk to the car, I think about the execution of those small fundamentals, the way that repetition allowed Concordia to make something very difficult look easy. What occupies my thoughts isn't all the home runs in the Mud Hens game or even seeing the Tigers' prospects play so well. Instead, it's a well-played ground ball or a player knowing how to advance the runner or an outfielder hitting the cut-off man. Little things. Nuance. Like appreciating the steadiness of Charlie Gehringer. Or realizing what your father was trying to say to you all those years you watched baseball together in the family living room.

Final Score: 11-6 Concordia

Four
COACH 'EM UP
May 6 – 10, 2018

Tecumseh Thunder U18
vs
Sarnia Braves Midget Major

Riverside Secondary School
vs
W F Herman Academy

Tecumseh Thunder U18
vs
Amherstburg Sr

Sunday, May 6, 2018

Tecumseh Thunder U18
vs
Sarnia Midget Major

Lacasse Park, Tecumseh ON
Game Time Temperature: 20°C

If the weather holds, today will be the first Canadian game of this project. Driving east along the Detroit River to Tecumseh, I kept looking at the sky, wondering how accurate the rain forecasts of rain would be. As I parked in the teachers' lot at the school next to the field, I could hear AC/DC's "Thunderstruck" from inside the car.

There are about twenty people here. It's chilly in the shade but almost warm in the sun. No anthem is played, the game just starts. I'm starting to really like Lacasse Park with its worn bleacher seats, painted a fresh green every off-season. There's a basic but decent scoreboard. The dugouts are wire cages with a bench. There is no entertainment here today. No mascots. No pep squad. No walk-up music, only music between innings. I am grateful for the lack of spectacle. Today it's just baseball.

A young woman announces the batters, only using the visiting players' first names. "Now batting: Greg." I hear the Sarnia players laugh at this. And then she says, "Now batting: Drew." People are actually watching the game today; it's likely mostly parents and grandparents in the crowd.

Last night I wore a lily-pad-green gown to a Scottish Country Dance ball. My curls were pinned up and I felt like a Jane Austen character, strathspeying with gallant suitors. Today, the humidity has made my curls unruly and they're tucked under a ball cap. My feet, dangling off a bleacher seat, move in time to the Scottish rhythms lingering in my head.

"Every pitch, two steps. 1-2. I don't want to see you flat-footed. Two steps, set your feet."

The Sarnia infielders lean in, listen to their instructions, move to where their coaches want them on each pitch. Repeat the fundamentals. Think about the possible plays before they happen. Burn it into their subconscious, into their muscles so that their reactions become automatic when the ball is hit. The stream of instructions and encouragement is constant from the Sarnia bench just to our right, down the first base line.

Earlier in the weekend, I had marvelled to Dale that pitchers and catchers could remember the ever-changing secret signals. "Some people," he replied, "would find it equally amazing that you can remember and do eighteen different dances in one night." Baseball doesn't come naturally to me the way that jigs, reels, and strathspeys do, but I think about advice I give to new dancers who are frustrated because they don't know whether to focus on their footwork or where they need to go in each dance. "Keep dancing," I say, "One day it will all fall into place." The same logic might be true for learning about baseball.

I return my attention to the infield. The hitter in the on-deck circle says "Heads up!" as a foul ball caroms off the backstop beyond the grandstand. A player lopes over to pick it up, stopping to talk to a friendly black lab on the way back to the dugout. I miss the rest of the at-bat because I'm watching the dog.

There are now about forty people here, mainly family and friends. The players are all seventeen- and eighteen-year-olds and— since they're playing at the Midget Major level—some of the best baseball players in Southwestern Ontario. Many hope to go on to play college ball at some level or, at the very least, play on one of the strongly competitive local Senior Men's teams. The calibre of play is much better than anything I ever saw growing up in rural Alberta, partially because of the population density and the longer playing season, but also because of sustained community interest in baseball in places like Tecumseh and Sarnia.

By seventeen I was trying to navigate my way through my first year of university. I was no longer living in the same town as my father and baseball wasn't high on my list of priorities. I hadn't played since I was fourteen—on a bantam team that played only against the nearest towns—bowing out when the sport became too serious. Not that I was ever very good anyway—a pitcher without great velocity, a catcher who let too many balls get past him, and a passable first baseman who couldn't hit a lick. Organized baseball was, for me, never as much fun as the games of move-up we played at recess and after school, baseball that expanded and contracted as kids would come and go, ending when it was too dark to see the ball. By the time we were fourteen, few players took our organized games seriously, despite the best efforts of our coach, Charlie Chapman, who tried both yelling and cajoling to teach us about fundamentals and strategy. But none of us listened. To us, he was just this old crank rambling on about keeping our feet moving and watching out for the bunt.

A few days ago, I was talking to a colleague about this project and my work on the Chatham Coloured All-Stars. "You must really love baseball," she said. When I said, "I do," she pondered for a minute and then said, unapologetically, "I don't know how you do it. Baseball is *so* boring. Nothing. Ever. Happens." I didn't know what to say other than, "I get that," which I hope she didn't interpret as "I think so too," which I don't.

As I left her office, I thought about what my mum always said to people who complained about how the prairies are so boring compared to the Rockies: "You just need a lesson in looking." My mum never really trusted people who couldn't see the beauty of the prairies. Our car trips were tutorials in looking and seeing the splendours of the open fields and vast skies. The prairies take work. You need to know to watch how the wind moves the wheat like waves, how the swaths of birds glide in the expanse of the sky, and how the sun and clouds cast shadows on the fields.

As Tecumseh come to bat in the second, I hear the Sarnia coaches joking about all the scouts here this afternoon, teasing their players about who might be watching. They have an easy rapport with their players and the players have a clear respect for their coaches that we never had for Charlie.

The first batter walks and, after two passed balls, ends up on third base with no outs. With no program to reference, I have no idea who stands on third or who is on the mound. Right now, they're all anonymous, echoes of every young player I've ever watched, their actions creating a palimpsest over all the games that came before. As I watch, that anonymity seems to deepen not only my ambivalence about who wins, but my focus on the game itself.

The next batter hits a shallow fly ball, but the center fielder can't make the catch, the ball ticking off his glove and falling to the grass. The run scores, putting a man on first with no outs. A stolen base and wild pitch move him up to third base. Still no outs and Sarnia's pitcher seems more than a bit rattled by the way this inning has unfolded.

A slow walk by the coach to the mound. A few soft words to settle his young starter down. A glance around the infield, a single clap, a calm "Let's go," and the Sarnia coach is back in the dugout. The pitcher gathers himself, goes to work on the next batter. Swinging strikeout on a high fastball, followed immediately by a second strikeout. Two outs. After a walk and a steal, there are runners at second and third, but a fly ball to left field ends the inning.

Calm down. Don't let what happened with those first two hitters get under your skin. Pitch like you can. I can't know, but this is the mound conversation I imagine. 1-0 Tecumseh after two innings.

Boredom, with my mum, was never an option. If you found something—anything—dull she sent you back to look at it properly. Everything had a hidden value if you looked for it. If you watch baseball in this way, you'll notice there is never a passing second in baseball that doesn't contribute to the larger narrative of the game. It's easy to see the significance of a walk-off home run but, more often than not, it's the fraction of a second that makes the difference between a strike and a home run. Or a change in the wind or the position of the sun that makes the difference between a caught fly ball and a hit.

Sarnia is back up and the announcer continues in her way: "Now batting: Jack." I hear the players hoot, like "Jack" is the funniest word they've ever heard. The inning is over quickly. The Sarnia coach instructs his pitcher, "Worry about the batter. Worry about the batter," and then his wild pitch advances a runner on base. The center fielder drops a fly ball and the advanced runner scores. "Time, Blue," says the coach, and he saunters to the mound. The next pitch is a strike. "Nice spot," someone shouts.

I watch the hitters in the on-deck circle swinging at the pitches thrown to the batter as if they were at the plate. Where I'm sitting right now lets me see a perfect triangle between the pitcher, the batter, and the on-deck circle. I'm eight feet away. I've never had this sort of view at an MLB game.

In the top half of the third, Sarnia get a double and a single from the first two batters, putting runners on first and third with no one out. #17 strides to the plate to a chorus of encouragement from the bench. "Your time, 1-7. C'mon, kid"—but he watches as strike three whizzes by and there is one out. #5 up now and one of the Sarnia coaches has to yell from the bench to remind him to look to the third base coach for signs. Wild pitch and the run scores from third, while the other runner advances to second. Two walks then load the bases with one out.

#20 up to hit for Sarnia. Hawk. Hawkeye. Hawker. His nicknames become a kind of chant, the collective hope for a hit or wild pitch or error. Anything to give Sarnia the lead.

Hawk hits the ball to the left side of the infield, but it's fielded by the shortstop on a tough, in-between hop, quickly flipped across his body to second, and then relayed to first, a throw the first baseman is able to dig out of the dirt. A 6-4-3 double play to end the inning and get Tecumseh out of a bases loaded jam. 1-1 going into the bottom of the third inning.

Six batters later the score is 5-1 for Tecumseh. End of the day for the Sarnia starter. The new pitcher, #23, is a tall, lanky right-hander who throws much harder than the starter did and with much better command. His first batter is a strikeout looking on a fastball on the low, outside corner of the strike zone. His fastball seems to get even better in the fourth inning, prompting the Sarnia coaches to shift the infielders towards third base with a left-handed hitter at the plate, yelling, "Do you think he's going to pull it?" Not a chance.

A ball goes foul and when the player goes to retrieve it, he has to negotiate with the dog who found it. It's the same black lab I watched before. Back on the field, Sarnia executes a nice double play—so nice that the grandparents and parents of the home team murmur their approval.

For the uninitiated, baseball can seem like a sport where nothing happens. Between innings, I consider whether my mind wanders because my colleague's assessment of baseball is correct. Or does my mind wander because there are so many things to watch and so many pieces in play, both on and off the field, that it's impossible to focus on just one? I head off my frustration with my wandering mind with the advice I give to new dancers: "Keep dancing. It will all come together eventually."

The score is 6-2 Tecumseh and there's a runner on second with two outs when Hawk comes to the plate for Sarnia in the top of the sixth inning. He digs in to the batter's box, eager to get a hit and pass the baton to the next player in the lineup, to at least tie the score before the rains come. Instead of getting a hit, though, he gets struck on the hand with an inside fastball. Hawk swears loudly and, as he runs to first, throws the bat hard towards his own dugout. From the bench I hear, "Not necessary. Not necessary." The tone is no longer teasing, but reproving. As much as they are trying to teach these young men how to play the game of baseball, they are also attempting to teach them how to carry themselves. How to be in the world. Hitting into a double play and getting hit with a pitch are just as much part of the game as getting a single or catching a fly ball in the field. I wonder if Hawk will see that, if he'll listen to his coaches with more attention than we did with Charlie.

Just as a fly ball to right field ends the top half of the sixth inning, the rain starts to come down. The rumble of thunder can be heard in the distance.

Final Score: 6-2 Tecumseh, game called for rain.

Tuesday, May 8, 2018

Riverside Secondary School Rebels
vs
W F Herman Academy Griffins

Riverside Baseball Park, Windsor ON
Game Time Temperature: 23°C

It's odd to be alone at Riverside Park awaiting the game between the Riverside Secondary Rebels and the Herman Academy Griffins, but Heidi couldn't get away from the office and I didn't want to miss the chance to see a high school game. As I sit, thinking about how long it's been since I was at a ballpark by myself, I listen to the Riverside coaches telling the players their positions for the day and where they'll hit in the batting order. Clad in short-sleeved black tops and grey pants, the players sit in a circle around the coach in front of their squat, chain-link dugout, listening. His final words are, "And take turns getting the foul balls." A dozen spectators, almost all parents, sit on lawn chairs or on the low metal stands that flank either side of home. The perfect circle of the reddish-brown dirt infield and the vibrant green of the spring grass, the beneficiary of the last few weeks of rain, contrast the blue of the cloudless sky. Herman takes the field for the first inning and, coach's instructions over, the first Riverside batter steps to the plate. I'm surprised to see that he carries a wood bat.

The Herman pitcher, a left-hander wearing #25, sits the first two hitters down with a strikeout and a ground ball to second. There's no PA system, no lineup cards. Only the numbers to identify this swirl of young men. The pitcher throws hard, mostly for strikes, and it's clear already that the Riverside hitters are going to have trouble with him. After a two-out single, the Herman coach yells, "Worry about the batter. Don't worry about the runner." Don't get rattled. Do what you know you can do. With only the scantest glance to first, the pitcher looks in to the catcher and fires home. Weak ground ball to second base. Inning over. He's big for his age, an intimidating presence on the mound. The green of his sleeveless top must make him look like the Hulk to the Riverside players.

In the bottom of the third, the Riverside hitters are faring no better against the Herman starter and Herman is already up 2-0. Good players, even at this level, can hit a fastball that doesn't have some kind of movement. His doesn't move and they still can't hit it. I wonder how better players his age—say the Tecumseh or Sarnia players we saw on Sunday—would do against him.

#59, now up for Riverside, swings late, mutters, "That was bad."

One of the parents behind home replies, "Why'd you swing then?"

"The pitch wasn't bad. My swing was bad." Like every one of his teammates.

The next batter bails out of the box on two inside pitches that are both expressively called strikes by the home plate umpire. He swings his body towards third base, stabs out his right hand, and emphatically yells, "Strike three! You're out!!" As if the day wasn't bad enough already for the hitters.

Herman is up in the third with another two runs in when I hear one of the Herman players yell to one of the women in the crowd, "Your kid broke another bat."

"He broke all of his. Whose bat?"

Instead of a reply, the batter's teammate turns to her, laughing, says, "He needs to get a job."

Through the fourth, the Riverside hitters continue to bail out on pitches that end up called as inside strikes. Fear—and the Herman pitcher—are inside their heads. As he walks off the mound at the end of the inning, the third baseman waits for him by the foul line. As his teammate mimes legs shaking and laughs uproariously, the pitcher smiles and shakes his head as he walks toward the dugout, accepting pats on the back and the coach's handshake. His day is done. Four innings, one hit, no walks, and no runs allowed. Between innings, I hear one of the mothers explaining to her neighbour that the Herman pitcher is going to Northern Kentucky University on a baseball scholarship to play outfield and occasionally pitch. This summer he's playing first base for the Windsor Selects. His name is Noah Richardson.

Riverside can't score in the fifth, but with another new pitcher into the game in the sixth, Riverside manage to put two on the board. The first two outs come quickly, on a ground ball to the shortstop and a strikeout looking. But an error by the third baseman, he of the shaking legs, keeps the inning alive, setting up an RBI triple by the next batter. Then, on a ball that barely gets away from the catcher, the pitcher fails to cover the plate and the second run scores, prompting the Herman coach to yell, "You guys gotta talk out there!" The final out is a strikeout, the batter grousing loudly at the home plate umpire about not only that call, but his strike zone all game. Borderline inside pitches were called strikes, but they were the entire game, and for both sides. You have to adjust to the way the strike zone is being called.

4-2 Herman going into the bottom of the seventh inning, the final inning in high school games and the last chance for Riverside. Unfortunately for Herman, it's then that their pitcher loses the strike zone, walking both of the first two batters, while the catcher allows ball four to get away from him both times. As I watch the Herman pitcher struggle, a voice from the past surfaces, reminding me exactly what is happening. In my mind, I hear Charlie Chapman yelling, "You're posing, not throwing!," and under my breath I find myself muttering that same phrase. First and third with no one out. The Herman coach has seen the same thing and is out to make a pitching change.

The new pitcher comes in and throws strikes. A strikeout for the first out, but the ball again eludes the catcher. The runner on first runs to second and then never stops, forcing the lead runner to come home instead of retreating to third. Caught in a rundown, he's eventually tagged for the third out. Instead of runners at second and third with one out, the baserunning error means that there is now a runner at third with two outs. A strikeout ends the game.

Final Score: 4-2 Herman

Thursday, May 10, 2018

Tecumseh Thunder U18
vs
Amherstburg Sr

Lacasse Park, Tecumseh ON
Game Time Temperature: 21°C

The cold has returned. That's all I can think as we walk, shivering, into the park for this Essex County Senior Men's League game. As I walk up the steps of the ancient grandstand, its coats of green paint peeling down to worn gray wood, I notice a sign bolted to one of the risers admonishing, "NO SPIKES ALLOWED IN THE GRAND-STAND." I hunch into my jacket as I watch Amherstburg in their bright red jerseys and sparkling white pants take infield before the game. They're a mix of younger guys, mid-twenties, former high school athletes still vaguely in playing shape, and older men whose former athleticism is more hidden, beginnings of beer bellies masking the ability to scoop a hard grounder at second before making the pivot and throw to first. Experience versus youth tonight.

There's a chilly wind and I count fourteen people in the stands, including us. Again, the game just starts. No anthem, no ceremony.

Since the last game, I've been thinking about how to be more deliberate in my baseball watching. This week I dusted off Koppett's *The Thinking Fan's Guide to Baseball*, which has been on my bookshelf, unopened, for nearly a decade. Perhaps this is painfully obvious to everyone else, but I did not know—or at least did not phrase it so clearly to myself at any point—that baseball is based on a round object hitting another round object. This fact of physics is at the core of everything. And that the only thing a batter can do is hit it squarely. After that, everything else is a consequence. It's odd that something so obvious can also be mind-blowing.

In our first years in Windsor, we went to a lot of baseball games with Dave Burke. We would often have whole sections to ourselves. Dave and Dale would gently tutor me in the finer points of the game, either by directly pointing things out and teaching me how to keep a scorecard or indirectly, as I listened in on their conversations about the game. I remember when Dave pointed out the Thome shift and I marvelled that I'd never seen it before. Once he'd shown it to me, I saw it every time after that. When I asked, "What is the manager telling the pitcher?" Dave paused and said, "I think he's saying, 'Don't suck, okay?'" From that moment on, I've always assumed that's basically what they're saying. It's Dave's voice I hear as I count out the players during the first game of the season to remind myself of the nine num-bers of the positions to use on my scorecard: pitcher-catcher-first-base-secondbase-thirdbase-shortstop-leftfield-centerfield-rightfield. When there's a grand slam home run, Dave's voice bursts into my head: "Colour that box in!" I'm not entirely sure when or why I stopped actively trying to learn more about baseball. I do know that baseball got much less interesting around the same time that I stopped trying to learn new things.

Through one inning the teams seem evenly matched, no runs scoring despite the Amherstburg pitcher giving up two walks in the bottom of the first. As on Sunday, the PA announcer is calling out only the first name for the opposing team. "Now batting, #17, Mitch." It's a source of endless amusement to the Amherstburg bench, but to me it's a bit unsettling, this stripping of identity from the visitors. Maybe it's working, though, as Amherstburg once again fail to score in their half of the second.

Bottom of the second. There are runners on first and second, one out, and two runs already in when Ardi Kelmendi comes to bat for the Thunder. It's the third time I've seen him this week, since he plays not only for the Thunder Midget Major team, but also for his high school team, Riverside Secondary. Like his teammates—from

Massey High School, Tecumseh Vista Academy, Brennan, St. Anne's,
Kingsville, Holy Names, Villanova, St. Joseph's, Sandwich, and Ken-
nedy—Kelmendi is among the best high school baseball players in
Essex County, and, like them, he'll play on multiple teams over the
course of the summer. Right now, he watches a wild pitch skip past
the catcher, allowing the runners to advance.

My colleague's comment last week about baseball being boring
continues to wend its way through my thoughts. I'm wondering if
saying, "Nothing happens in baseball" is like when people say, "Why
don't poets just say what they mean instead of writing all these hidden
meanings." Having taught English, I've encountered the notion of the
"hidden meaning" dozens and dozens of times and given my share of
lectures about the relationship between language, meaning, and form.

But I also recognize that unless you know what to look for, you can
only go so far in understanding a poem. If you're not aware of diction,
metre, form, the poetic tradition, sound, and language, then poetry is
just words on a page. If, for example, you look at a few lines of poetry,
say, John Donne's "Holy Sonnet 14," you can see a deliberateness in
his choice of words:

> "Batter my heart, three-personed God; for You
> As yet but knock, breathe, shine, and seek to mend;
> That I may rise, and stand, o'erthrow me, and bend
> Your force to break, blow, burn, and make me new."

It's probably not an accident that he relies on single-syllable words
(only three of the thirty-eight words have multiple syllables) or that
he uses hard sounds (batter, heart, knock, seek, that, break) and soft
sounds (breathe, shine, mend), and lots of words that start with "B."
If you only look at the words for what they say—and not, for example,
how they sound—you're only seeing part of the poem. Similarly, if you
only look at pitching as something that enables or prevents home runs,
you're only seeing part of the game.

I feel compelled to confess that while I'm not overly fond of Donne,
this poem often pops to mind when I think of batters at the ballpark.

In fact, I've even considered writing a poem about Curtis Granderson that starts "Batter—my heart!"

The strike zone has begun to elude the Amherstburg pitcher, the wild pitch just the worst sign of it. Rather than load the bases, he finally throws a strike on a three-ball count. Unfortunately for him, Kelmendi singles up the middle, the scorched ball barely missing the pitcher on its way to center field. As he contorts away from the batted ball, I flash back to a ball that our friend Dave Burke, pitching in a men's league for Woodslee, could not avoid. I wasn't there that day, but in my mind, I see Dave dropping to the mound, unmoving, his brother rushing in from the bench. I see the players trying to attend to him. The ambulance and the paramedics. The operation. His worried family. The steel plate he now jokes about. And, finally, Dave getting back on the mound. It's that last part I still find the most unbelievable. Not that he got hit in the head. Not how deathly serious it all was. But that he managed to overcome the fear, to throw a baseball towards a bat from sixty feet six inches away.

The Amherstburg pitcher wasn't hit, of course. I don't know if he's ever been hit, but I do know he's had at least one close call. The fear is there, just like it is with the hitter every time he steps in the batter's box. A single that barely missed him scores two runs to make it 4-0. How will he react? K. K. Maybe that single was a wake-up call.

Until this project, I'd never really given much thought to all the invisible work behind those MLB players who make everything look so easy that we take their skill for granted. It's like my friend John, the comedian, showed me time and time again—stand-up comedy isn't just standing up and being funny. It's years of practice, weeks of reworking, and hours of refining that make those twenty minutes work, seemingly without effort. The key to understanding anything—poetry, comedy, or baseball—is noticing what you've never thought about before.

As Koppett writes, "crowds invariably react [to fielding] incorrectly. The plays usually cheered loudest are not nearly so difficult as many others that go unnoticed." Here's where the artistry of noticing becomes important. If you're only watching for home runs or a favoured team's victory, you're going to miss a lot of the game. Just as Alice Walker writes in *The Color Purple*, "I think it pisses God off if you walk by the color purple in a field somewhere and don't notice it," I wonder if the baseball gods get pissed off if you don't notice a perfectly executed bunt.

By the end of the third inning, it's 9-0 and Kelmendi's single is long buried on the scorecard. It's an impressive lead for this young Tecumseh team, though going by the look on their coach's face, it's hard to tell they're ahead at all. No jokes or gentle teasing. No sense that he's happy with what he's seeing. Just the business of baseball.

After all three Amherstburg batters strike out in the third, they finally manage to get a man past first base in the fourth inning. Third base. No outs. Sac fly to center field to score Amherstburg's first run of the game. After the ball is thrown back to the pitcher, the Tecumseh coach has him throw to third base, claiming that the runner left early, but the home plate umpire calls the runner safe. The coach is incredulous and starts chirping at the ump. "That's six blown calls in two days!" I turn to Heidi, see her curious look, and shrug. Tecumseh are up 9-1 and it's a men's league game in early May. The biggest surprise, though, is that the coach isn't ejected from the game.

As much as I try to focus on pitch movement, I am frequently distracted by a girl behind me who has talked non-stop since first pitch. She has pulled me into long, winding tales about her job, her apartment, her car, her dog, her brother's car, her student loans. When the conversation switches to hernias, I take this as my cue to refocus on what Koppett taught me in this morning's chapters: "Acquiring the raw materials is the science part of pitching, and so is the constant problem of keeping all deliveries in good working order [. . .] Only then comes the art, the process of deciding what to throw when, and where. The tactics and the thinking begin here." As I watch through my new Koppett lens, I come to comprehend that this game is more than the 9-1 score. And that the Tecumseh coach is probably trying to get his pitchers to be deliberate for each Amherstburg batter. And that Kelmendi didn't just go up to the plate without a plan or an idea in the same way that Donne didn't just let whatever words came to mind simply fall on the page. Koppett says, "Far and away the most important thought of all, however, is: what pitch do I *want* to hit? This is where the artists are separated from the purposeless stick-wavers." I can see why going into the ninth with a 1-0 score could be considered dull. Or why it could be, if you know what you're looking for, the most amazing game you've ever witnessed.

But it's not a 1-0 game tonight. It's 10-1 for Tecumseh in the fourth, and if you believe the theory that scoring is the most exciting part of a game, this should be a great game. But it's not. Sometimes it feels like I'm just logging hours at the ballpark, which is also part of this project—watching and learning from games at all levels. Much of baseball is exactly what these young players are doing—refining and reworking their skills and their understanding of the game to become, as Koppett says, artists instead of purposeless stick-wavers.

In the bottom of the inning, things go from bad to worse for Amherstburg. The new pitcher, their third of the evening, might as well be throwing batting practice the way the Tecumseh hitters are seeing his fastball. By the end of the frame it's 14-1 Tecumseh and the only question is how quickly the top of the fifth can be played before the ten-run mercy rule can be invoked. I want desperately to get out of the cold; I'm not so much rooting for Tecumseh as for the end of the game.

I'm up on my feet, walking in place, and swaying to keep warm as Tecumseh take the field. The first batter walks—the first all game for a Tecumseh pitcher—and I find myself muttering under my breath. But then a crisply executed 6-4-3 double play gives me renewed hope. An easy ground ball to the second baseman should end the game, but the ball goes right under his glove. Never got low enough to the ground, either with his glove or his body. E4. The coach won't be happy, even up 14-1. Finally, though, a fly ball to center field ends the game and we shuffle to the warmth of our car.

Final Score: 14-1 Tecumseh

Five

MICHIGAN
AND TRUMBULL

May 13, 2018

Great Lakes Intercollegiate
Athletic Conference Tournament

Ashland University
vs
Davenport University

Northwood University
vs
Davenport University

Sunday, May 13, 2018

Ashland University Eagles
vs
Davenport University Panthers

Police Athletic League Field, Detroit MI
Game Time Temperature: 52°F

Even though it's mid-May, I've got my puffy coat zipped up to my nose and I'm grateful for the hot coffee from the Detroit Institute of Bagels on Michigan Avenue. There are probably a hundred people here this morning to watch their sons, brothers, and boyfriends. It's definitely a partisan crowd and the parents mostly seem to know each other. They are chatting amongst themselves in the stands and bantering with their kids on the field. They know the nicknames of players. They start heckling umps early in the game. "What is *wrong* with you?" "Bad call. You are bad." This is our first tournament and there is a palpable change in mood from the other games we have seen this year.

We meant to be here two days ago, the Friday of the tournament pencilled into our schedule of games, but once again the weather conspired against us. Despite the heavy rain, Davenport beat Tiffin 11-6 and Northwood beat Wayne State 3-1, their second losses eliminating both Tiffin and Wayne State from the tournament. Grand Valley State was then eliminated on Saturday, which left Northwood undefeated and Ashland and Davenport with one loss each. They will meet today in game one, with the winner advancing to the championship game against Northwood.

Most of the crowd is wearing either Davenport red or Ashland purple. Heidi and I are both in black coats, zipped up tight against the morning chill. I'm glad to see Ashland again, but it doesn't matter to me who wins today. Heidi and I and the four umpires on the field might be the only people in the park who feel that way.

The two teams make short work of the first inning—a lead-off walk, followed by three groundouts for Ashland in the top half and two strikeouts and a lineout to the shortstop for Davenport in the bottom half. In the top of the second, Alex Huard, Davenport's third baseman, charges a ground ball, snagging it on a high hop and throwing on the run to first for the second out of the inning. With no runner on first, the subsequent double is harmless as he is stranded on second by a strikeout that ends the top half of the inning. In their half of the second, Davenport goes down in order. No score after two innings.

I've seen enough different kinds of baseball in the past six weeks to know that these guys are pretty good. I'm starting to recognize fielding abilities as a marker of quality and skill, not just hitting. The fielding is faster, more confident. Plays that would have seemed pretty miraculous in Lacasse Park seem routine here.

Ashland goes in order in the top of the third, but Davenport gets something going in the bottom of the inning. Walk. Stolen base. Davenport fans yell at the home plate umpire about a hit batsman. Batter to first on a walk anyway. Runners on first and second. Ground ball to short. Toss to second. Relay to first. 6-4-3 double play. Runner on second advances to third. Single scores the run. Caught stealing ends the inning. 1-0 Davenport after three innings.

In the top of the fourth, Ashland manages two singles, including one to lead off the inning, but again fails to score. As I watch Ashland's scoring attempts, I think about the Q&A session before last night's performance of *The Summer King*—the opera about the Negro Leagues catcher, Josh Gibson—at the Detroit Opera House. The composer, Daniel Sonenberg, was asked why baseball lends itself to narrative, to which he replied that in baseball the situation changes after every pitch. So do the possible outcomes of the next pitch, a story that unfolds differently every time, an almost infinite branching of narrative possibility. In the majors, a leadoff hitter who reaches first base scores about 38 percent of the time. This is not, of course, the majors, but at this level there's still a good chance—likely about one in three— that the runner will score. But Connor Barleben, the second hitter, swings at a 1-1 pitch and flies out to center field, thereby creating a new situation with a new set of possibilities. But what if Barleben had got a hit instead of flying out to center field? Or hit the ball to the right side of the infield, as I was taught and Dad would have expected, in order to advance the runner? If not a sacrifice, then what if he had shown more plate discipline, an important emphasis in the way the game is taught today? What if he had been patient at the plate, able to get himself into a 2-1 or 3-1 count instead of swinging at the 1-1 pitch? In that hitter's count, would he have got a pitch that he could drive rather than loft? What if he did get the pitch he wanted and simply got under it? Who knows what might have happened if he had not swung at that first pitch—there are many possible outcomes.

Family members are watching the game with deep investment in the final outcome. There's a definite sense that there's more at stake here than just a win or a loss. How someone's kid plays today might determine something bigger for him in his life. By comparison, Dale and I are watching with engaged indifference. The scout behind us is watching for something else entirely. At the end of the inning, I hear him on his phone saying, "I've seen what I needed to see. I'm heading out." He leaves and I am curious what he saw. We all want something distinct from this game. What's not obvious to me is what I want from the game—both today and from baseball in general.

The moms are particularly engaged, more so than the dads. A mom behind me is, I think, cheering for her son, although it's hard to tell because she's cheering for every player on the Davenport team as if he were her son. "Barrel it up here, 7. You can do it, kid." "Come on kiddo. Stay on it. Stay on it."

As I listen to the chatter around me, no one is talking about their car or their brother's car or hernias. People are talking about the game.

"Come on, base hit, right now," says Davenport Mom. There's a bad bounce and an out at second. Score is still 1-0 Davenport in the bottom of the fourth. There's a level of concentration here that I haven't witnessed at most Tigers games. People are watching pitching, catching, and fielding; they are paying attention to many more details than just the score.

The parents have a level of understanding about the game that still lets them admire a great catch or a beautiful pitch from the opposing team. There's an implicit understanding that the opposing pitcher is someone else's son. Aside from comments toward the umps, the parents are keeping the tone respectful and generous.

Krystien Johnson-Battilana, the right-handed pitcher for Davenport, is back out for the top of the fifth inning. He stands with his right foot on the rubber, facing third base, hip towards home plate, glove and pitching hand raised to his chin. He then starts his motion, both hands dropping to his belt while his left knee rises level with his hip. As he strides forward, his right arm is drawn behind his shoulder and directly over the top in an easy, fluid motion home. Only two strikeouts so far, but not a lot of hard contact. Like the slow roller to the second baseman off the bat of the leadoff hitter. One out.

After allowing a walk and a single, Johnson-Battilana comes back with a strikeout. Two on, two out. A single by the designated hitter, Carson Mittermaier, ties the game and leaves runners at first and second, prompting a visit from the Davenport pitching coach. As they huddle at the mound with the catcher and infielders, "Eye of the Tiger" plays over the PA system. Barleben, the on-deck hitter, uses his bat as an air guitar, strumming dramatically, seemingly oblivious to his surroundings. Maybe it's a way to clear his head before he bats in a tied elimination game. Maybe he's just a young man having fun at the ballpark.

Conference over, the guitar once more becomes a bat and the song only an echo. Two men on, the focus shifts back to the confrontation between pitcher and hitter and to all the possible outcomes. When potential becomes reality, Davenport walks off the field, a groundout to second base ending the Ashland scoring threat. Three quick outs for Davenport in the bottom half of the inning and it's 1-1 after five innings.

Davenport Mom knows how to watch the game with all its nuances. She sees everything. She's on top of every pitch, every swing, every catch, every moment of the game. "Nice pitch. Keep 'em comin', keep 'em comin'. There we go. There it is. Beautiful pitch. Go get him, kid. Go after him. Go on. Fire it in, kid. Keep 'em comin'." I wish I had Davenport Mom in my office sometimes, saying, "Keep 'em comin'. You got it, kid."

It's still 1-1 and this is the most evenly matched game we've seen this season. Although the score is low, this is the antithesis of nothing happening.

There are two outs in the top of the sixth when the ball is chopped up the middle, just over the outstretched glove of the pitcher. The second baseman, Nolan Bryant, charges and scoops the ball near the ground, throwing in stride to just get the batter at first base. One more tough chance converted into an out.

A man who is quite clearly a scout sits to our left, his stopwatch and notepad clear for all to see. It's hard to know who he is here to observe, but I don't see a radar gun and he's not charting pitches, so my guess is one of the hitters. I'd like to ask, but I can't get up the nerve. I doubt if he would tell me anyway.

The Northwood players are sitting behind home plate, waiting to see who they will play. Three of them—likely all pitchers—are sitting near us as one of them charts the locations and types of pitches thrown. A different kind of scouting as they get ready for the upcoming game.

Chris Slavik is still pitching for Ashland, with six strikeouts already. Unfortunately for him, the third baseman boots a grounder from the first batter. E5, runner on first base. After a wild pitch moves the runner to second, the go-ahead run scores on a one-out infield single. Slavik is pitching as well as he has all game and he never allowed a hard-hit ball in the inning. But sometimes that's not enough. Sometimes one of your fielders can't quite make a play.

Sometimes your grip isn't quite right and you throw the ball in the dirt when your catcher was expecting a fastball up. Sometimes a hitter is able to get a toe on the first base bag just ahead of an underhand toss from the pitcher. Sometimes those possibilities collide and you give up a run, and your team is suddenly down 2-1 with three innings left.

It's silent in the park because everyone is concentrating fully on what's happening on the field. I can hear an announcer calling the game from the press booth: "Here's the pitch. A curveball" and I feel like I'm in a sports movie, the way the voiceover happens so you know what's important. As I try to think about how I can watch baseball more deliberately, I am reminded that there's no commentary, no analysis when I'm watching baseball like this and that I need to do it for myself.

Single plus a fielding error. Single. Runners on the corners for Ashland in the top of the seventh. Grant Wolfram, a lefty, in to pitch for Davenport as Austin Eifrid steps into the batter's box for Ashland. Eifrid hits a shallow fly ball and as I watch the center fielder settle under it, I think there's no way they send the runner from third. But Alex Niecikowski is off as soon as the ball hits Zac Wilson's glove. Maybe it surprises Wilson as much as it does me because his throw skips in front of home plate and the tying run scores easily.

"Keep working 3-6. You got this, kid."

I don't know if it's one of the parents in front of us calling to the pitcher, but it seems to work, as he gets the next hitter to roll a weak ground ball to first base for the second out of the inning. An intentional walk to Mittermaier puts runners at first and second base, allowing Wolfram to pitch to Barleben, who has already made outs twice in the game with runners on base. Barleben is also a left-handed hitter, whereas Mittermaier hits from the right side. Since Wolfram is a left-handed pitcher, he theoretically has the advantage against a left-handed hitter. It's the percentage play to walk Mittermaier here, to stack the possibilities in your favour. Any smart manager would make the same call. No question. But in a 2-2 count, Barleben gets a pitch he likes and doubles to left center, scoring two runs. A surprise twist to the story.

Davenport Mom is cheering for the new pitcher. "Fire it in there, fire it in. Keep 'em comin', keep 'em comin'. Way to throw smoke, buddy. Good pitch. Good pitch. You got this guy." As it turns out, the pitcher doesn't have this guy. The next pitch flies deep into left field scoring two runs. It's now 4-2 for Ashland. But Davenport Mom isn't deterred. "Come on 3-6. You got it, kiddo. You got it." The runner advances on a passed ball. A nice final pitch gets them out of the inning. I'm starting to love Davenport Mom. She is relentlessly hopeful and positive and I'm still not sure who her son is. The world needs more Davenport Moms.

Middle of the seventh inning as the Sam Roberts Band's "Detroit '67" blasts from the speakers at the top of the concourse. I look out over the city skyline and think about Willie Horton leaving the locker room at Tiger Stadium, driving towards 12th and Clairmount on July 23, 1967. Standing on the hood of his car in his Tigers uniform as he tried to calm people down during the riots. I think about my father. The ghosts of baseball. I briefly wonder again if the history means anything to these players, their parents—to anyone but me today. Maybe they all just see it as a neutral site, a convenient location to play out the end-of-season tournament. I wonder if they realize everything that has happened to and in this city. The ways baseball matters and the ways that it doesn't. All of their cheering, all of their partisan invective at the umpires, all of that passion for their teams is layered on top of more than a hundred years of Tigers baseball. Detroiters embracing their teams, yelling support—hoping, celebrating, commiserating. The ghosts of baseball past settle in with me to watch the rest of this fascinating, and increasingly tense, game.

No runs in the bottom of the seventh or the top of the eighth. In the bottom of the eighth, Slavik comes back out to pitch for Ashland. With a man on second, Brian Sobieski hits a hard shot back up the middle, a ball that strikes Slavik hard in the right shoulder and ricochets away from him. It's a scary moment as the trainers rush out to check on him and, like every other time I see a pitcher hit, I flash back to Dave and to the fear that every pitcher must live with every game. Slavik looks not to be very badly hurt, but still comes out of the game. Pat Carlozzi, a left-hander, comes in to pitch for Ashland.

Davenport loads the bases. Pitcher throws 2 balls and 1 strike. The Davenport bench is cheering him on. Davenport Mom says, "Come on 3. Any way you can, kid. Come on, 3." He is walked. "Make it yours, kiddo," she tells the next batter. "Be patient. Hit or walk, hit or walk."

Carlozzi gets a mound visit from his coach. A right-hander and a left-hander warm up in the bullpen. The mound visit seems to settle him down so he can get outs, but Davenport is able to tie the game with consecutive sacrifice flies by Petravicius and Huard. In the ninth, each team brings just three batters to the plate and the score remains tied at 4. Extra innings in the best game we've seen this year.

The first Ashland batter in the top of the tenth is out on a fly to second and I record "F4" in my mental scorecard. I find myself cheering for Davenport because I like Davenport Mom so much. She's cheering for the pitcher now: "You got 'em, kid. You got this. Fire it in there." The pitcher throws a strike and then there's a runner on first. Ashland gets a double. The ball skims the line to the edges of right field. The shortstop catches a nice flyball. No one advances. The winning run is on third base and they're intentionally walking the next batter with two outs. Bases are now loaded. Not only is the park silent, Detroit itself seems to have been silenced. The pitcher winds up. It's 2 balls, 2 strikes. Now 3 balls and 2 strikes. "Win it here, kiddo! This is what you live for." He strikes him out and I let out a holler. Somehow, I've become partisan. This game reminds me of what I love about baseball.

In the top of the tenth, with runners on second and third and one out, Anthony DiPonio, Davenport's shortstop, makes an over-the-shoulder catch on a high pop fly for out number two. Since Andrew Click is a right-hander, the Davenport coach has him intentionally walk Michael Rogers, a left-handed hitter, so that he can pitch to Niecikowski, a right-handed hitter, with the bases loaded. Once again, it's the percentage play. As the at-bat works its way to what feels like an inevitable full count, the tension inside the park is palpable. Everyone is watching the game, hanging on every pitch. Click sets for the 3-2 pitch, a fastball that Niecikowski swings through. A fist pump and a yell from Click as he walks off the mound.

The first Davenport batter is up and Davenport Mom says, "Take the hop if he's going to give it." The first batter is out F7. "Make it yours," she says to the second batter, "Find a way on here." Someone's dad yells, "Make him work. Make. Him. Work." The second Davenport player strikes out. The third batter is out 5-3.

No runs in the bottom of the tenth or in either half of the eleventh as the tension continues to build.

The first Ashland player gets a single. The second batter strikes out. Davenport Mom has left her seat and is now watching closer to the field but I can still hear her calling to the pitcher. The third batter is out F8 and I catch myself clapping. Dale seems amused and surprised by my sudden partisanship. The fourth batter singles, a long drive into right field, and the runner advances to third base. The runner on first is picked off trying to steal for the third out. Dale explains to me why this is bad base running.

DiPonio's leadoff single in the bottom of the twelfth brings the Davenport crowd to their feet, the red now outweighing the purple as morning turns to afternoon. A sacrifice bunt advances DiPonio to second base. Wilson is intentionally walked to put the double play back in order. A ground ball will still get Ashland out of the inning, but a walk to Aaron Fadden loads the bases and brings up the first baseman, Jacob Buchberger.

With the bases loaded, Carlozzi is back to the full windup, facing home, glove in front of his face, pivoting towards third and then firing home in one compact motion. Buchberger digs into the right-hand batter's box and takes the first pitch for a ball. The Davenport fans are all standing, most with their hands up around their faces, as if in prayer or, perhaps, in actual prayer. The Ashland fans seem shrunk into themselves, hoping against hope for the double play ball that will usher in a thirteenth inning. Carlozzi goes back into his motion, releases the ball towards the plate. Buchberger uncoils his bat, its barrel snapping out to drive the ball down the left field line and beyond the black plastic tarp of the outfield wall.

A home run ball silently soars over the wall in far left field, securing an 8-4 victory for Davenport. I take a photo of the batter crossing the plate into the arms of his entire team. In so doing, I have captured a moment of sheer, wordless bliss. Nothing compares to the thrill of watching such a feat. As half of the parents storm the concourse to celebrate, the other half slouch down the stairs to find their sons. I imagine them trying to find the words they'll need to say. Dale and I, on the other hand, are the only ones still sitting in the stands watching everything unfold. In my notebook I write, "Hello baseball. I'm back."

Final Score: 8-4 Davenport

Sunday, May 13, 2018, later

Northwood University Timberwolves
vs
Davenport University Panthers

Police Athletic League Field, Detroit MI
Game Time Temperature: 61°F

I sat in the car for a bit between games, wondering how Davenport will do after playing twelve innings. I have to admit I was also wondering how I would do after watching that game. When I go to art galleries, I usually stay until a piece of art moves me to speechlessness. I've learned that I can't process much after that. Will today's game be like that?

When I meet up with Dale in the bleachers, Davenport looks a little tired and dusty, while Northwood looks well-rested, their powder-blue uniforms pristine and fresh as they take to the field.

The Northwood bench is loud. The bench players roar encouragement at the two strikeouts by their pitcher, Jake Gross, that open the game, the noise reaching a fever pitch with the first baseman's running throw to end the inning. When their catcher, Brian Dombrowski, doubles in the bottom of the first, the entire team erupts, most of them standing on the top step of the dugout, barely contained by the imaginary line that separates bench from field of play. Even the subsequent two groundouts to shortstop can't dampen their enthusiasm. They know that with one more win they will be conference champions.

There's much less to cheer about in the second inning, though, as three straight hits—a Buchberger triple and Austin Petravicius single, capped by an Alex Huard home run to left—make the game 3-0 Davenport. From behind me I hear, "Well, they just had twelve innings of batting practice." Three, maybe four minutes and the calculus of the game has changed completely. More leeway for Davenport and their depleted pitching staff. It's not exactly desperation, but there is certainly a sense of urgency for the Northwood bench that wasn't there in the boisterous first and that becomes ever more heightened as they fail to get a base runner in either the second or the third.

Despite the tension that seems to seep from the bench and the many Northwood fans in the park, it's still early in the game. Six more innings. Eighteen more outs. An hourglass measured in opportunities rather than grains of sand.

The scoreboard is hard to see from the angle I'm at so I'm watching the ump for balls and strikes. I start trying to compare my calls with his. I'm doing okay, but it's hard to maintain this level of attention for two games in one afternoon. I focus on the field, but am soon distracted by the stylized font on the Davenport uniforms. My thoughts drifting to an imaginary discussion over font choice. Is this typography by committee? *Who* argued for this font? And why? Will this go down as the "Great Font Fiasco of '18"? If I were the kind of person who yells in public I might call out, "Hey. Davenport. Nice serif font on your uniforms!" I wonder how many people would nod like dashboard dogs in agreement without lifting an eye from the game. Or, more likely, how many would crane their necks to get a good look at the type of person who trash talks a team about their font in a tournament when there are two outs and the batter's got a 3-2 count. Also, I realize I've just become a Davenport supporter so I keep my thoughts about their font to myself.

By the time they've ceded six of their precious outs, Northwood are able to tie the game on a home run in the fourth and a bases-loaded single in the fifth. 3-3. Cue the noise from the Northwood bench.

My notes form a record of the next two innings—Top 6: Ж, F8, F8; Bottom 6: Ж, 1-3, 6-3; Top 7: F9, 1-3, BB, F7; Bottom 7: K, 6-3, 4-3—in scorecard notations that evoke the bare facts of what happened. Strikeouts, flyouts, groundouts. But these symbols don't record the way Sobieski watched strike three go by in the top of the sixth, frozen in place by a curveball he wasn't expecting, Ernie Harwell's voice in my head saying, "He stood there like the house by the side of the road, and watched it go by." They don't record the grace of a shortstop moving to his right and throwing on the run, or an outfielder taking the measure of a high fly ball and moving to just the right spot. They don't record how Justin Palmbos, the Davenport relief pitcher, pitches to the low part of the strike zone to set up a high fastball for a swinging strikeout in the bottom of the seventh. They don't record the mounting tension of a 3-3 tie after seven innings.

Everyone else is concentrating deeply on the game. I am pretty certain there isn't another person in this whole park who has noticed this font choice, let alone spent two entire at bats thinking about it. After a moment of watching pitching, I become distracted by a Timberwolves player skillfully juggling a Snickers bar between his hand and his clipboard beside the dugout. I find I'm still thinking about fonts. And how I'd like a Snickers bar. I'm not me when I'm hungry.

Nolan Bryant leads off the Davenport eighth with a double. I glance over at Heidi and wonder what she's thinking, what she's feeling about the air of tension in the park. I wonder about the young man on his phone who I overheard saying, "I'm at the ballpark where

Tiger Stadium used to be. I just wandered in and they're playing." Is he still here? Did he get caught up in this beautifully played game? Did he pick a team to support as he watched? Or is he like us, trying to refrain from having a rooting interest in the outcome of the game? Runner on second with no outs. Odds lean heavily towards Davenport taking the lead. Everyone here feels something different about this chance, about this new set of possibilities. As with any good story, I just want to see what happens next.

Bryant sees that Zac Wilson's line drive to left will not be caught and begins to sprint from second. The fielder plays the ball on one hop and fires a throw that skips perfectly in to the catcher at home plate. The ball is there in time, but the catcher cannot hold on to it, and Bryant scores on a half tumble, half slide that leaves him sprawled across the plate. 4-3 Davenport with a good chance to add on at least one more run. But with Wilson on third base and two outs, Northwood's right fielder, Miles Hardy, dives to his right and just manages to snare what looks to be a sure single from Petravicius in the webbing of his glove. I might be imagining it, but I can almost feel the collective exhale from the Northwood fans.

I get caught up in the game until I hear Michigan people talk about hot dogs. My friend, a retired linguistics professor, tells me that bodies of water—oceans, lakes, and rivers—have historically created distinct linguistic features. Every time I cross the Detroit River, I see what she means. You can often tell which side of the river people are from simply by having them say two words: hot dog. Is it "haught daug"? Or "hat dahg"? An Ontario friend told me about playing Taboo—the game where you have to get your team to say a specific word without using words listed on a card—with a guy from Michigan who was getting angry because the Canadians kept guessing "leprechaun." The Ontarians heard "small, green, hat" when he was saying "small, green, hot." The answer was "jalapeno." My thoughts of Snickers bars have been replaced with veggie-dog cravings.

Bottom of the ninth, still 4-3 Davenport. Last three outs for Northwood this game. Three more outs to get for Davenport. If Northwood loses, each team will have one loss and will have to play again, later in the afternoon. So it might not be the end of our day or the days of these teams.

E5. Single. Runners on first and second with no outs. A sacrifice bunt will move the runners up to second and third, and mean that the tying run could be scored on a fly ball to the outfield (and that the double play is no longer in order). But it will also mean that Northwood has used up one of those last three outs. To bunt or not to bunt. I imagine my father and Kurt both expecting the third base coach to give the sign for the bunt. It's what I expect as well, one of those fundamental plays that are much easier in practice than they are when you're one run behind in the ninth inning of a conference championship game. Noah Ingram moves in to the batter's box and, as Palmbos throws his pitch, squares around to bunt, just far enough in front of the catcher that his only play is to the second baseman who is covering at first. One out, runners on second and third. The Davenport coach moves the infield in to try to prevent the run from scoring, but a walk loads the bases. Infield back to double play depth. Kyle Ziegler at the plate. On the 2-0 pitch Ziegler swings weakly at a pitch inside, yielding a very shallow fly ball to center field. As I watch it fall, I can't imagine it being deep enough for Northwood to send the runner. But as the ball settles into Wilson's glove, McClelland takes off from third. Wilson's throw is up the line, arriving at the catcher just as McClelland begins his head-first slide across the artificial turf that passes for dirt around home at Police Athletic League Field. F8 sac fly to tie the game.

That brings up the righty Hardy. I grab my program from under the seat to check his batting average: .235. At this point, I'm expecting extra innings. The first pitch is a ball, up and away. Foul to the left, followed by a called strike on a low fastball. 1-2 and Hardy has to protect the plate, swinging at anything that might be close in case it's called a strike by the home plate umpire. Palmbos sets, checks the runners, and comes to the plate with a high fastball. Hardy manages to just nick it to avoid the strikeout and keep the count at 1-2. A ball in the dirt. On the 2-2 count Hardy swings, the barrel of the bat connecting solidly with the ball, propelling it into center field and Northwood to the conference championship. An improbable ending to the story.

The Northwood players flood from their dugout, piling on their unlikely hero where he stopped just after rounding first base. As they celebrate, Palmbos takes off his glove and slumps to his haunches between home plate and the mound, staring off into the middle distance in disbelief. Several teammates stop to pat him on the back before Buchberger walks over from his position as the cut-off man behind the mound and pulls Palmbos to his feet, enveloping him in a hug that's as meaningful to me as the home run he hit earlier in the day.

Final Score: 5-4 Northwood

Six

ARE YOU
FROM VIRGINIA?

May 17 – 18, 2018

NCAA Division III Regional Tournament

College of Wooster
vs
Wabash College

La Roche College
vs
Ithaca College

Adrian College
vs
Otterbein University

Marietta College
vs
Wabash College

Otterbein University
vs
Ithaca College

Thursday, May 17, 2018

Driving to Adrian MI

Thursday morning and we're on the road, I-94 churning under our tires, talk of the tournament we're speeding towards and the smell of hot coffee filling the car. The NCAA Division III Mideast Regional in Adrian, Michigan—a double-elimination tournament hosted by Adrian College, with the winner going on to the Division III World Series just outside of Appleton, Wisconsin—is the only NCAA postseason regional tournament to fall within our one-hundred-mile radius. For us, it will be a full immersion in baseball, with five games over the next two days. And we would have missed it entirely, if not for a message on Monday from Chris Wainscott, who's active in the Windsor-Essex County baseball scene. We're learning to roll with the unexpected. At least this time it's not the weather.

We reach Ann Arbor, turn south off I-94 on to state Highway 23 for a few miles before cutting across on Ridge Highway, the road that will take us to Adrian. I listen as Heidi tells me about what she's been thinking as we begin to lean in to this summer of baseball. I tell her that a lot of my recent thinking has been about how the situation of a game changes with every pitch, and how the players are constantly forced to react. I've been thinking about the rhetorical idea of kairos—right timing—in relation to baseball, about how the right play is always dependent on the situation. Kairos is here bounded by the precise and ordered rules of the game, and requires situational thinking that's not as messy as where rhetoric happens, in the real world where context is much more complex. Still, baseball provides a branching, kairotic narrative that, if you pay attention, is always new, yet, at the same time, intensely familiar. Maybe that's why I've kept coming back to baseball. Maybe that's what I'm searching for this summer, in tournaments like this one, in places like Adrian.

Thursday, May 17, 2018

College of Wooster Fighting Scots
vs
Wabash College Little Giants

Nicolay Field, Adrian MI
Game Time Temperature: 79°F

As we approach the stadium, we are greeted by a series of gigantic photographs depicting Adrian College Baseball above a list of the years they won their conference, appeared in a Regional, or went to the Division III World Series. Below the photos, a four-foot version of their mascot, a menacing yet cartoonish bulldog in a crewneck sweater, leans against an outsized brown and yellow "A." This likeness, as well as stylized pawprints in school colours, appear all over campus and throughout the town.

It's sunny and warm—nearly shirtsleeves weather—as we move to our seats on the first base side of Nicolay Field, just past home plate. A few days ago, we tried to see some high school baseball in Windsor, but the fields were unplayable messes, green and brown bogs that will need many days like this one to dry out. Here, though, the green and brown carpet of artificial turf has drained perfectly and, as the College of Wooster and Wabash College finish infield practice, I can see that the rains have had little effect. Ringed around the outfield from the right field foul pole to left center, past the scoreboard in straightaway center, are a series of banners commemorating past accomplishments of the Adrian College baseball program. Signs for local businesses pick up where the banners leave off and extend to the left field line. Meijer. Carlton Lodge. Jimmy John's. Slusarski Excavating and Paving.

Players from Shenandoah sit all around us, eating sandwiches, talking to family or teammates, waiting to see which of these teams they will play tomorrow. Since they beat Marietta 3-2, Shenandoah will face the winner of this game, while Marietta will face the loser in an elimination game. Later today, Ithaca will play La Roche, while Adrian will play Otterbein. A Shenandoah player a couple of seats down from me gets ready to chart pitches while his teammates lean back on their elbows in relaxation. Wabash supporters sit on this side of the diamond, directly above their team's bench, while Wooster fans congregate on the third base side.

Driving here, I was struck, as I often am, by the differences within our hundred miles. The built environment in Michigan is subtly but distinctly different—the street signs are a slightly different green and have a thicker Helvetica font than those in Ontario, the lampposts are more uniform, and the roads are slightly wider. Moreover, there are no signs for "varmint control," nor pristine barns painted that particular shade of brick red in Essex, Lambton, Kent, and Middlesex Counties.

Bro-country music from the ballpark PA fills the stands with images of jacked-up tailgates and the ubiquitous trinity of babes, beer, and trucks. There is a festival atmosphere and people are settling into rituals. I'm grateful for the covered stands so I don't need to worry about sunburn. This is an impressive facility: the seats are comfortable and there are cup holders, like at an MLB park. The stands are filled with parents and other teams in the tournament trying to get a sneak peek at the competition. Most of the women here have "Team Name Mom" shirts. I am an outlier in a black sundress, just here for the baseball. I'm not sure whether I am imagining suspicious glances or not.

By chance, we have chosen to sit in the Wabash section. The Wooster fans and parents are on the other side of the field. The Wooster parents are very loud and engaged. The announcer asks that we all refrain from profanity and derogatory comments and that we provide a supportive environment for players, officials, and fans. He then announces, "As the national anthem was played this morning, it will not be played again." The game simply starts.

The Wooster players, in their brown jerseys, white pants, and brown caps with yellow bills, take the field as this afternoon's home team. Jared Wolfe, the Wabash leadoff hitter, walks to the batter's box, his grey uniform with its red lettering still pristine before the game's opening pitch. As Chandler Dippman, today's starting pitcher but the team's regular third baseman, sets down Wabash in order, I try to absorb the fact that they are called the Little Giants.

I am particularly intrigued by Wooster's team name, "The Fighting Scots." Does "fighting" refer to intra-Scots feuding or a unified Scots front? I wonder if this team is similarly legendary in their tendency to hold multi-generational grudges.

A hit batter and a throwing error put runners on second and third for Wooster in the bottom of the first inning. Both the Wooster bench and their fans are loud and boisterous, confident that they will win this tournament and advance to the Division III World Series. As of today they are ranked fourth in all of NCAA Division III, the only team at this Regional in the top ten. They clearly expect to win and when Dan Harwood, second in Division III in RBIs, singles to score both baserunners, there is a sense of inevitability from the bench and the stands. Loud inevitability. One inning in and it's already 2-0 for Wooster.

Between innings, the announcer tells us to be vigilant to keep our community safe: "If you see something, say something." This statement seems at odds with this pristine, idyllic collegiate park, filled with baseball parents on an early summer afternoon.

With two outs in the second, Wabash manage to cluster together two singles and a double to get on the board. Singles in the second and third score two more runs for Wooster to put them back up 4-1 after three innings.

Meanwhile, after the cluster of hits in the second inning, Dippman has settled in to his rhythm. He's not overpowering—the Shenandoah player with the radar gun tells me he's topping out in the very low 80s—but his control is exceptional and the Wabash hitters can't seem to figure him out, producing weak ground balls and high fly balls for easy outs. As he comes to the mound in the top of the fifth, I move to stand directly behind home plate so I can get a better angle on his motion to home. He begins facing the hitter, his glove over his face, right hand inside as he grips the ball. The batter can only see his eyes as he begins to unfurl his lanky frame at the start of his motion, pivoting towards third in two steps, setting his feet, and delivering the ball to the catcher. To the first batter, Dippman throws a fastball for a called strike, followed by two swinging strikes on a changeup in the dirt and a fastball on the inside corner. K. A similar mix of fastballs, curves, and changeups from a variety of arm angles produces a second strikeout, but this time the catcher can't come up with the ball in the dirt and the hitter reaches first on the wild pitch. But Dippman is able to settle down, get a weak grounder to second and an infield pop-up on a slow curveball to end the inning. The Wabash hitters are guessing and off balance, and still down 4-1 after five innings. I walk back to Heidi and the thinning crowd of Shenandoah players as the Wooster fans applaud the final out.

Part way through an inning, there was a stoppage in play because the third baseman's belt broke and another player ran out to give him his own. The ballgame stops as he rethreads his replacement belt. When he's done, play resumes and the crowd cheers. I add this to the list of things I've never seen before at a baseball game.

The Wooster team has a funny rally cry—sort of like a bird, which doesn't quite make sense to me. If they're the Fighting Scots, it should be a Groundskeeper Willie curse. Or a jovial "Heauch!" On the other hand, what sound would a Little Giant make? I have so many questions. And none of these questions, I note to myself, have anything to do with baseball. I shake myself out of my mascot reverie and remind myself it's the final inning. Wabash still has a chance to start something that will tie it up.

By the time I resume standing behind home plate in the top of the ninth, the score is 4-2, Wabash scoring on a single-steal-single sequence in the sixth. Dippman is still on the mound and I'm back to take some photographs and video to supplement my notes. He opens with a strikeout, but the ball gets away from the catcher, caroming a bit towards the Wabash dugout. The first baseman yells, "Outside! Outside!" as the catcher retrieves the ball, indicating which side of the bag to throw the ball.

As I pull out my iPhone, crouch behind the plate, and position the lens in the center of one of the fence's diamonds, I hear a voice say, "Is he yours?" I turn to see an older man sitting in the front row, directly behind me, one leg folded over the other, fingers interlocked around his left knee. He's wearing a blue windbreaker, his white hair peeking out from beneath his baseball cap.

"Pardon me?"

"That pitcher. Is he your boy?"

I blink, try to process what this man is saying and why he thinks that the Wooster pitcher must be my son. Taking photos, but not with a professional camera, so I must not be covering the games as a photographer. No radar gun or pitch chart, so I must not be a scout. I quickly realize that the next best guess would have to be that I'm family and, as I begrudgingly admit to myself, I am about the right age to be Dippman's father. Groundout to third for the second out.

"No, no. He's not mine. I don't have anyone playing this weekend. We're just here to see some baseball."

He nods, doesn't say anything else. I can tell he's surprised by my answer, but also happy that baseball alone is enough to draw someone to the park on a beautiful spring day in Adrian, Michigan. At least that's what I imagine as I walk back to my seat and the final out of a complete-game win for Chandler Dippman.

Final Score: 4-2 Wooster

Thursday, May 17, 2018

La Roche College Redhawks

vs

Ithaca College Bombers
Nicolay Field, Adrian MI
Game Time Temperature: 77°F

The late afternoon sun is shining on the field, but we're in the shade of the bleachers on the third base side of home plate. A cool breeze blows and I pull on my jacket against the chill as I look out over the park from this new angle. The field, the dugouts, the press box are all immaculate, better than anything we've seen outside of professional baseball, with the exception of the University of Michigan. I see why Adrian are hosting this Regional.

We're in the midst of the La Roche College parents in their red La Roche Baseball jackets and hoodies and caps. They are there en masse, prepared for an afternoon of baseball, coolers of food and drink arrayed around them as they talk about the upcoming game, about La Roche's chances this year. Two years ago, they won this tournament and went on to the Division III College World Series. From the snatches of conversation I catch before the game, the parents seem to think they have a chance to advance again this year.

After spending the last game thinking about mascots, I am trying to focus more on what's happening on the field. My mind, however, keeps coming back to the 1934 Chatham Coloured All-Stars and, in particular, to a photo I scanned from a scrapbook borrowed from a relative of Boomer Harding. It's Boomer on the Bevan Trophy-winning hockey team in the Junior City League. I have long studied the racial barriers in 1930s Ontario, but this photo threw me for a loop. Abstractly knowing he was the only Black player on this team is totally different from actually seeing him stare out of a photograph as the only person of colour on a team of twelve. This was 1932. Tonight, I look around the field and the stands and notice that while there are some

African-American players and parents, the vast majority are white—in approximately the same ratio as Boomer's hockey team photo.

La Roche take the field to begin the game. Tre Thomas takes the mound for his warmup pitches, the bright red of socks worn high to the knee matching the red of his jersey and cap. A right-hander, Thomas is the first African-American player we've seen this weekend. His parents sit in the front row, near the screen, gently encouraging him as he gets ready for the first blue-and-gray clad Ithaca batter.

Ball. Ball. Ball. Swinging strike. Ball. Lead runner on base. But Thomas is able to settle himself down with a pop-up to short followed by two swinging strikeouts. I can already see he has a live arm and that there's a lot of action on his fastball, the sound of it hitting the catcher's mitt like beautiful music that echoes across the park.

The La Roche contingent clap and yell their approval as the teams switch places for the bottom of the inning. On just the second pitch, Jonathan Spina doubles. It's a great chance to score the first run and the La Roche crowd knows it.

"Anyway, anyhow. Get 'em on, get 'em over, get 'em in!"

"Say hey, 4. C'mon, kid"

Joe Professori strides to the plate. A single scores the run. That, or any other hit, is, of course, the ideal outcome. The La Roche parents yell for it, while the Ithaca supporters, scattered throughout the crowd in the bleachers on either side of the field, cross their fingers for a strikeout that will ensure that the runner stays on second base. But as Professori digs his cleats into the right-hand batter's box, I hear the voice of my father as he leans in to me: "Hit it to the right side. Move the runner over. Do your job." It's the baseball I knew growing up. The baseball you hardly ever see any more in the majors, where that kind of contact is anathema to the current focus on power and launch angles. That emphasis makes statistical sense at that level of play, where the potential reward of a home run outweighs the risk of a strikeout or fly ball. At this level, though, no matter what, the player in this situation needs to make sure he moves the runner to put the potential run on third base with less than two outs.

Professori takes the first pitch, never really makes any effort to offer at Jake Binder's fastball, but instead takes its measure, stores up information. On the 0-1 pitch, Professori hits the ball to the right of second base as Spina breaks for third. Out 4-3, but he's done his job. Spina then comes in to score on a ball the shortstop can't handle, the run scoring because Professori was able to move the runner over. Dad would be pleased.

This is a long day of baseball and my gaze shifts to the small, white poodle wandering around our shared row in the stands, looking a little bored. He too is showing his team allegiance by sporting a red La Roche harness and leash set. Both his parents have #redhawknation t-shirts. His mom is wearing a Redhawk visor while his dad has a camouflage hat and a camera with a lens the size of a loaf of marble rye. He looks like a birder, and in some ways, he is: he's observing the La Roche Redhawks in their natural habitat. Like some birders, he has an imitative call that he sounds with regular frequency: "Get 'em on get 'em over get 'em in." The poodle yawns. He's seen this all before. He settles in for a nap, impervious to repeated cries of "Get 'em on get 'em over get 'em in. Get 'em on get 'em over get 'em in."

Aside from a few standard NCAA announcements between innings, there are no promotions, contests, or gimmicks: there is only baseball. That being said, this is not, by any stretch of the imagination, a passive, impartial crowd here for the love of a good game. They're not only here to see their boys win big, but to see the other parents' boys lose. Things seem a little more personal than in other games we've seen.

Leading off the bottom of the second inning, La Roche's Dylan Urban hits a ball to the first baseman. It should be an easy toss to the pitcher for the out, but the first baseman bobbles the ball just enough for Urban to be safe. It's already the third error for Ithaca. A steal by Urban and the third baseman's second error of the game put runners on the corners. Binder manages to induce a double play ball, but the error that put the man on third comes back to haunt Ithaca. 2-0 La Roche after two innings. Everyone in the park knows that it could be far more lopsided already.

In the awkward silence following an Ithaca error, Camouflage Hat Dad shouts down to the La Roche player at bat, "We believe. You gotta believe," pauses and then adds "Get 'em on get 'em over get 'em in."

Although I have no reason to cheer for either of these teams, I find myself sliding toward Ithaca: I admire the parents' unwavering faith in them as the errors accrue. I wonder which parents have the son with two out of the four errors. Having watched MLB almost exclusively until this summer, I had no idea teams could get so many errors. MLB errors were, for me, difficult to spot and mostly seemed like a penalty for a bad break. Some of the errors from the past few weeks have been cringeworthy, but they're also part of the game.

In the top of the third, Austin Hoffman fields the ball deep in the hole, a 2-2 pitch off the bat of Jack Lynch that seems destined to be a hit. Hoffman never gives up on it, though, as he calmly collects the ball, plants himself, and steps into the throw, a rocket to first that barely beats Lynch to the bag. One out and everything seems to be going right for Thomas. He's locating his pitches, keeping the Ithaca hitters off balance, and getting great defense behind him. But then he walks Andrew Wollner on four pitches and Domenic Boresta on five. Suddenly there are runners on first and second with only one out. He manages a first-pitch strike on the next hitter, but his second pitch is too far inside, hitting Jake Generali to load the bases.

The La Roche coach signals to the umpire that he wants to come to the mound. He needs to calm his young sophomore pitcher down. He's lost the strike zone and appears more rattled with every pitch. I think back to Dippman's performance for Wooster in the first game, all the baserunners he allowed and how it never seemed to faze him, never seemed to shake his demeanor. Ten hits against him, but no walks. He was always around the strike zone and never seemed in danger of giving up many runs, never seemed bothered by pitching with men on base. Thomas, on the other hand, pitches like he's unhittable at times, but is clearly prone to losing control of the strike zone and letting that lack of control get inside his head.

The poodle's camouflage-hatted dad has just bought him a bunless hot dog and the poodle rouses himself from his nap, his whole body wriggling with delight and gratitude. The Redhawk's pitcher is throwing mostly balls. Seven in a row and he's just hit a player and the coach makes a visit to the mound.

The coach walks back to the dugout as the La Roche fans murmur their encouragement. "Settle down, kid. You got this." A sacrifice fly to left field scores the run. Midway through the third, it's 2-1 La Roche. The game is far closer than it should be.

It's the bottom of the third and the catcher, Shane Roebuck, is at bat. "That's ball four. Take your base, Shane." Despite it being the eighth pitch of the at-bat, he has to be reminded that it's a walk.

The guy I've mentally started calling La Roche Dad turns to his friend, says, "He's taking math next semester." He's a stout man, wears a La Roche hoodie, a Tilley hat perched on top of his shaved head framing the goatee that frames his face. I don't know if it's his son, the son of his friend, or someone else's. It doesn't seem to matter. They all laugh, not out of meanness, mind you, but out of what seems like a genuine affection that comes from spending so much time together watching their sons play ball.

After a fielder's choice from the first baseman to the shortstop erases Roebuck, Jay Novak singles, putting himself on first base and Hoffman on second. A wild pitch moves the runners up to second and third with two outs. The La Roche crowd sense that this is their chance to take command of the game again.

"Come on, 2-8."

Johnathan Melendez singles to score both runners. La Roche has four runs on only three hits and lead 4-1 after three innings.

As was the case with the first game, today it's again assumed that we have a boy in the line-up and I can tell we're getting scoped out to see which player is our son. Dale stands to take a picture of the pitcher and the man beside us says, "That your kid?" That we have no child on the field surprises people. "You're here just to watch baseball?" "Yes, sir." Silence. I sense this answer raises more questions as I can tell we're still getting scoped out. People seem suspicious that we'd just drive here to watch baseball. I find it unusual that this is so unusual.

Thomas is back out for the top of the seventh inning. He's only given up three hits and has six strikeouts, but there have been times when his command of the strike zone has disappeared. Like the third, when Ithaca scored a run without getting a hit. Or the sixth, when he gave up a rare single and then hit a batter to put two men on base. Unlike the third, he was able to settle himself, shake off the nerves so he could locate his fastball away to the left-handed hitter, inducing a weak fly ball to left field for the final out.

Wollner, the first hitter of the seventh, swings at strike three, a ball in the dirt from Thomas that Roebuck isn't able to catch cleanly. He quickly picks up the ball, but Wollner eludes the tag as he leaves the box. Roebuck takes two shuffle steps to his left to create the right angle for the throw and fires to Melendez at first base for the out. Textbook fundamentals. The kind of play you'd want to show to a young catcher.

Dale leans over and kisses my cheek. "Thank you," he says. "For what?" "Doing this project with me." I shrug as if it's no big deal. "It's kind of like a dream come true," he continues, "watching all this baseball." While I'd like to be home right now, I tell myself there will be other summers to garden and read books on my porch while being serenaded by cicadas. This is a summer of baseball.

Now that the Redhawks are more firmly in the lead, the La Roche parents have quietened down. I have put aside my notebook to let the pleasantness of the late afternoon wash over me. I am neither hot or cold, not afraid of frostbite or sunburn. This isn't the most interesting game I've seen but it's certainly not the least. I simply am here, on a summer afternoon in May, watching a baseball game with the person I love most in the world, who is loving this summer more than any other. He is concentrating on the pitching. I pat his hand and give it a squeeze. He smiles and resumes watching the end of the game.

After a bunt single and a walk, the coach watches Thomas throw one more ball before he's pulled from the game with runners on second and third and two outs. He's only surrendered one run, as long as Jake Seymour can get the last out of the inning. It doesn't look good when Seymour walks the bases loaded, but Sam Little hits a chopper back to the mound, a ball Seymour himself takes to first for the final out.

Seymour strands a pair of baserunners in the eighth, and Shane Emrich comes in to get the save in the ninth. The La Roche parents applaud the effort, gather their coolers, make plans for dinner. Tomorrow their sons will play the sons of either the Adrian or the Otterbein parents.

Final Score: 5-1 La Roche

Thursday, May 17, 2018

We leave the athletic complex for the break between games, a brief respite from the baseball bubble in which we've immersed ourselves. We heed the outfield advertising and drive the short distance from campus to Jimmy John's. I recognize a few people from the tournament—mainly parents from Ithaca and La Roche—others in search of food that isn't popcorn or hot dogs. I wonder if they're still thinking about baseball, if the distance of their bodies from the ballpark has meant a distance for their minds from the game.

As I eat my sub in this brightly lit restaurant in a strip mall in Adrian, Michigan, part of me is still sitting behind home, simultaneously on both the first and third sides of the plate. It's like I'm seeing the two games laid over one another. Dippman's control in my left eye. Thomas' velocity and movement in my right. The loud confidence of the Wooster contingent in my left ear. The steadying encouragement of the La Roche parents in my right. Neither game was really that close—it felt like a foregone conclusion fairly early on in both games, with Wooster and La Roche clearly the better teams—but it was oddly mesmerizing to watch that inevitability. The two games echo through my mind even as we walk back to the car and the Adrian-Otterbein game that will cap off our day, adding another layer of pitching, of defense, of fundamentals. Another layer of parents. Another layer of baseball.

Thursday, May 17, 2018

Adrian College Bulldogs
vs
Otterbein University Cardinals

Nicolay Field, Adrian MI
Game Time Temperature: 70°F

Back at Nicolay Field, we climb the steps to the bleachers along the first base line, but the stands are jammed with Adrian fans. It's a sea of brown and gold, and there are no seats to be had. We retreat, head to the third base side, and are barely able to find a place amongst the Otterbein supporters. It's Friday night, Adrian's first game of the tournament, and the atmosphere feels charged in a way that is completely different from the two games we saw this afternoon. Officially, however, Otterbein is the home team tonight. As the crowd settles in, the Cardinals catcher throws to second base, signalling the last of Stevie Yuran's warmup throws, as Zack Zschering strides towards home to lead off for the Bulldogs. The game is about to begin.

Dale and I got married after a whirlwind few weeks. It seemed like a good idea at the time and time has proved us right. When we first met, I could never have imagined that one day I would be sitting next to him in rural Michigan for my third baseball game in under twelve hours. I cannot think of a single instance where he has guided me poorly; it has always made sense to follow him. And so here I am, watching the fifth and sixth teams of the day.

In its first half-inning, this game seems faster, more precise than the other two. The local Adrian team are playing so the stands are filled with a wider array of fans. The locals are here supporting their team but

there are also a lot of Otterbein parents and families. There are people in lawn chairs alongside the edges of the field and others on blankets on a hill past centerfield. Two and a half innings into this game,
it's apparent that these two teams are more closely matched than the
others we've seen today. Between batters, the Bulldogs snap the ball
between bases. I am developing a great affection for the "Snap! Snap!"
sound of a ball hitting a glove, something I could never hear through
the din at Comerica Park.

It's the bottom of the third and Tommy Parsons, the right-handed
starter for Adrian, is throwing smoke, mixing in just enough curveballs and changeups to keep Otterbein off balance. He's working with
a one-run lead courtesy of a couple of singles and a wild pitch in the
top of the second inning. Like Yuran, Parsons pitches quickly, taking
little time between receiving the ball from the catcher and going into
his motion. Behind Parsons, the fielders are always on the balls of
their feet, a choreography of bodies arrayed across the diamond in
their grey road uniforms and black caps, socks all worn high like a
team out of the past.

After striking out Pat Birrer, Otterbein's designated hitter, on a
low fastball, Parsons gathers the ball from his catcher, Frank Resto.
Parsons slides his right foot against the edge of the first base side of
the pitching rubber and brings his hands to his chest, ready for the
next hitter.

Mitch Stotler steps into the left-hand batter's box, takes a couple
of quick cuts, and readies himself for the pitch from Parsons. Fastball right down the heart of the plate that seems to freeze Stotler,
the slap of the ball into the catcher's mitt reverberating in the still
of the evening. The next pitch is fouled down the right field line, but
since there is almost no foul ground in the outfield, Tristin Richardson has no play. Fastball up around Stotler's shoulders. Breaking
ball in the dirt. On the 2-2 pitch, Stotler takes a good fastball that's
just above the strike zone. Good eye. 3-2 and Stotler is able to foul
off a changeup. Foul tip on a 3-2 fastball, but Resto can't hang on.
Finally, on the eighth pitch of the at-bat, Stotler hits a short pop-up
to the third baseman. No hit in the end, but still a good at-bat for
Stotler, the number nine hitter, as he was able to take close pitches

and foul off a couple of two-strike pitches to stay alive. In the end, though, the pitch selection—both type and location—made it difficult for him to do more that extend the at-bat. Parsons is pitching well.

By the time Otterbein comes to bat again in the bottom of the fourth, Parsons and the Bulldogs have a 3-0 lead after scoring two runs with two outs in the top of the inning. Around us, the Otterbein parents seem slightly worried. A man with a shaved head, wearing an Otterbein University hoodie sits in the front row of our section, looking increasingly unhappy as the game unfolds. To our right, one of the fathers cups his hands around his mouth and yells, "Come on, Cards. Get the bats out!" The tentative cheers and clapping pick up as the first two Otterbein hitters single off Parsons, bringing Justin Feltner to the plate with no one out.

In this situation, especially with the way Parsons has been pitching, I have no doubt that the Otterbein coach will have Feltner try to bunt the runners over. As Parsons goes into his motion, Feltner squares around, pulls his top hand up slightly on the handle, and attempts to cushion the ball with the barrel of the bat. It's a good bunt, down the third base line, far enough in front of the bag that the third baseman has only a play at first base. Dugan Darnell charges the ball, but can't field it cleanly. E5. Everyone is safe.

With the bases loaded and no one out, Parsons goes back to pitching out of the windup as Tim Snyder comes to the plate. Adrian will concede the run for a double play ball, but a strikeout would be even better. Every player on the Adrian bench stands on the lip of their dugout, as they have been all game. Behind us, one of the Otterbein parents yells, "Trade places with him. Come on!" The tension is starting to build, as a hit will put Otterbein back within a run.

On the 0-1 from Parsons, Snyder goes the other way, a shallow pop-up to right field. On contact, Richardson breaks to where he thinks the ball will land, calculating its trajectory as he has on countless fly balls since he first put on a glove. But this time the distance is further than Richardson can cover, even with a dive at full extension. The ball glances off the tip of his glove, scoring two runs for Otterbein. Parsons is able to pitch around a couple of other baserunners, but the damage is done and the inning ends with the score 3-2 Adrian. It's a whole new ballgame.

After marvelling at an Otterbein outfielder's impressive catch, I see tonight's game is more complex than others we've gone to these past few weeks. Batters are bunting. Pitchers are making batters swing. The fielders are attempting and making gutsier plays. I think this leads to more interesting baseball because, when the players are more skilled, they can make more things happen within the narrative of game.

It's been a long day of baseball and I get up out of my seat and go for a little walk around the park. I'm standing by the edge of the stands, watching people watch baseball. There's a slightly chilled breeze. Unlike me, most of the parents have an array of collegiate attire with them to account for all the possible temperatures. I pull on my jean jacket, with its Jane Austen pins, over my sundress. The sun is almost set, painting the sky aquamarine with swaths of grey, fuchsia, and violet. Standing by myself, I am struck at the loveliness of it all. Hundreds of people watching the same thing, but watching it differently. In these days of on-demand, streaming video, watching something happen live in a crowd strikes me as a rare and special thing. No one knows what will happen next. We are all witnessing the events unfold together. I have no idea who is going to win—there are no pages to flip through to the end or fast-forwards or Google spoilers—or even announcers to tell us what we're seeing. Baseball takes its time to reveal itself and it is not a game for the impatient. Baseball is a game that takes as much time as it needs. As much as I've felt like an outlier at this tournament, moments like this remind me that while we all might be here for different reasons, we're all here because of baseball.

As Parsons takes the hill again for the bottom of the fifth, there's a cold wind blowing through the park, reminding me that it's still May in Michigan. Day games might be beautiful, but the nights can still carry a bite. I'd like to put on my hoodie, but it's in the car and I don't want to miss anything.

The inning opens with an infield single, putting Parsons into the stretch with Tyler Thompson on first base. Thompson takes a big lead, dancing off the bag, forcing Parsons to throw over several times, even as he strikes out the next hitter. It's clear that the runner on first is bothering Parsons. When Luke Barber, the cleanup hitter, takes the first pitch he sees over the Meijer sign in left, I wonder how much the distraction at first affected Parson's ability to locate his pitch.

After a pop fly for the second out, Parsons walks Feltner and Snyder. When Birrer hits an easy ground ball to the third baseman, Parsons appears to be out of the inning only one run down. Darnell sets himself, his body low to the ground to prevent a bad hop, looks the ball into his glove, and throws it past the outstretched glove of the first baseman, allowing the third run of the inning to score. E5. A ground ball to second ends the inning, but Adrian now find themselves down 5-3. I doubt Parsons is much longer for this game.

I think back to the beginning of this project, when, soggy and cold, I worried what I'd gotten myself into. I smile to myself, remembering one of the first conversations I ever had with Dale where he talked about his trip to Chicago. I mentioned the paintings I'd like to see at the Art Institute of Chicago, and he told me about going to a Cubs game. I asked, "Is that the park with all the ivy on the walls?" We've since been to the Art Institute and to Wrigley Field numerous times, each of us embracing the world of the other. And now I'm in Adrian, Michigan watching my third baseball game of the day with him.

Standing at the edge of the grandstand, I witness a home run and it's now 5-3 for Otterbein. It's still anyone's game. I make a mental list of all the scenarios that could happen and realize that my guesses are as good as anyone else's. If I ignore the cell phones in people's hands, if I ignore the lights in the field, the fancy scoreboard, tonight could be any day in the past hundred years. There's something about the way this game transcends time.

Standing alone, surveying the field, watching the game unfold, the sun has nearly set. I think, "I like this." This revelation is comforting. Over the past year or two, I've been loath to wonder aloud if I still like baseball. Tonight I've realized I don't just like a team or a player, the ballpark, or the experience of watching baseball. I like the game. I return to my seat and smile at Dale. He smiles back between pitches.

Top of the eighth and Colin Hoffmann, the fourth pitcher of the evening, comes on for Otterbein, the 5-3 lead still intact. He'll face the eight, nine, and one hitters—Resto, Torrento, and Zschering. It looks like a sure out when Resto hits a short fly to the second baseman, but Stotler loses the ball in the lights. By the time he's able to locate it, the ball is dropping to his right and Resto is standing on first base. The Otterbein parents are in disbelief, livid at this mistake by Stotler. From the intensity and volume of the comments, it's clear that his parents must not be sitting near us. At least I hope they're not.

Aaron Ajrouche comes on to pinch run and, like Thompson in the bottom of the fifth, takes an aggressive lead, daring Hoffmann to throw over. After a couple of tosses to first, Hoffmann finally comes to the plate, but he's so concerned with Ajrouche stealing second that he fails to pause before the pitch. Balk. Ajrouche to second and then to third on a flyout to right field. Zschering's single scores the run and it's 5-4 Otterbein. The error has cost them, making Stotler the most unpopular person in the park, at least among the Otterbein supporters.

When Gunner Rainey, the Adrian left fielder, flies out to center field, there are two outs and a man on first. Hoffmann can still get out of the inning with the lead going into the ninth inning. But most of the Otterbein parents don't see it that way, muttering still about the "stupid play" that opened the inning. From one of the dads, a curly-haired man sitting directly behind us, I hear, "Come on, Colin. Settle it down." He clearly knows baseball, has been encouraging the players throughout the game, making smart comments, joking with the other dads, but he never once said anything about Stotler's error. Unlike the other parents, he seems to realize that errors are part of the game. His calm tone seems to rouse the rest of the crowd from their murmurings and pull them into the moment.

Zschering takes his lead. Every time Hoffmann throws over to first, the entire Bulldogs bench yell "Back!" in unison, a chorus accompanying the action on the field. Every one of them is poised on the edge of the dugout, hanging on every action on the field. When Zschering steals second, the bench roars. The tying run is in scoring position.

That brings Brady Wood to the plate. Hoffmann's first two pitches are called strikes. One more and he's out of the inning with the lead. Ball. On the 1-2 pitch, Wood pulls the ball to left field, a flare double that slices away from the left fielder. Zschering scores and the bench erupts, barely able to keep themselves from spilling out of the dugout. The game is tied, but Adrian still have a runner on second and a chance to take the lead.

When Hunter Hayes singles to left, Wood charges around third and stomps on the plate before chest-bumping the bat boy who has come to retrieve Hayes' bat. The bench empties to meet him as he runs back towards the dugout. Above this scene, in the first base stands, the Adrian fans are ecstatic, hollering and cheering for the go-ahead run. Around me, the Otterbein parents sit in stunned silence. 6-5 Adrian going into the bottom of the eighth inning.

This game is quickly turning into one I imagine I will list among my favourites of this summer as it exemplifies what's good about the game of baseball. I don't want to fall into that nostalgic reverie about the purity of the sport, but tonight's game—and all the games today—have been about the game and not about "the ballpark experience." I notice that every single time the ball leaves either pitcher's hand, the crowd goes instantly silent. People are here to watch baseball. True, they're here to watch their sons, brothers, grandsons, and boyfriends play baseball—but they're all watching the game.

Tonight I tried to focus my attention on what *doesn't* happen in a game as much as what does happen. Someone doesn't get on base. Someone doesn't catch a ball. Someone doesn't make a double play. Maybe learning to see baseball anew is learning to notice all the small, remarkable things that happen—or don't happen—every second of the game.

I'm surprised that Parsons is still pitching for Adrian in the eighth, but as I watch him dust Birrer with three pitches—a foul ball and two swinging strikes—I realize that he is still throwing serious heat. Over years of watching MLB, I've become accustomed to seeing the pitch count on the scoreboard, but there's nothing like that here. Still, it feels as if he's thrown a significant number of pitches.

After a groundout to second, Ben Beachy hits the ball to left field, held to a single by Rainey's leaping grab of a very high hop off the lively turf. If he doesn't make that play, Beachy has at least a double, if not a triple, the tying run in scoring position. But that play negates part of the threat, gives Parsons a better chance to get out of the inning. Beachy takes his lead, but he's leaning too far. Parsons throws the ball to Hayes, whose sweep tag brushes Beachy's hand before he can touch the bag. The Bulldog bench erupt as Parsons bounces off the mound, pumping his fist several times as he leaves the field with his 6-5 lead intact.

Adrian score five more runs in the top of the ninth, the Bulldog players loud and boisterous for every walk, bunt, hit batsman, balk, error, and hit. By the time Otterbein comes up in the bottom of the inning, all tension has leaked from the park, replaced by elation or depression, depending which set of fans or players you're observing.

As I'm turning over the events of the game in my mind, I notice that Parsons is back out on the hill. Otterbein used seven pitchers and Parsons is still out there. As Tyler Thompson walks to the plate, the curly-haired Otterbein father behind me yells, "Come on, T-Square!," desperate encouragement that feels more defeated than hopeful. It's a good at-bat, a nine-pitch battle, but it ends in a ground ball to the second baseman. It takes Parsons only three more pitches to get the final two outs.[1]

As we gather our notebooks, I listen to the Otterbein parents still grousing about the play in the eighth, the ball that Stotler lost in the lights. The curly-haired man can't seem to speak—he seems crushed by the weight of the loss. His wife, on the other hand, can't stop talking about how it was Stotler's fault they lost. True, they did look to be in control until that point, but even with the run, Otterbein was still up by one. It wasn't the decisive moment of the game and his teammates needed to pick him up. Stotler didn't give up Wood's double or Hayes' single to lose the lead. He didn't single-handedly surrender five runs in the ninth. He wasn't the reason Otterbein weren't able to score a run in either of the last two innings. He's just the scapegoat, a convenient target for a game gone wrong.

Final Score: 11-5 Adrian

Friday, May 18, 2018

The final out of last night's game was at 11:05. By the time we got to our hotel it was nearly midnight. As we were checking in, we ran into parents from Otterbein still reeling from the loss, pointing to an error that started the "wheels falling off." They seemed upset, heartbroken, angry. We were all tired. And I was hungry. The desk clerk told us the only food options were packaged sandwiches from the nearby gas station or the 24-hour McDonald's down the road. Filet-O-Fish it would have to be. Eating well on this journey is proving difficult.

At the hotel, the curly-haired man recognized us, asked who our team was, and, by extension, where our son goes to school. I told him we were just there to watch baseball. "And you don't have kids who play?" I said no, describing instead a bit about going to see games within a hundred miles of Windsor.

"How many games?"

"We're trying for fifty."

"And you're not following any particular team?"

"No, just watching baseball."

"That sounds like a great summer."

"It is. It really is."

He began to smile, clearly intrigued by the idea of baseball that wasn't also tied to obligation.

This morning we make our way down to the breakfast area. It's already filled with people in a variety of team colours. Ithaca. Marietta. Wabash. Otterbein. The curly-haired man greets me as we pour our first coffees of the day.

"How about that pitcher for Adrian last night?"

He seems to have moved past the loss, eager instead to talk baseball, to compare notes on what we both saw.

"Amazing," I reply.

"After he gave up that home run in the bottom of the fifth, he just stared into our dugout. I wasn't sure if he was angry at himself or angry at Luke, but I thought he was done."

"Agreed. I can't believe he was still out there for the ninth."

A man in an Ithaca shirt, coffee already in hand, interjects, "How many pitches do you think he threw?"

"Had to have been at least 140."

I nod agreement, add, "I'd love to find out."

"Me too. That was gutsy pitching—too bad it was against us. Sometimes you just have to tip your cap and move on." He tilts his head towards the man in the Ithaca shirt. "I guess we've got you at noon today."

"That you do."

We all share a smile and wish each other good luck, echoes of last night's game still lingering, the promise of another day of baseball on the horizon.

Heidi and I take our plates to an empty table, sit down to eat, and begin talking about yesterday's games. Next to us, an older man, white haired and wearing a Wooster vest, asks if our son plays for Shenandoah. "No," we reply, telling him about the one hundred miles, the fifty games. How we're trying to figure something out about baseball by immersing ourselves in it for the summer. He's excited about the project, tells his daughter about what we're doing when she sits down to eat.

What I don't tell him, because I'm just beginning to understand it myself, is that I'm learning to watch the game again and, in the process, falling back in love with baseball. I don't think that would be happening if I were still tied to one team, or even one kind of baseball.

This morning, again, it was assumed we belonged to a team and people were surprised we were here just to watch the games. Some, not a lot, seemed interested in this book project. A man at breakfast said, "I assumed you were with Shenandoah." As we walked to our car, I said to Dale, "You know Shenandoah is in Virginia, right? We were just "Y'all from Virginia'-ed." When we moved to North Carolina for work, we couldn't figure out why people kept asking if we were from Virginia. Someone gently told us that this meant, "You're not from here, are you?" Eventually I realized what they were saying was, "You're outsiders." Maybe I should replace my sundress with a Team Name Mom t-shirt to avoid suspicion.

Friday, May 18, 2018

Marietta College Pioneers
vs
Wabash College Little Giants

Nicolay Field, Adrian MI
Game Time Temperature: 63°F

Though it's sunny and bright, the wind is cold as we make our way back into Nicolay Field for Wabash versus Marietta, the first of our two games today. Both are elimination games.

Wabash, in their grey, red-trimmed uniforms, take the field for the first inning. Cody Cochran, a right-handed senior, is on the hill this morning for the Little Giants. He begins his motion facing third, hands at his belt, knees slightly bent. When he comes to the plate, it's straight over the top with little wasted motion, just a quick stride towards home. Simple but effective as he strikes out three Marietta hitters in the first two innings. He's not fast like La Roche's Thomas or Adrian's Parsons. He's more like Dippman from Wooster, but with more offspeed stuff, fooling the hitters rather than over-powering them. Jim Price, the radio colour commentator for the Tigers, would almost certainly say that Cochran is using his whole arsenal and understands the art of pitching.

This game is our fourth in twenty-four hours, an island of base-ball I'm glad to inhabit. You'd think it would be hard to readjust to yet another new game, but by the time Cochran walks off the field at the end of the second, I've settled back in. It takes a couple of innings to get the feel of each game, to find the rhythm, but then everything except what's on the field melts away.

It's a weekday and I'm checking and responding to email every few minutes. There's something wrong with the online registration site for the conference I'm organizing. The caterers need to know whether we want muffins or fruit trays. Both? Do we need vegan muf-fins? Dale has given up asking, "Did you see that?" I'm not watching baseball well. I worry I'm not making decisions about refreshments well either.

Every time I focus on the game, I catch myself wondering what time it is back home. Though only a hundred miles away, Adrian seems different enough from Windsor that I feel like I must be in a different time zone, which, of course, we are not. The boulevards are wide and the downtown seems thriving with small shops and businesses. The houses are almost all are made of wood, not brick, and have the stateliness of a bygone era that never expanded into Ontario. As we drove through town last night, I noted the presence of a well-stocked toy shop and busy little diners amidst the roadside signs advertising firewood, gun sales, and animal traps. My mind is everywhere but on the field. I feel like I'm doing nothing well. Official workday hours will be over soon. I'm hopeful my phone will stop pinging with queries about muffins.

By the top of the fifth, there's still no score thanks both to good pitching and some great fielding, most notably Eric Chavez's running scoop, complete spin, and perfect throw to first to get the third out for Wabash in the third inning. As Cochran retires the side on two fly balls to left field and a pop to the catcher, I realize that he's been using his curve and changeup to set up his fastball. He's pitching backwards. I've seen it pointed out on television, understood the concept, but never before have I been able to identify it on my own. Sitting so close to home plate, watching so many games so intently—especially all of these games at the same level in such a short span of time—is changing the way I watch pitching, allowing me to pick up on nuances that were previously lost on me.

The crowd is fairly sparse but lively, it's mostly families in the stands. There's an allegiance to your school, or your child's school that I don't often see in Canada. Your alma mater seems to be a larger part of your identity in the United States than in Canada. I Google Marietta College and learn that it's one of America's thirty-seven "Revolutionary Colleges," institutions with origins reaching back to the eighteenth century. Established as an academy in 1797, and founded as a college in 1835, Marietta has an enrollment of just over 1,200 students and fields twenty-two varsity teams. Schools of this age are very rare in

Canada, and none that are as old or as big have twenty-two varsity teams. I also pause to reflect on the fact that Jane Austen was working on her first drafts of *Pride and Prejudice* when Marietta College was first formed.

Scott Oberhelman gives up a double to Sean Roginski to open the bottom of the fifth. Marietta's coach doesn't hesitate in walking to the mound to replace his starter. Oberhelman has been pitching around baserunners all game, but I'm still a bit surprised he's so quick with the hook. Dalton Wiggins comes in to pitch, but he keeps falling behind in the count. When he does begin to throw strikes, the ball finds the heart of the strike zone and Wabash pounds the ball for five hits and four runs. 4-0 Wabash after five innings.

Dale has just pointed out to me that the Wabash pitcher is "throwing backwards," something I've never heard of before and would not have noticed on my own. I envy Dale's ability to focus and see the game in ways I cannot. When 4:30 rolls around, I feel I can be excused from not answering email. I toss my phone in my bag, zip it up, and, for good measure, put it a few feet down the row.

Marietta is getting something going with the help of a few fielding errors, overthrows, and the like. The Pioneers bench and their fans are waking up. From this seat and this angle, I can really see the pitches and I can tell that this is where the real game is happening. Typically, it seems that people watch pitching in terms of what the batter does. But I realized today that you can also watch baseball by looking at what the pitcher does to the batter.

Cochran is back out to pitch the eighth inning for Wabash with a 4-0 lead. Trent Castle leads off the inning for Marietta with a single, which brings up the catcher, Brady Cottom. Two curves miss the strike zone to make the count to 2-0, prompting the Wabash coach to signal that he wants to visit the mound to talk to his starter. Cochran comes back to run the count to 3-2, but Cottom hits a shallow pop-up to right field that eludes both the outfielder and the second baseman. Runners at first and second with no outs. When the count goes to 3 balls and no strikes on the pinch hitter, Shane Fetsko, noise begins to swell from the Marietta dugout. But Cochran is able to come back, locating enough pitches to get Fetsko swinging on a fastball just outside the strike zone. After a flyout, Cochran walks Chris Petrucci and is done for the afternoon, up 4-0, but responsible for all three baserunners.

I turn to the man sitting next to me, his Wabash Baseball hat worn low over his eyes. "He stopped being able to throw his curve for strikes," I say.

"Yeah, once that happens, he's done. Been that way since he was a freshman. If he can't throw the curve, his fastball isn't worth a damn."

When Moffett sprints out in the eighth to try to close for Wabash, I smile at his little hop over the baseline on his way to the mound. Moffett is full of rituals. He balances his feet behind the pitching rubber. Takes a deep breath. Touches his hat. Steps past the rubber. His glove hand quivers. He assumes his stance. Winds up. Throws. Repeats. I never would have seen these if I hadn't put my phone away.

Final Score: 4-2 Wabash

Friday, May 18, 2018

Otterbein University Cardinals
vs
Ithaca College Bombers

Nicolay Field, Adrian MI
Game Time Temperature: 68°F

As the Wabash and Marietta teams make their way from the field, they are quickly replaced by Ithaca and Otterbein players. Bats and helmets are lined up in the dugouts, ready for the coming game. Players stretch along the baselines, play catch in the outfield. Each team takes infield practice. Coaches meet with the home plate umpire to exchange lineup cards. As Emmett Dunn takes to the mound for his warmup pitches, the Ithaca infielders take ground balls from the first baseman while the outfielders toss the ball lazily between them. I wave to the curly-haired dad from Otterbein, who's sitting to our right, even with first base. It's warm and sunny, but I feel like I'm in a fog of baseball I don't want to leave.

This is the fifth game we've been to in twenty-four hours. I'm a little tired—but I'm settling in. I summon Davenport Mom and tell myself, "You've got this kiddo! You got it." A lady just came to talk with us about our project. The man at breakfast told her about it and she was interested in learning more. Her son plays for Otterbein, but he's likely not playing today. "The seniors are a special group," she says, almost wistfully, "This is their game." Listening to her talk, I'm reminded that collegiate teams have players who have been together for four years and who have made deep commitments to the team and each other. Unlike MLB or minor league ball, they can play knowing that none of them will get traded. These relationships are visible and obvious when you see the players in the dugouts or during warm ups. I contrast these players with the Mud Hens who seem, when I'm having a cynical moment, more like a group of independent contractors wearing the same uniform.

Otterbein scores two in the first and another in the second before Dunn is lifted for a relief pitcher. He is the picture of disappointment as he walks slowly to the bench, head hung low, eyes to the ground. More players from the College of Wooster filter in to seats behind us as Tyler Hill throws his last warmup pitches.

In the bottom of the second, Ithaca score two to bring themselves within a run. I turn to a couple of the Wooster players sitting behind us and ask them about sliding on the turf infield.

"Is there any give?"

"It's softer than dirt."

"Yeah, and you slide further. We have the same infield at home, but our grass is real."

Though I've seen this kind of infield in several parks now, it still seems like an oddity to me, so different from what we played on as kids or what I've watched for most of my life. But I haven't seen a bad hop all weekend, the balls caroming predictably off the ground and into fielder's gloves. And the turf burn I imagined you'd get from sliding into second or home is not what the players describe at all. Different than what I've known, but in the end perhaps better, especially when you're trying to play baseball in spring in Michigan.

Ithaca scores again in the bottom of the third and the game is tied at 3. A double play on a scalded liner to the third baseman gets Ithaca out of a jam in the top of the fourth. A ground ball to the Otterbein third baseman ends the Ithaca threat in the bottom of the fifth. A fly ball to left field with runners on the corners helps Otterbein navigate out of the danger in the bottom of the sixth. Still tied after six.

In the bottom of the sixth, I chat with a lady outside the restrooms who saw me writing notes all tournament. She asks who our team is and I tell her why we're here. Intrigued, she tells her friend about the project and the friend says, "There's baseball in Canada?" She gives it some thought and adds, "I thought you all just played lacrosse." We talk about where we're from and the friend says, "Wait. Canada is less than a hundred miles from here?" I'm not sure if she's more surprised or scared. I walk back to my seat and imagine making a bumper sticker that says, "Canada: We're closer than you think. Sorry about that." Then the announcer says "cahn-fidence" and "lap tap computers." Canada seems far away again.

The Wooster players are talking about last night, about Parsons' complete game. I overhear one of them say that he threw 146 pitches.

"Really? Shit, that's a lot of pitches."

"I wonder what he had left by the end."

I turn, say, "His fastball had as much jump in the ninth as it did in the first. It was something to see."

The player who's charting pitches looks up from his work, adds, "Well, I can't imagine that he pitches again this weekend."

Meanwhile, in the top of the seventh, Tyler Thompson and Luke Barber single to put runners on first and third. As Connor Brett strides in to hit, the Otterbein crowd bellow nervous encouragement, hands clasped near their faces as if in prayer for the go-ahead run. They know it's win or go home.

Brett runs the count to 2-2. Hill checks the runners and begins his delivery, a fastball that Brett lifts into center field. Matt Carey, the center fielder, settles himself under the ball's descent, ready to launch it towards home. As soon as the ball hits Carey's glove, Thompson breaks from third. From my right I hear the curly-haired father yell again, "Come on, T-Square!" Everyone else seems to draw a collective breath, unable to exhale as both Thompson and Carey's throw move inexorably towards home plate and Wollner, the waiting catcher. The throw arrives on one hop just as Thompson is about to cross home. It's a good slide, but Wollner angles his body in front of the plate and tags Thompson to prevent the run. A murmuring groan sounds from the Otterbein parents, air leaking from their shared hope. Record it as an 8-2 double play to end the inning and preserve the 3-3 tie.

I miss a vital play because I'm eavesdropping on a conversation between visiting team families. One of the moms recounts how she asked a hotel clerk what there is do here in this town other than watch baseball: "He said, 'Well, you can go to Cabela's and watch the fish in the aquarium.'" All the parents laugh. Another mom laments the lack of high-end outlet shopping. There's a pause in play and Journey's "Don't Stop Believin'" echoes across the park just long enough for Dale and me to belt out "South Detroit." I'd like to be on my porch now. This is a lot of baseball.

It's still 3-3 after seven, eight, nine, ten innings. This is by far the most evenly matched game of the tournament. Both teams have had multiple chances to score in the seven innings since Ithaca tied the score in the bottom of the third, but timely pitching and good defense have stopped every threat. It's compelling baseball, but as I look around at the Otterbein and Ithaca contingents, I wonder if they're able to enjoy it, able to appreciate the quality of the game and the drama unfolding in front of them. A few of the parents can barely watch, the tension too much for them. Win or go home. I'm glad I'm just here to watch baseball.

The rain that's been lightly misting for a couple of innings picks up as Ithaca take the field for the top of the eleventh. Stotler leads off with a triple and, as I glance over at the cheering Otterbein parents, I wonder if the triple cancels out yesterday's error. Has he redeemed himself in the eyes of the curly-haired man's wife? I suspect it will depend on whether or not he scores.

Jack Morello, pitching his fourth inning for Ithaca, walks to the back of the mound and readies himself to face Ben Beachy, the Otterbein shortstop. As Morello throws his first pitch, he slips on the brown artificial surface, falling on his chest. Ball one, but not the run-scoring wild pitch it could have been. The turf is slick and it's clear that gaining purchase isn't easy right now. There's little the grounds crew can do either—since it's not dirt, Quick Dry won't help. Morello can only ask for time, run to the dugout, and change into a pair of shoes that will give him better traction.

It's starting to rain. The potential winning run is on third with no outs. It's slippery on the field and the pitcher just wiped out on the mound. They stop the game while he changes his cleats.

After this short delay, Morello checks on Stotler at third, then delivers the 1-0 pitch. Beachy gets enough of the bat on the ball to lift it just over the shortstop's head and into left field for a bloop single. Stotler scores. The Otterbein fans roar their approval. Has he now done enough for them to forget last night?

Morello tries to collect himself as Thompson walks towards the batter's box. He didn't throw a bad pitch to Beachy, but, because of its timing, its kairos, the bloop has the same effect as a hard line single. He has to put it out of his mind, focus on the next batter, make sure Otterbein doesn't score another run. Even before I actually hear it, "Come on, T-Square" echoes in my head. The curly-haired man and the rest of the Otterbein parents know how important another run would be. Thompson needs to move the runner over to second base.

Thompson squares to bunt as Morello goes into his motion, but isn't able to lay the bunt down the third base line. He doesn't get on top of the ball, but pops it instead into foul ground, just past the outstretched glove of the Ithaca third baseman. Another chance.

Morello sets, checks Beachy's lead at first, throws home. This time Thompson gets on top of the ball, pushing it down, but he's not able to deaden it enough or direct it down one of the foul lines. Instead, the ball turns into a soft grounder to Morello, who realizes he has time to go to second to force out the lead runner. The shortstop takes the throw from Morello, steps on the bag, and fires to first, just in time for the out. Double play. Instead of a runner on second with one out, the bases are now empty with two outs. A pop-up to the third baseman ends the inning. The crowd sings along as "Sweet Caroline" plays over the PA during the inning break. Otterbein are up 4-3.

Ithaca are down to their final strike when Carey hits a two-out single to score Webb Little in the bottom of the eleventh. I can't help but imagine what might have been if Thompson had been able to lay down that bunt. What is the curly-haired dad thinking right now? What are the Otterbein parents saying to each other? A ground-out to second means the game is still tied as we head to the twelfth, though you wouldn't know it from the defeated body language of some of the Otterbein fans.

Top of the twelfth and Morello is still pitching for Ithaca. From the velocity of his fastball, it's hard to tell it's his fifth inning of relief. His 3-2 fastball is too much for Barber, Otterbein's cleanup hitter, who swings through the pitch for the first out. Brett can't catch up with Morello's fastball either. K for the second out. A fly ball to center field ends the inning.

The only Wooster player who remains is the one charting pitches. The rest have moved beyond the first base grandstand to the open area near right field. The Shenandoah players are there as well, all of them watching as they await their upcoming game. It's been well over three hours since this game began and the later it goes, the more every other game today will be pushed back.

John Kopicky, the Otterbein pitcher, is out for his sixth inning of relief. Fly ball to left field for out number one. Kopicky's first pitch to Wollner spins him out of the batter's box. Fastball high. Foul straight back. Fastball high. Called strike on a fastball on the inside edge of the strike zone. 3-2. Wollner manages to foul off Kopicky's offspeed pitch and then walks when the next pitch is high. One on, one out for Domenic Boresta, Ithaca's leadoff hitter. As Boresta pulls around to bunt, Kopicky's pitch hits him squarely in the back. Runners on first and second, one out. The rain is once again coming down hard as the Otterbein coach walks out to make a pitching change.

No matter how this game ends, it will be a heartbreaker.

Even from distance, the anxiety from the Otterbein fans is palpable. No sound comes from that part of the stands. Some can barely even look at the field as Ethan Doty gets ready to pitch to Cam Fuoti. The Ithaca players are all assembled at the rail of their dugout, literally hanging on every pitch that Doty throws. On the 1-1 pitch, Feltner blocks a curveball in the dirt to prevent the runners from advancing, but can't do the same two pitches later. The wild pitch puts runners on second and third. The rain continues steadily as Fuoti strikes out swinging.

Two outs and the lefty Webb Little is up. Fastball high. Foul straight back. Little pumps his bat through the bottom of the strike zone, readies himself for the next pitch. Foul straight back again. One more strike and Doty will be out of the inning. Ottberbein are so close to having another chance. Curveball that Little fouls off his leg. There's almost no noise in the park as Doty delivers the 1-2 pitch. Little hits what looks like a routine ground ball to the shortstop and I think we're headed to the thirteenth. But as Beachy attempts to field the ball, he slips on the wet turf, and though he tries to make the throw to first from his knees, it's too late. Wollner score and the game is over.

Otterbein, the tournament's number two seed, lose another heartbreaker and are headed home. As we walk towards the car, I avoid the curly-haired father, not knowing what to say.

Final Score: 5-4 Ithaca

Seven

CROOKED NUMBERS

May 20 – 27, 2018

Port Lambton
vs
Wallaceburg

Villanova
vs
Brennan
(Windsor and Essex County
Secondary Schools Athletic Association
High School Playoffs)

Tecumseh Green Giants
vs
Tillsonburg Old Socks

Sunday, May 20, 2018

Port Lambton Pirates
vs
Wallaceburg Warriors

MacDonald Park, Port Lambton ON
Game Time Temperature: 16°C

I don't want to be here, in this car, driving to Port Lambton. It's not that I don't want to watch a baseball game. Not that at all. It's just that at the Division III tournament, Ithaca play Wabash later today, with the winner playing Wooster in the championship game. That's where I want to be—in fact, I watched some of the Adrian-La Roche game on my phone when we got home yesterday—but I think Heidi has almost reached her saturation point. Giving myself over to the rhythms of the tournament for a couple of days was magical, the world falling away, even more fully that it does for a single game. I didn't care who won any of the games in Adrian or at the GLIAC tournament in Detroit last weekend and that lack of rooting interest was freeing, letting me focus on the game for its own sake. I feel different coming out the other side of these tournaments—something is shifting in the way I watch baseball.

As we drive north on Highway 40, the lush farmland streaming past the car windows, I wonder about what the baseball will be like in a Western Counties League game. Almost certainly, it won't be played at the level we've seen over the past week, but it's still baseball, whether played at Nicolay Field, Comerica Park, or at a diamond in Port Lambton. Today's game is as important as any other. I try to readjust, pull myself back into the moment. Time to focus on what we're moving towards rather than where we've been.

Yesterday, I was up at 5 am to watch the royal wedding with Griff and Julie and today I was up early to try and do some gardening. I know Dale was tempted to go back to Adrian but there seemed to be an unarticulated understanding that I needed three hours alone in my garden this morning, weeding and listening to the birds, not thinking about baseball at all.

I am starting to see that there is a difference between "going to a baseball game" and "watching a baseball game." Watching a game studiously takes a different kind of energy. It also feels like work—albeit rewarding and satisfying work. It was hard to get into the car again to spend a day—on a holiday weekend day at that—away from home with pen and notebook in my hand.

I feel better once we hit the highway. The fields are starting to turn green with the newly arrived warmth. For whatever reason, I do the driving in Canada and Dale in the United States. Today it's Dale's turn to consider the crops in the fields as our parents and grandparents did on the prairies. We don't always talk about Dale's dad and my grandfather, but I feel like they're often in the car with us and almost always with us in the bleachers. My grandfather didn't say a lot, but he saw everything, whether in nature or a ballpark.

The ballpark is a block east of the St. Clair River, the dividing line between Canada and the United States, carved out of a field on the edge of town. Beyond the park on the first base side is a large building that houses equipment storage, a concession, bathrooms, and a team clubhouse. Three small bleachers ring the area behind the newly constructed backstop. A skatepark sits directly behind the home plate bleachers, on the edge of a fallow field. The ballfield's dirt is meticulously raked and the grass is beautifully manicured. The players mingle near covered dugouts before Port Lambton take the field for the start of the game.

About fifty people are ranged around the park, in the bleachers and on lawn chairs down the left field line, friends and family here to cheer on the hometown team. Children chase each other, stop back at their parents to get money for hot chocolate or hamburgers. Beyond the right field foul pole, eight people watch the game from a house's large porch. A cheer goes up from those distant seats when Port Lambton score a run.

It's the Sunday of the Victoria Day long weekend and it's cold. I wish I'd worn more clothes. This is what Canadians like to think of as the unofficial beginning of summer. Needless to say, we all feel a little ripped off. It's supposedly 16° C but there's a cold wind coming off the lake and it's overcast. I'm sitting under two blankets. Two moms behind me talk about it being the May 2-4 Weekend and how they're not doing anything interesting. One says, "These weekends get lamer every year we get older, don't they?" and the other smirks and nods. They make enough allusions to suggest that watching this ball game does not fall into their "something interesting" category.

The dugouts are chain-link rectangles with corrugated steel roofs. When Wallaceburg are fielding, there's only one guy left in the dugout. There are a few people watching the game, but most only seem to watch when their loved one is at bat. The fans in the stands are almost exclusively wives and children, used to spending their Sundays this way. The wives and mothers talk to each other, with one eye on their kids and the other less intently on the field. A kid next to me just shouted, "Come on, Dad! Hit the ball." The batboy for Port Lambton is about as tall as the bat and members of the team need to tell him when to go get it. A few little girls are dressed in baseball uniforms. Players talk to their families through the fence; a dad barks orders to his sons from the on-deck circle, telling them to behave.

On the field, it's clear that Port Lambton are the better team, despite it being a much smaller town, a mix of men in their twenties and thirties, guys who have clearly played baseball most of their lives. In the field, only the third baseman appears out of shape, more suited to beer league softball than to handling scorched balls down the third base line. Wallaceburg, on the other hand, is comprised mainly of this type of player.

In the first, the Wallaceburg first baseman barely moves on an RBI single to his right, while later that inning, the center fielder is unable to get any kind of read on a routine fly ball. Both would have been nearly sure outs at any other level we've seen this spring. It's hard to tell what the Wallaceburg pitcher is throwing, but it seems to be variations on a low-velocity fastball, along with a curve that doesn't seem to break. Whatever it is, the Port Lambton hitters aren't fooled, banging out six hits and scoring four runs in the first.

A lot of the guys on both teams look like Dale and are about the same age. I wince when they slide, knowing their bodies don't bounce back like the college kids' do. It's 4-0 for the Pirates, who have seven hits to the Warriors one. I think this is going to be a long game.

In front of me, a grandmother watches her son playing for the Warriors. She has brought four kids ranging in age from about one to ten. She explains the nuances of pitching and fielding to the kids as she plies them with snacks and hugs as needed. This half-inning she's found a missing shoe, negotiated the purchase and sharing of a bag of chips, and prevented a toddler from putting a handful of dirt in his mouth without missing a pitch or a play. She's my new base-ball-watching hero.

In the top of the fifth, Port Lambton turn their second 4-6-3 double play of the game, this one on a ball that the second base-man can't handle, but that deflects perfectly to the shortstop, who's running to cover second. He steps on the bag and has time to make the throw to first. Laughter ripples through the crowd as the umpire calls the batter out. Smiles and backslaps as the players run to their dugout.

The grandmother is answering the kids' questions about the rules and has suggested a few times that they play baseball when they get home. She tells them about how she used to play when she was a girl. I'm not sure if the kids are listening. I want to tap them on the shoulder and whisper, "Listen. One day you'll want to know this." But I don't.

It's now 6-0 in the bottom of the fourth. The batboy has been replaced by two little girls, who seem a little older and a little more seasoned in their work. If a ball leaves the park, everyone yells "Heads up!" because no one is really paying attention to the game. Judging from how often the players wander up to the fence and talk to people in the stands, it would seem that even the players are a bit bored. They too are complaining about how cold it is. The crowd chatter is minimal but I notice here—as in Windsor—people call the players "boyce"— not boyz. "C'mon boyce!"

One of the grandkids knows the name of the pitcher and he hollers at him. He's watching strikes, encouraged by his grandmother. A player of Dale's age slides into base—needlessly, I would say if I were his wife. I cringe, imagining her helping him hobble back home saying, "You didn't need to slide. You were going to be safe." The guy seems okay and I am relieved on behalf of wives everywhere.

By the last of the seventh and the end of the game, the score is 9-1 for Port Lambton. It has by no means been the kind of well-played game I hope to see every time I come to the park, the kind of game we saw several times in the two tournaments this week. Games like this one, though, remind me that everything about baseball is hard—from pitching to fielding to hitting to running the bases—and it's that difficulty that makes the well-played games so special. Still, there were moments of great beauty—grounders perfectly played, balls in the dirt blocked by catchers, curveballs that fooled hitters, pitches taken the other way. And there's beauty, too, in watching guys who just want to play baseball. No one here is playing to get to the next level. They're playing because they love the game, because they don't want to give it up to play beer league softball. Not yet.

As we get ready to leave, a few of the Port Lambton players walk to the equipment building to retrieve rakes and a tarp for the mound. There's no grounds crew here, no one to take care of the field other than the players themselves. No one else to raise money for a new backstop. No one but family or friends to run the concession stand.

Walking back to the car, I think about baseball and the texture of a Sunday afternoon in a small town.

Final Score: 9-1 Port Lambton

Wednesday, May 23, 2018

Villanova Catholic Secondary School Wildcats
vs
F J Brennan Catholic High School Cardinals

(Windsor and Essex County Secondary
School Athletic Association Playoffs)
Cullen Field, Windsor ON
Game Time Temperature: 18°C

"This is the nicest day we've had to watch baseball," says Dale. It's 9:25 am and there's a cloudless blue sky. When we arrived at the ballpark, Dale and I became spectators 14 and 15. Although I've lived in Windsor for nearly eighteen years, this is the first time I've been to Cullen Field, which is part of Mic Mac Park, nestled between the Ojibway Prairie Provincial Nature Reserve and some large industrial complexes. I hear birds and the hum of factories.

It's warm, but not yet hot. A bit of a breeze. Though I'm here with notebook and pen in hand, it still somehow feels like I'm playing hooky from all the writing obligations I have this summer.

The field has been freshly mowed, the grass an emerald green, vibrant and lush from spring rain and lustrous with the morning dew. As the Villanova coach hits ground balls to the infielders, it's clear they're having problems gripping the ball, their throws to first often skipping ahead or wide of the mark.

"Don't aim the ball. Let it fly. If it sails on you, it sails on you."

Don't aim the ball. Charlie's voice echoes in my memory, those practices forty years collapsing into now.

Sitting in this ballpark on a mid-week morning, tucked away from city streets, feels like finding a secret garden. I'm struck by how little the players are, especially after watching so much college ball. They seem more than just a few years younger. This is the only game we've been to where most of the players are shorter than the umpires. A player comes running over to a mom seated nearby, his cleats clanking on the metal risers, to see if she has any water. He's polite and grateful as she sends him away with two bottles of bright blue Gatorade.

I'm amused at how the pitcher's cap pops off his head with almost every pitch. I'm not sure if this is the kind of thing John meant when he said "You should see something new every baseball game." But still, I note it.

I know by the sound the wood bat makes that the ball is foul. It's not the solid crack of a double or the no-doubt thunk of a home run. It's more like a hard tick, the ball glancing off the wood, never making solid contact. And then, almost before the ball hits the ground beyond the fence down the third base line, I hear the Villanova coach yell, "I need somebody on that, please!" People in the stands point to where the ball lands. Bring it in. Make sure we have enough balls to play.

The next pitch is a ball and suddenly Villanova have runners on first and second with only one out. From the third base dugout, I can hear the Brennan coach reminding the infielders to turn the double play on a ground ball if they can, but to make sure they get at least one out. I see the other Brennan coach motioning to the outfielders, moving them in slightly with the pitcher up next. The first base coach leans in to the runner on first, reminds him not to take a lead that's too big. To tag up on a fly ball. To hustle on a ground ball. From the coach in the dugout, I hear, "One out here. Give me a good at-bat. Battle up here." Coaches constantly reminding players of the possibilities, and their responsibilities, in each scenario.

The Villanova pitcher manages a squib back to the mound, a kind of swinging bunt that moves the runners to second and third. It's not a hit, but it's a decent at-bat, at least moving the runners over and leaving them with a chance to still score. The runners also did their jobs by getting good jumps and giving the pitcher only one play: the sure out at first base. The pitcher fielded the ball cleanly and understood that trying to get the out at second was too risky. Everyone did what they were supposed to do, what their coaches had reminded them to do.

I've been watching a Villanova player wandering around on the other side of the ballpark fence for some time looking for a ball. I can see his frustration growing. Eventually, he trots back to the dugout. His report that he cannot find the ball is met with a resigned shrug. There seems to be a tacit acknowledgement that sometimes you need to sacrifice a ball to the weeds. If there were an index determining what level of baseball a team plays, whether or not they care about finding foul balls would certainly be one of the major factors demarcating their status.

This is a game where I'm able to hear almost all of the baseball chatter. The coach standing near third base shouts, "I believe in you" to the batter, #24, and his faith is rewarded by a double. He then tells the batter, now the runner, to watch for a passed ball and move up. But, the third out happens and he's left on base.

Scanning today's crowd, I think about Stacey May Fowles' book *Baseball Life Advice: Loving the Game That Saved Me*, where she talks a lot about gender and MLB. Fowles' book made me realize that, with the exception of the Tigers and the Mud Hens games, there has been a near equal split between genders in most of the crowds at smaller games we've attended. Occasionally, women—mothers and grandmothers to be specific—have outnumbered men. And when the moms and grandmas are there, they are *present*. They watch each pitch and see each play. They're smart, vocal, loyal, and they *know* the game. I think about Wallaceburg Grandmother and Davenport Mom. Do they watch major league baseball when they're not watching their kids?[1] I can't imagine either of these women would be lured to a major league park by offers of "Pink-it-and-shrink-it" team merchandise or the condescending "Baseball 101 for Women" events Fowles describes.

Fowles' book has made me wonder if what I've perceived as a waning interest in baseball is, in actuality, a waning interest in Major League Baseball. I've come to appreciate the unspoken assumption at parks like this that, if I'm in the stands, I'm here to watch baseball.

Down 3-0 in the bottom of the fourth, Villanova have something going—runners on first and second with no one out. The Brennan coach positions the infielders, reminding them of their responsibilities on the bunt. The second baseman yells to the shortstop, "I got bag," indicating he'll cover on a throw to second from the catcher. It's part of the constant chatter, the conversation of the game. Up close, as we are today, just to the first base side of home, I hear it all.

The batter squares himself around, pulling the corner fielders toward the plate in anticipation of the bunt. At the last moment, however, he pulls the bat back, letting the pitch travel to the catcher. The runner on second breaks for third, and with the third baseman moving towards home, easily steals the base. Because of the third baseman's responsibility on the perceived bunt, no one had bag—by using a fake bunt, Villanova introduced an unexpected possibility and took advantage of the anticipation of Brennan's fielders making the correct play on a bunt. The bunt sign now off, the batter swings away and hits a ball past third base, scoring Villanova's first run.

After an error on the shortstop puts runners at second and third, Villanova have another excellent chance to score. Hit. Sacrifice fly. Wild pitch. Even a slow roller to the right side might score the run.

Villanova Coach: "Lot of confidence in you right now."

Villanova Bench, after a couple of balls: "He doesn't want to come to you."

Umpire: "Players in the dugout. Players in the dugout. The top step is in play."

Villanova Bench, after a deep sac fly to left field: "That's the way. That's the way."

By the bottom of the fifth, though, I can see the slump in the Villanova players, heads down as they walk off the field for their turn at bat. And I can no longer hear them talking to each other, silenced by the 5-2 score. The Villanova coach clearly sees what I see, hears the same silence I do.

"Come on, boys. I want to hear a lot of chatter. Get in the game. I want to hear everyone. You gotta want it."

Be in the game. Support your teammates. Don't give up.

Two walks, a single, a balk, and an error: Villanova score two to get back within one run. The Villanova players run to take their places in the field for the top of the sixth. All of them are talking—to themselves, to each other, to the coaches. I look over at the Villanova bench. The coach claps his hands, yells, "Hey, let's have some fun!"

There are more mistakes in this game than I've seen before this season: a runner at second who should not have tried to steal, two bad fielding errors, and a balk. These are costly. On the other hand, this game is a learning experience and, as my friend Alec said the time I didn't tighten the lid of my water bottle before putting it into my book bag: "You'll only do that once." And he was right.

The Brennan parents are still unhappy about the balk call in the bottom of the fifth, adamant that the pitcher stepped off the rubber. Their relationship with the two umpires working the game is, shall we say, strained, and it doesn't get any better when Brennan bats in the top of the sixth. Almost every called strike is accompanied by booing and increasingly livid protests from a few of the Brennan contingent, seated just on the first base side of home. I glance over, try to catch a glimpse of who's yelling. There are assorted mutterings from a number of people, but most of the commentary is from a heavyset man with a goatee, wearing black pants and a Blue Jays jacket, his cap on backwards. From the way he's yelling, I assume he has someone in the game.

The breaking point for the home plate umpire comes when the man takes exception to a called strike and yells, "They're all kids out there. Be fair!"

"Shut your mouth or you're going home."

When the man won't stop yelling, the umpire points at him and jerks his thumb backwards. Out. As in out of the game, out of the park. He asks the Brennan first base coach to ask the fan to leave, says they won't restart until the man departs. At this, the Brennan coach throws up his hands in exasperation, both at the umpire and,

I think, at the father in the stands. The umpire won't listen to the coach's arguments about how he can't control the fans. The man has to go.

Finally, the man stomps out of the park to the soundtrack of his own expletive-laden tirade. None of the other Brennan parents seem at all upset to see him go.

I smile looking at the players—a few years age difference at this stage in their lives makes a huge difference in terms of size and strength. Right now, there's a little lad twitching nervously on first, watching the batter, waiting to run. The first baseman is a large, lumbering fellow, nearly twice as big as the runner. Earlier, I saw a younger player get high-fived for his fielding efforts only to be nearly knocked off his feet by the enthusiasm of his older, larger teammate.

Villanova score a run in the bottom of the sixth and the game is tied at 5 heading into the final inning. With a man on first for Brennan in the top of the inning, one of the Villanova moms near us yells, "Turn two, boys!" On the very next pitch, the Villanova shortstop gloves a grounder near second base, steps on the bag, and fires to first for the double play. As the players run off the field, their excitement is palpable, their mood bolstered by a fine defensive play, their chatter focused on getting the winning run. The prophetess of the double play claps her hands, turns to her neighbour, says, "You never know with baseball."

Listening to a baseball game in a ballpark is like standing silently amongst the trees in nearby Ojibway park. When you actually stop and listen, the silence you thought you were hearing reveals itself to be a diverse group of sounds. "Here we go!" "I want everybody in the game. *Everybody*." "Come on, kid," one kid yells to another. "You gotta want this." "Gotta go to work, right here." "Right on it. Right on it. Right on it." "I want to hear some chatter going on" and a player responds, "Let's get some chatter going."

"Every guy up. Every guy in the ballgame right now." The coach hardly needs to say it any more. The Villanova bench are ready to boil over as the hitters put on batting gloves and retrieve bats from the rack in the dugout.

A walk and a double put runners at second and third with one out. The Brennan coach opts for an intentional walk to load the bases, putting both the double play and the force out at home in order. Yelled reminders from the base coaches to the runners. There's nothing subtle now, no hand signals, just a series of reminders of what to do if X, Y, or Z happens. An infield fly for the second out. Now all the runners have to worry about is not getting picked off and to run as fast as they can at the crack of the bat.

Bases loaded, two outs, and who should stride to the batter's box but Villanova's starting pitcher, inserted back into the game under high school rules. When he walked off the hill after the third inning, he looked completely lost, crushed by having given up three runs on no hits and putting the team's playoff hopes in jeopardy. When he singles for the walk-off win, his teammates mob him at first base, their playoff hopes resurrected.

Final Score: 6-5 Villanova

Sunday, May 27, 2018

Dale is away on his annual guys' trip and I'm preparing to head out on my own to a baseball game, since I was unable to attend the Riverside/ Herman game last week. I spent much of last night online trying to decide which game to attend. You'd think it'd be easy to find out what games are happening on any given weekend, but even this librarian finds it challenging to get accurate and up-to-date information. When I saw Woodslee's Oriole Park listed as the venue, I knew I'd found my game. Oriole Park is the ball field I love most in the world, and the game has the added bonus of being at 10 am. It's going to be a very warm day and I'll be happy to avoid the afternoon sun.

I've enjoyed—needed, really—a few days without baseball, time to garden and read a novel. Attending today's game is partially about math: it will my nineteenth, meaning we need to go to thirty-one more before Labour Day to reach our fifty-game goal. This summer has been the closest I've ever been to obsessive behaviors.

I'm nervous to be flying solo. Can I watch a game without back-up? Can I rely on myself to see everything that needs to be seen at a baseball game? It's as if I'm back at my driver's test, where I had the disconcerting realization that the first time I was actually driving without a teacher, I was being examined. Or, as my driver's ed teacher said, "Examinated." Today I feel like I'm going to be examinated at baseball. Although I've consciously not kept a scorecard for most of the games we've been to this year, I'm going to bring my scorecard book to help me pay attention to the details of the game itself.

Sunday, May 27, 2018

Tecumseh Green Giants 35+
vs
Tillsonburg Old Sox

Oriole Park, Woodslee ON
Game Time Temperature: 24°C

If anyone ever says the phrase "idyllic baseball park," my imagination instantly summons Oriole Park. This isn't a place you'd just happen upon. You need to know to turn off County Road 46 at the church, then pass the graveyard and the school to find it, nestled between stands of trees and cornfields. I'm not sure what makes this park so magical for me. Is it that I've never been able to find it without a map, making it seem like a baseball Brigadoon? Or that there's something eerily beautiful about the light on the field, no matter what time of day or evening? Maybe it's that the air is so still that the only sounds you hear, aside from the occasional lawn mower or barking dog, are the sounds of baseball.

When I pull up in the school parking lot across a narrow road from the ballpark, the umpires have just arrived. I follow them across the road and find a spot on the three-level bleachers in the shade. A young woman and I smile at each other. Together, she and I make up two-fifths of the crowd. A mother and two young girls are on the other bleachers.

As I sharpen my pencil, and enter the date and time of the game in my scorecard, I hear Chris Wainscott—a colleague from the University of Windsor—and the umpires comparing notes about aging bodies. This is a tournament weekend and they've played a lot already. Chris is on the Tecumseh team. He stops by to say hi, adding, "I hope you brought a sense of humour with you. It's going to be a mess. We're a team of old fat guys. I smell like Bengay and I have ibuprofen coursing through my veins." I smile and wish him luck.

Players are rolling up the tarps covering the mound and plate and one of the players is marking the field with chalk. At first base he stops to survey his line and comments, "Looks like a blind snake did this." I hear Chris say "I already regret today." A Tillsonburg infielder replies, "We're not here for good baseball" and players on the field laugh. It's so quiet that I can hear the joke repeated in each dugout and the ensuing chuckles.

Watching the game, I still feel like I'm waiting in the car for my driver's test examiner with her crumpled raincoat, tightly clenched clipboard, and "You will invariably disappoint me" demeanor. As they tell you in driver's ed, don't focus on the examiner, focus on the road. I tell myself, don't focus on the chapter you'll need to write, focus on the game. I enter a double, a bunt, a wild pitch, a tag out, an F5, and a strikeout into my scorecard. I watch pitches. I record each batter. I'm proud of myself. I've watched two whole innings and not missed a play. I could pass a quiz on this game. I can do this!

But then I drop my pencil and have to retrieve it from under the bleachers. And I miss a play, or maybe two, and I have to ask the smiling young woman what happened. She didn't see either. She seems nice, and it appears her husband is on the team. Normally I would chat with her, but I'm being a serious baseball watcher today, focusing only on the game. I leave a few blanks in my scorecard because I saw a dog on a walk and he was very cute. His owner throws a stick and the dog returns with an even bigger stick. After the dog vanishes from sight, I tell myself, "Be better next inning."

I'm a little tired, and I catch my mind wandering across the field. I notice another dog in a yard on the edge of left field doing his morning reconnaissance. One of the little girls on the other bleachers is refreshingly non-partisan: she cheers for everyone who gets a hit. I notice that an ump just laughed at a pitch and one of the infielders shouted "Eephuuuussss." I wonder if this is the first Eephus pitch I've ever seen in real life and am thrilled at this possibility. Another mom has just arrived with four little girls and a basket of activity books to amuse them. They look like nesting dolls in a line as the books and crayons are distributed. And all of these details make me smile and miss two more at-bats. I ask my bleacher mate what the score is and she doesn't know either. It's a new inning. Chris comes by and chats. I ask him what the score is and even he doesn't know. He asks someone else. There is some debate about the score but no one seems very certain and no one seems to mind.

I talk some more with my new friend. Her name is Katie and her husband plays for Tecumseh. She tells me she's one of the few wives who goes to every game. She's expecting a baby in the fall and wears a shirt that has "Future baseball fan" written across her belly. She asks what I'm writing down, and I tell her about the project. We talk some more and realize we have friends in common: two degrees of Windsor.

I like Katie, and I try to both talk to her and watch the game, but do neither very well. I imagine the baseball equivalent of my driver's test examiner making judgmental notations on her clipboard about how I'm watching the game: "Fails to execute proper notation of double play"; "Unable to merge making a new friend with watching action on the field"; "Erroneously gives right of way to extraneous conversation instead of observing location of pitches."

Katie asks about my scorecard and about some of the calls. She describes how she loves going to baseball games, the experience of being in ballparks like this one and Comerica Park. Above all, she loves watching her husband play. She confesses she doesn't always understand all the rules of the game, but still she loves baseball. I smile at Katie—not only because she's so effortlessly happy—but because she has just articulated something that's been elusive to me all summer: there are multiple ways to watch baseball and enjoy a game. There is no quiz. No pass or fail. No certificate of achievement. You just need to find what makes you happy about baseball and watch it in the way that brings you the most joy. I very consciously put my pencil away, close my notebook, and keep chatting.

The rest of the game unfolds in rather underwhelming ways and then suddenly it is over. I gather my things and say goodbye to Katie. On the way to my car, I run into Dave Burke, who's playing in the next game. It seems right to see Dave here because we used to come to this park to watch him play. Because he was one of my formative baseball tutors, he's been on my mind a lot this summer. I say, "Do you remember the last time Dale and I were here?" He laughs, saying, "I know exactly what game you're talking about." We reconstruct a game where two outfielders on the same team started throwing punches at each other in the middle of an at-bat. Dave forgot that one of the mothers in the stands got involved, but remembers the team was from Michigan.

The morning coolness is giving way to enveloping heat and I wish Dave good luck on the game and say goodbye. As I start my car and wait for the air conditioning to kick in, I realize I know the final score is 6-4, but not who won. Somewhere in my mind, my inner baseball "examinator" protests loudly. Somewhere else in my mind, my conversations with Katie silence that voice. There is no test at the end of a ballgame.

Final Score: Uncertain

Eight
A STUDY
IN CONTRASTS
June 1–3, 2018

Woodslee 35+
vs
Harrow Sr.

West Side Woolly Mammoths
vs
East Side Diamond Hoppers

Detroit Tigers
vs
Toronto Blue Jays

Friday, June 1, 2018

Woodslee Orioles 35+
vs
Harrow Sr. Blues

Oriole Park, Woodslee ON
Game Time Temperature: 19°C

After work tonight, we were both tired. Dale said he'd be happy to stay home as, I think, would I. But we're still worried about making our fifty games after all the rainouts this spring. Spending most of our non-working hours going to baseball is starting to feel normal.

The thermometer says it's warm but the wind is cold. On our way to Woodslee, we stopped at the Dairy Freez in Comber for supper and a bit of their famous ice cream. It's been so hot lately that it's hard to imagine being this chilly. Driving to Oriole Park for the second time in a week reminds me of the very early days of my baseball watching in Windsor. We would often come to this lovely park after work to see Dave play on perfect summer evenings.

Friday night in Woodslee. Not even really a town. More like a crossroads. Gas station. Church. A few houses. And a ball diamond surrounded only by trees and silence. The light standards are still surprising, an intrusion of the artificial in this pastoral setting. Since we last attended a game here, there's a new backstop and small bleachers behind home plate. When we first started coming, we had to bring our own lawn chairs, but other than that, little has changed in the last sixteen years. Coming here makes me think about what Mark Kingwell wrote in *Fail Better*: "Any park, with that magic square of ninety-foot spans arrayed around the plate and the mound, contains the universe of baseball." Not only the universe of baseball, but its soul.

For a few years, we'd drive out once or twice a summer to see Dave play and to just let the rhythm of the park wash over us. But then Dave got hurt and we stopped coming, even after he started to pitch again. After that, my experience of live baseball shrunk almost exclusively to the Tigers. Without Woodslee, Major League Baseball became synonymous with baseball for me. As we have watched games this summer—in Detroit and Toledo, Windsor and Tecumseh, and all the other places within one hundred miles of our house—I have come to realize that this focus on the Tigers obscured so much of what I love about the game. And even though we're already twenty games in and even though Dave's not playing tonight, coming back to Woodslee feels like coming home to baseball.

There are seventeen people here—brothers, sisters, mothers, wives, girlfriends, children. A Woodslee player is looking for balls by the side of the road. Two more balls have landed there while he's been looking. Another ball bounces over the backstop and a Woodslee player picks it up. He lines his fingers up with two seams, lifts his arm like he's about to throw a fastball, but instead carries it back to the dugout in that grip.

A few more fans trickle in. A man sits alone right behind the plate in the top row of the bleacher seats. He and Dale give each other a nod that I'm coming to recognize as the gesture that says, "Hello fellow connoisseur of the game. I shall leave you in silence but perhaps we can compare notes about pitching later."

No score in the bottom of the third and Woodslee are up to bat. The Orioles' starting pitcher lays a perfect bunt down the third base line and gets all the way to third on a two-base throwing error. Heads-up baserunning. I flash back to a similar throw from the

Woodslee shortstop in the top of the inning, a ball in the dirt that the first baseman expertly scooped on one hop to save the error and get the out. For a 35+ team, Woodslee are very mobile and, on defense, they know where to position themselves. No help from coaches here. Back on offense, players who will not be up to hit right away act as first and third base coaches, helping the baserunners to keep track of the ball and gauge whether to try to advance or retreat.

#11 strides to the plate.

"Come on, kid."

"Get a hit, kid."

No coaches, but they're still calling each other kid, just like they did in high school.

#11 homers. 2-0 Woodslee.

A new pitcher enters the game for Harrow in the bottom of the fourth inning, with the score still 2-0 Woodslee. He's got some zip on his fastball, but his warmup tosses are wild. I'm not sure I would want to stand in against him and am not really surprised when he opens with a walk, the runner then taking second base on a pickoff throw that gets away from the first baseman. On a lineout to the second baseman, Harrow should double the runner off second, but there's no one there to cover the base. From what I've seen tonight, it's a play Woodslee would probably have made.

A Woodslee batter gets to third on an overthrown ball to first. A home run scores two for the Orioles and you can hear someone's leaf blower from across the field. There's a couple who have set up lawn chairs where their yard comes up against the left field fence. I watch a dog trot around and eventually settle at their feet. I just saw a double play—a rare thing at this level.

By the top of the sixth inning, the score is 8-0 Woodslee. The wind is cold and all twenty spectators are simply hoping for outs. If I weren't in shorts and a golf shirt, I would be fine, but it was warm all day. I forget that nights in early June don't always stay warm.

There's a bit of muted chatter on the field, but compared to some of the college games we've watched—the benches absolutely alive with talk, with cheering on their teammates—it's like being in church. Even the infield is almost silent, apparitions calmly fielding grounders from the first baseman.

An error and a single put runners on first and second for Harrow, but a strikeout looking means they fail to advance. A single then loads the bases with only one out, the best chance by far that Harrow has had all evening. There's still no chatter in the infield, nor are there coaches here to admonish the players to talk, to get in the game. But I can tell by the way that they set themselves before the pitch—ready to move laterally, charge a slow roller, or play a big hop—that they've internalized all those years of coaching. Each has an inner voice that says, "Keep focus. Stay in the game."

The ball is chopped in front of the mound. I see the catcher flip off his mask, field the hop, and fire the ball to first before shuffling back two steps, his foot touching the plate, his body extended like a first baseman, ready to receive the return throw. Double play. 2-3-2. Beauty under the lights.

It's the bottom of the sixth and I am so cold my handwriting is shaky. It's 8-0 for Woodslee and now I'm just hoping for outs. I've been colder a million times more than I've been warm this project.

The game ends. The Woodslee and Harrow players shake hands, meeting near the mound. I hear a couple of the Woodslee players say, "Good job, boys" to the Harrow players as they clap them on the back. They're guys who spend their free time keeping up this beautiful little park—their universe of baseball—so they and the kids of the community can play. And so people like me can try to find their way back home to baseball.

Final Score: 8-1 Woodslee

Saturday, June 2, 2018

West Side Woolly Mammoths
vs
East Side Diamond Hoppers

Jimmy John's Field, Utica MI
Game Time Temperature: 72°F

We didn't plan to be in Utica, Michigan tonight. We planned to be home, afternoon game between the Tecumseh Thunder Juniors and Underwood Orr already in the books. When we got to Lacasse Park, however, Underwood Orr were nowhere to be seen. On the field, the Juniors were wrapping up practice.

I asked a couple of the coaches about the game, but they didn't seem to know anything about it or particularly care that I was asking. From what I could finally gather, instead of a game today, there are two games tomorrow, despite what the website said. We got back in the car and drove home to check schedules. After some searching, we realized that we could go to a United Shore Professional Baseball League (USPBL) game tonight. Changing plans on the fly is a big part of this project and not only because of the weather.

But here we are, walking up to Jimmy John's Field, a park purpose-built to host the USPBL, an independent, four-team professional league consisting of the Birmingham-Bloomfield Beavers, the Eastside Diamond Hoppers, the Utica Unicorns, and the Westside Woolly Mammoths. All teams play on this field, with games Thursday to Sunday (plus the occasional Tuesday or Wednesday) from early May to early September. The team names are placeholders, a way to differentiate one from the other, a fiction to anchor the teams and the league in the real and imagined geography of Metro Detroit. During the course of the season, players are only ever visitors in name, batting first but going through their routines in familiar surroundings. For most adults here tonight—and even, I suspect, for most children—it doesn't matter which teams are playing. What

matters is that there will be baseball. For once, I won't be the only
one in the park who doesn't care which team wins.

As we walk to the ticket window, I see the towering black-and-
white photos that dominate the top portion of each of the park's
three front pillars. Jackie Robinson, Eddie Stanky, Pee Wee Reese,
and Spider Jorgensen in the Dodgers dugout on the day of Robinson's MLB debut. Ted Williams mid-swing. Babe Ruth examining
a bat as one of his Yankee teammates looks on. As your eye moves
down, the photos give way to a dark brick façade, an evocation of
the way the old ballparks used to look when men like these played
in them. Red, white, and blue bunting is draped over the railings that
peek between the columns. The park and the league have only been
around since 2016, and yet everything about the walk to the entrance
is meant to connect you to the history of baseball, to nostalgia for
a time that most people at the park would never have known. You
don't come here to see the Unicorns or the Diamond Hoppers or the
Woolly Mammoths or the Beavers. You come to see baseball. And
while what's on offer might not be Jackie or the Splendid Splinter or
The Babe, the USPBL wants us to see it as part of the same tradition.

Our tickets tell us that tonight the Woolly Mammoths are playing the Diamond Hoppers. Westside versus Eastside.

We walk along the outside of the grandstand, along the third
base line, surveying the park before taking our seats. There's a covered beer garden and a picnic area past third base and further on,
to the right of the foul pole, is a playground and wiffle ball field.
On a berm beyond the right field wall, people lounge on blankets
while kids tear up and down its length. Across the diamond, there
are more picnic areas and covered spaces in which fans can mingle.
At field level, underneath the grandstand, there's restaurant seating
with full table service. Above this area, between first and third base,
there's room for 2,000 patrons; in total, the park holds 4,500. All the
amenities of a modern ballpark, but on a smaller scale.

It would be difficult to find a more bizarre juxtaposition of baseball
from last night's game in Woodslee. As we walk into the park, there's a
sign announcing tonight's game will have a Bob Seger theme. Behind
the left field fence, a Bob Seger tribute band, Bullet Detroit, serenades

us from a sound stage; we're told they'll play between innings and after the game, too. When the players are announced, they run out onto the field, each holding the hand of a child. The national anthem is sung, and children in the outfield hold up an American flag nearly as big as the outfield itself. Kiss' "Detroit Rock City" plays as we wait for first pitch. By the end of the first inning, I notice that every player's walk-up music is a different Bob Seger song and I wonder if there are enough songs for both teams. I am surprised that there are. The whole scenario feels like the setting of a T Coraghessan Boyle novel.

Our seats are behind the plate, about ten rows up, but it feels higher since the seating is stacked on top of the main-floor restaurant. Around us are mostly families. A few of the kids have Woolly Mammoths or Diamond Hoppers hats, but most wear a cap from their own Little League team, a Tigers cap, or no cap at all. The mascots wander the sidelines, stopping for pictures, getting high fives from kids and adults alike. An excited buzz runs through the crowd as the Diamond Hoppers take the field.

Tyler Palm steps to the mound and begins to take his warmup pitches. At 6'8", he's a commanding presence and even in his first few throws I can see that his fastball has some zip. As he unspools out of his windup, the ball looks even faster out of his right hand because of his height. One of the few players on either roster from Michigan, Palm played college baseball at Oakland University, just up the road in Rochester. Palm was undrafted in 2017, so it was either sign on with an independent professional league or forego the dream of playing in the major leagues.[1]

Palm's first inning: two strikeouts and a groundout to second base.

Unlike Woodslee, where you can hear a lawn mower down the road or a dog barking in the neighbouring yard, there are no moments of silence here. In fact, there's a concerted effort to fill every second with noise. When there are no game sounds, the crowd is urged to sing "Daaaay-o" or is commanded "Everybody clap your hands!," to which the crowd responds dutifully with a respective "Daaaay-o" or a "Clap. Clap. Clapclapclap!"

In front of me are a white couple, two African-American parents with a little boy, and two South-Asian parents with a little girl about ten years old in a white, glittery party dress. This is the South-Asian family's first game and they ask me to take a picture of them. I happily focus their smiling faces against the backdrop of the field. I have never seen a child as excited to be at a baseball game as this sparkly little girl.

The South-Asian woman in front of us, here with her husband and daughter, tells the African-American woman next to her, here with her own husband and son, that this is their first baseball game. I don't mean to eavesdrop, but even as I try to concentrate on my own notes, I find myself pulled into their conversation, wishing I could ask them what they think of it all. What better way to introduce people to the game than what's on offer today. Inexpensive. Entertaining in ways that both kids and parents can appreciate. But at the core of the experience is baseball. Engaging, well-played baseball. And despite all the distractions in this ballpark, people are extremely attentive to it—far more than is usually the case at Tigers games—clapping and cheering for good plays from both sides, appreciative of the effort these young men are making on a gorgeous early-summer evening.

The USPBL Dancers dance to a Bob Seger song performed 1950s style. Half the dance squad are in the Diamond Hoppers' green and orange colours, the others are in the Mammoths' blue and red. This might be the first time I've ever seen an equally bipartisan pep squad. It takes me a while to process that there are absolutely no firm rooting interests in this game and in this league. People are just watching baseball. And having fun.

I wonder what Susan Jacoby—whose book *Why Baseball Matters* considers why MLB is having trouble attracting young viewers and fans—would make of this league. Although I know of a few baseball purists who would be outraged at the level of entertainment on offer here tonight, I think MLB could learn something from this league. Another thing the majors might learn from this league: the cheapest seats were lawn seats, at $6 each. Although you could buy $20 and

$35 seats, our $12 seats are quite decent. We'd looked at going to a Tigers game tonight but comparable tickets were $40 apiece.[2]

The last time I was at a USPBL game, I spent a lot of time deciding which ball cap to buy. Eventually, it came down to the mascot — as a Canadian, I liked Birmingham Bloomfield's Buzz the Beaver. Tonight, I might cheer for the Eastside Diamond Hoppers because I think that whoever thought of naming this baseball frog Ribbi is a genius. I imagine few people here pick their team allegiance according to neighbourhood. It probably comes down to which colour scheme you like and whether you like woolly mammoths, beavers, frogs, or unicorns best. Or, maybe you don't cheer for a team at all. Maybe you just cheer for baseball.

After a bloop single to open the bottom of the fourth, J J the Bat Dog retrieves the bat from home plate and brings it back to the Diamond Hoppers dugout. He goes out again after a flyout to center field, but this time chases the ball on the throw back to the infield before retrieving the bat. The perils of employing a bat dog, I guess.

A walk and a foul pop to the third baseman brings Gunnar Buhner to the plate with two outs and runners on first and second. On a 3-1 count, Buhner hits a hot grounder down the third base line. Off the bat, it seems like a sure single to at least load the bases, but David Kimbrough II goes down on one knee to scoop it off the grass before getting up and stepping on the bag for the fielder's choice to end the inning. 4-1 Diamond Hoppers after four innings.

The game is a finely choreographed onslaught of distractions. A pre-recorded baseball organ plays "If You're Happy and You Know It" and the crowd claps in the appropriate places without interrupting their conversations. There's Bob Seger trivia on the big screen. J J the Bat Dog is carrying a basket of bottled water and towels to the umps. Rows 5 and 6 have won cupcakes and cannoli. A four-year-old from Grosse Pointe has been selected to race Ribbi around the bases. As they round each base, Ribbi slows his giant plush webbed feet to a moving standstill to give the wee lad an edge. The little Grosse Pointer is ecstatic to have beaten the odds and the crowd goes wild. Or maybe they go wild because John McAdams has been named "Beer Batter of the Game." If he gets a hit, there are $5 craft beers from Brooks and Sherwood. This ballpark knows how to appeal to all types of fans.

I think about last night's game, where there were no announcers, no gimmicks, no music—just baseball. While the other games we've seen on this project have been interesting and engaging, tonight is the first time I'm actually having fun engaging in the distractions instead of worrying about how often my attention is taken away from events on the field. There are many things that delight me: J J the Bat Dog, the little girl in the party dress who remains thrilled to be here, the dancing mascots, the hopeful fans when the Beer Batter steps up to the plate. I cannot contain my glee at seeing Woolly and Ribbi dancing together to Taylor Swift's "Shake it Off." I record them on my phone and watch it multiple times.

Mike McGee is out to pitch the bottom of the fifth for the Mammoths. I glance over at the radar gun as he pitches to the first batter. 92 mph on a called strike. Three pitches later, McGee gets the swinging strikeout. Batter two. Fastball at 92 for a swinging strike. Called strike on a 72-mph breaking ball. Swinging strikeout on a changeup at 80. Three more pitches and McGee has struck out the side on eleven pitches.

By the end of the sixth inning, people with smaller children have begun to drift home. "Cotton Eyed Joe" plays over the PA system. It's pleasant sitting here in the twilight watching young men play baseball. The air is just a bit cool now on this early June night, but I wouldn't want to be anywhere else or with anyone else, baseball washing over us. I think about all the games we've seen. The good plays, the sloppy plays, the different styles of pitching, the warmth, the cold, the fans, the parents, the blowouts, the close games. At all those games nearly everyone cheered for a team or a player, but tonight people are here just for the game and the experience of watching the game. Maybe that's why tonight feels so perfect, watching two teams with no history, no real geographic base. Two teams that are little more than different jerseys.

Tonight, no one is cursing out an ump. No one's dad will be asked to leave the stands. No one is calling for a coach to be fired. No one is still harbouring a grudge at the home team for not making the play-offs last season. No intra-parental tensions exist between teams. I didn't know how much these things had weighed on me this past month until I felt relieved by their absence tonight. Tonight—with its mammoths, beavers, unicorns, and frogs, its made-up neighbourhood rivalries and its borrowed nostalgia—might be the night when I feel closest to what I find beautiful about baseball. Indeed, a cynic would find fault with many things about this game and this league. But I grow increasingly tired of how often we kowtow to cynics and, in so doing, miss seeing the joy the little girl in the flouncy dress experiences in every single play. I add "spar-kly party dress girl" to the list of baseball watchers I want to emulate.

It takes a while for it to sink in just how good the baseball on the field really is. Just look at McGee's pitching. The five strong innings Palm threw—seven strikeouts, four hits, two walks, and only one run.[3] Kody Ruedisili's basket catch in the first. Kimbrough's scoop at third base. Moments of sheer beauty even in an 8-1 game like this one.

It's the top of the seventh and a few people have left or found other things to do in the park. There's a pretty constant hum of con-versation and chatter but most people are actually looking at the field in front of them as they talk. A man just said, "Come on, let's strike this guy out!," which might be the first remotely partisan thing I've heard all evening.

Tonight I'm also feeling confident in noting how good the base-ball is. And I wouldn't have been able to pinpoint why it is so good if I hadn't seen the games I've seen these past weeks. For reasons I can't quite articulate, tonight's game seems like a turning point. Maybe it's because we're nearing the half-way point of our fifty games. Or maybe I'm just settling in, finding my feet on this project, and learning to watch baseball differently. Maybe I'm just enjoying baseball again.

In the past weeks, while sitting in various ballparks waiting for the games to start, while sitting at red lights while driving to the games, while wandering back to the car to head home in the dark, my mind has often drifted back to the Chatham Coloured All-Stars and what our interviewees told us. They said that baseball was important because there wasn't TV. On the surface, this is a simple idea. Baseball was entertainment, yes, but it was also social, a way you could connect with each other, catch up with your friends, be part of your community. This USPBL game seems to be part of that tradition.

In the middle of the eighth, it's clearing out quickly; in part, because it's 9:43 pm and past the bedtime of 70 percent of the crowd.

By the time "Sweet Caroline" plays between the eighth and ninth innings, there aren't many people left in the park. All the families have gone home. Most of the couples have moved their date nights elsewhere. We stay, see the Mammoths score their second run. The Diamond Hoppers' victory song plays on the big video board in center field. Matt Derry conducts a field interview over the PA system with catcher and "Beer Batter" Josh McAdams, who got three hits in four at-bats and was named player of the game. We pack our things, share a smile, and stand for a minute looking out over the lights of the park.

Final Score: 8-2 Diamond Hoppers

Sunday, June 3, 2018

Detroit Tigers
vs
Toronto Blue Jays

Comerica Park, Detroit
Game Time Temperature: 64°F

Earlier in the week, I went to the Barrel House after my dance class and the Blue Jays game was on the TVs. My elation was instant when, out of the corner of my eye, I saw a player come up to the plate. I would know that stance anywhere, recognize the way Curtis' fingers tap at the bat as he waits for a pitch.

Today we're checking in with the Tigers again and, like our April 1 game, I'm a little shocked at how our Sundays have changed. In some ways, things aren't much different. I have my Tigers jersey on with "Granderson 28" on the back. We're drinking coffee on Broadway and eating muffins. We have books to read and I have my journal. But Curtis is a Blue Jay now and 1515 Broadway is gutted. The Wurlitzer Building—so long boarded up and protectively scaffolded—is now a heavily curtained space with a valet-parking stand outside and brass-mermaid pulls on the heavy doors. Dark and opulent, it's made to look like it's always been this way—but it hasn't. This "new" Detroit is here, but driving home from Utica late last night through a range of neighbourhoods, it's also evident that problems linger no matter how many stand-up espresso bars pop up in the downtown core. Is a Lululemon store better than an empty building? Downtown Detroit will be something people study, talk about, write about for years.

As we were driving home last night, we were talking about the game, this book, and watching baseball without rooting interests. It's odd to have gone from two games where we had absolutely no rooting interests to a game where I have deeply conflicted and contradictory allegiances: the Tigers and Curtis Granderson. I'll be cheering for the Tigers, my team. But I'll also be cheering for a single player on the opposing team, and for an American team over a Canadian team.

I know there'll never be a player as important to me as Curtis Granderson. I'm not sure whether he was what Stacey May Fowles calls my "gateway drug" to baseball, but I'm convinced you can only have a player like this once in your baseball lifetime.[4] Dale has gently reminded me that this might be the last season Curtis will play—he's nearing retirement age. If that's true, this might be the last time I see him play. I'm trying not to think about it.[5]

In many ways, it's another day at Comerica as we make our way through the turnstile and walk along the concourse, the sunshine and brilliant green of the field peeking through in snatches to our right. But since we were here last, we've seen eighteen games that didn't involve the Tigers. Eighteen games in which I had no stake in who won. Two months of trying to watch baseball in a different way.

Today feels different than I expected it would. I've kept an eye on how the Tigers are doing this year, but only in my peripheral vision. I know they've won four in a row and eight of their last ten, and that the Rally Goose—a hunting decoy one of the players brought to the dugout—has become their good-luck charm over that stretch. I know that they are overperforming, playing scrappy baseball through a lot of injuries. I know that some of the young players, like Jeimer Candelario and Niko Goodrum, are showing out well and that Michael Fulmer, who will pitch today, had a good April and a bad May. I know all of those things, just like I know that yesterday was the anniversary of Armando Galarraga's 2010 near-perfect game. The blown call on what would have been the final out of the game still rankles, but nothing like it did when it happened. At the time, I was livid, convinced that Jim Joyce, the first base umpire, had robbed someone on *my* team of an incredible achievement. If the same thing happened with Fulmer on the mound today, I'm sure I would be disappointed to miss out on seeing a no-hitter, but I can't imagine that level of emotional investment I had eight years ago.

As I watch the pre-game video, with its baseball cards and grainy action nodding nostalgically to Tigers history, I can't help but think of last night's game and the photos that lined the stadium's façade. And of the drive home, along Van Dyke, out of the suburbs and into the heart of Detroit, a road eerily lit in the fog. We passed abandoned buildings and empty lots a block or two on either side of this main artery, and then suddenly we were in Indian Village, a slowly gentrifying hipster enclave. It was a reminder that Detroit hasn't changed completely since we started going to Tigers games, that there are really two Detroits. Our way of seeing the city is not the reality for the vast majority of people who live here.

All the things I loved about the Tigers come back to me as I walk into Comerica Park. I'm overcome with nostalgia for all the previous Sundays Dale and I have spent here together over the past fifteen years. Unlike last night's game, there's no need to manufacture team history, loyalty, or nostalgia: it's all here. The video montage they play before the game almost brings me to tears. I do love this team. It also sparks feelings of guilt for not paying as much attention to the team as I once did. Will this project rekindle some of that spark for me when Opening Day rolls around next year?

The moment we pass the statues, I look at the outfield and spot Curtis right away. My heart sings to see him back in Comerica, even in a different uniform. I see the starting lineup and he's batting leadoff. It seems like old times and I am grateful to be here.

Being back in Comerica, especially the morning after that USPBL game, makes me realize that this way of watching the game that I'm trying to cultivate is not natural. Most people attend to cheer *for* a player, a team, or both. Watching in pursuit of a well-played game or beautiful play, or watching pitching for its own sake is not how people normally take in baseball. That's not to say that knowledgeable fans aren't interested and on the lookout for those things, but that they view them through the lens of their specific rooting interest, like my reaction to Galarraga's near-perfect game. People see us as oddities, our way of approaching baseball this summer as quite outside their own experience.

As a kid, I thought my father liked the Expos and the Blue Jays because they were Canadian teams. Maybe that was part of it, but I realize now he would follow whatever team he could see/hear because he just really liked baseball. He was, in fact, quite catholic in his baseball watching. Of course, all those days listening to the Cardinals and the Yankees on the radio or watching the Expos and Blue Jays, and later the Cubs on television, made him think in terms of a particular team in a particular year. Still, I think overriding this was his interest in the game. Maybe my desire to watch baseball without loyalty to only one team is just an extension of Dad's wandering baseball fandom.

Today we're sitting in section 327, which remains one of my favourite vantage points in the park. Here I can see the game unfolding, laid out before me like a giant chessboard. It was here that I really first learned about baseball with Dale and Dave, where I saw the Thome shift for the first time, where Dave taught me how to keep score. When we had our partial season tickets, I liked being close to the action and to the players ten rows up on the first base side. But today I'm happy to be back in my original space—it's quieter, more thoughtful. From up here, you can see how every player on the field responds to a ball in play. This vantage point gives the game a broader narrative sweep.

Just like when Dave, Dale, and I went to games, we have a whole row to ourselves. In 2003, Detroit's worst season on record, there were times when we'd have a whole section to ourselves. Vendors would just shout up to us instead of climbing the stairs: "Y'all need anything?" It's not quite that bad today, but it's close.

They've announced the attendance of today's game: 24,658. It's clear from looking around that attendance is counted by tickets sold, not turnstile clicks. It's hard not to make a connection between the number of people here today and the offer they're announcing on the big screen: for $39 you can get a seat for every home game for the entire month or, for $29, you can get standing-room admission. The offer would have been unimaginable ten years ago, but entirely plausible in 2003 or 2004. I guess that's the nature of baseball fandom. I'm reminded of an acquaintance who proudly proclaims his undying love for the Tigers when they win and then angrily tweets "I'm done with the Tigers!" when they lose. Looking around at the partially filled stadium, I see my friend isn't the only one who feels this way.

I recently read a news story noting that Tigers attendance has been steadily dropping over the last four years. Today, many of the fans here in Detroit are wearing Blue Jays caps and shirts, undoubtedly Canadians who have crossed the river to cheer on their team. A sizeable portion of the Detroit fans are also, like me, wearing jerseys celebrating Tigers of the past, instead of the present. Cabrera aside, section 327 looks like a bit of an All-Star team with Ordoñez, Rodriguez, and Verlander jerseys and t-shirts dotting the crowd. It occurs to me that my Granderson jersey is older than most of the kids in attendance today, and that he was never a Tiger in their lifetime.

Reading the names on my scorecard between innings, I think back to that old "Who's Your Tiger" campaign they had in 2007. Who would be my Tiger if they ran that promotion today? It seems wrong to think about this when Curtis is on the field—albeit in a rival uniform. But, if pressed, I'd probably go with Niko Goodrum. Or Nick Castellanos, though Dale keeps thinking they'll trade him and I just can't go through that again.[6]

The crowd is sparse and there's a lot of room around us in the upper deck on this overcast but pleasant afternoon. As much as I love being close to the game—whether in our old Tigers seats just past first base or behind home plate as we've been so many times in small parks this season—there is something beautiful about this view, the diamond and field laid out in front of us, with the backdrop of downtown Detroit beyond the confines of the park. You can see everything at once, watch the play as it develops. A double play becomes an intricate dance when seen from above, the moving parts synchronized so that it appears to require no effort at all. Iglesias setting himself, scooping the hot grounder, flipping the ball to Rodriguez at second. Rodriguez dragging his foot across the bag, firing the relay to the Goodrum at first, his body stretching in full extension as he catches the ball for the second out of the third inning. Set, scoop, flip, drag, relay, stretch, catch. The players make it seem automatic, but it is anything but. We know you can never assume the double play.

Curtis just caught a fly ball and I scored it, as I used to, F8, making the top loop of the 8 into a little heart. I smile and show it to Dale, who nods and then adds, "But he's playing left field." Aha. I erase it and make it F♥ and show it to him again with a self-satisfied smile to which he nods back. In my scorecard lexicon, it's patently clear that Curtis caught the ball.

Curtis is out 4-3 and he's the final out of the third inning. I clap but then suddenly stop. I have no idea how to react. What counts more? My Tigers fandom or my affection for Curtis? Or my distinct lack of affection for the Blue Jays? Somehow the non-partisan nature of the past few weeks has made the peculiarities of fandom visible in ways they've never been before.

Just now, I clapped for a nice 5-3 out and Dale said, "You know you just clapped for the Jays throwing Miggy out?" I feel completely disoriented.

There are other things that I never would have noticed before this season. Something as simple as Kevin Pillar ambivalently tossing a baseball to a fan in the stands has been made strange now that I've seen players scouring parking lots, overgrown grass, and ditches for baseballs so the game can continue.

Top of the sixth and there's still no score. To this point, Fulmer is only at sixty-one pitches and so has an outside shot at throwing a Maddux, a term that nicely captures efficiency for a pitcher. Coined by Jason Lukehart in 1998, a "Maddux" is a complete game shut-out in which a pitcher throws fewer than a hundred pitches.[7] With the emphasis on pitch counts and the ever-increasing use of relief pitching in the major leagues, complete games are rare in and of themselves, complete game shutouts even rarer. To see a Maddux would be something special.

Fulmer starts Aledmys Diaz with a fastball, but misses outside for a ball. He then gets the call on a slider on the outside corner. Diaz connects on the 1-1 fastball, a hot grounder that looks like it will go for a base hit through the hole between short and third. But Iglesias ranges to his right, corrals the ball in his outstretched glove, plants himself, and throws a perfect strike on one bounce to Goodrum at first for the out. That brings up Granderson. Fastball through the heart of the plate for a strike looking, followed by a changeup for a swinging strike. On the 0-2 pitch, Granderson hits a weak foul pop to the third baseman.

Sixty-seven pitches with two outs and Yangervis Solarte up to bat. Fulmer has him down 1-2, but misses with a changeup that is just low and a slider just inside to run the count full. Solarte fouls off a fastball at the top of the strike zone and then an inside fastball. The eighth pitch of the at-bat misses badly inside and Solarte draws the walk. Suddenly the pitch count is at seventy-five.

Three balls to Justin Smoak put Fulmer deep in the hole, in danger of walking a second man and putting a runner in scoring position. But a called strike and a foul ball bring the count to full and Fulmer's pitch count to 80. The 3-2 pitch is another 95-mph fastball—about the speed Fulmer has been throwing all day—but it's down the middle of the strike zone and straight. Major league hitters seldom miss pitches like that, no matter what the velocity. Smoak crushes a home run to right center and the Blue Jays lead 2-0. The shutout, the Maddux, and, in all likelihood, the complete game are no more.

There isn't a lot of chatter up here, but a down a few seats, in the row behind us, are a dad and his daughter. The dad looks like the owner of an indie record store, not at all like the typical baseball fan you might imagine. The daughter, about six years old, is wearing hipster jeans and a cool jean jacket with a flowery shirt. She is quietly snuggled up to her dad, rapt by the game unfolding beneath us.

He's explaining the game to her and has just broken down a suicide squeeze. He details why the Tigers attempted it and why, in this case, it failed. She nods. He points out that a fly ball could score a run right here. They sit in silence for a while. He tells her why he thinks the Tigers players need to stop swinging for the fences and just worry about getting on base. She asks questions I cannot hear but I notice he listens, carefully. He talks to her gently, like an equal, but still respectful of her childlike wonder at the world. I see him outlining not only how the game is played but also how to watch a game of baseball.

Captivated by this dad and his little girl, I cast my mind toward her future when she tries to explain to people, perhaps even to herself, what baseball means to her. And I know, at different points in her life, she will try to describe Sundays like these with her dad and with the Tigers. And whomever she talks to will never really understand, even though they might pretend they do.

Leonys Martin leads off the bottom of the sixth with a home run of his own to get the Tigers back to 2-1. As the ball settles into the outfield seats, the Rally Goose makes its first appearance of the day, a flying Canada goose superimposed over the home run sign on the video board that spans most of left field. I crane my neck to glimpse whether the original Rally Goose has made an appearance in the Tigers dugout, but I can't see. The season is long and the players find ways to amuse themselves, but this time it has caught the imagination of the fans, somehow seeming to capture the spirit of this overachieving team. Maybe Martin's home run and the cry of the Rally Goose will spark the offense.

Castellanos hits the ball to the warning track, but it doesn't carry in the still cool air of early June. Later in the season that might have been a home run. Cabrera, the next batter, is visibly upset when he's called out on strikes, taking off his batting helmet and yelling at Laz Diaz, the home plate umpire, with such vehemence that I'm surprised he's still in the game. A walk to Candelario, but Sanchez, the Blue Jays starter, is able to strike out Goodrum for the third out. 2-1 Blue Jays after six innings.

I know there's a million-to-one chance that this dad or his little girl will ever read this book and a two-million-to-one chance they'll know I'm writing about them. If they do, I hope they know that seeing them together and listening to their conversations has started to clarify so much of what I've thought about what baseball means to me. I still can't articulate what it is they've shown me, but I know it's about love. And hope. And how baseball can bring those two things together.

It's 8-1 for Toronto and the sun has just come out from behind the clouds. I watch Curtis in the outfield. I stare at the Detroit skyline. I turn my Tigers cap inside out. Dale looks over and says, "I think that's the most hopeful rally cap I've ever seen." It's baseball. Anything can happen.

Final Score: 8-4 Blue Jays

Nine
MIDDLE INNINGS
June 7 – July 1, 2018

Windsor Selects
vs
Windsor Stars

St. Clair Green Giants
vs
Lake Erie Monarchs

London Majors
vs
Barrie Baycats

Thursday, June 7, 2018

Windsor Selects
vs
Windsor Stars

Cullen Field, Windsor ON
Game Time Temperature: 26°C

Tonight there's an announcer at Cullen Field. When we arrive, he's introducing the umpires and the starting line-ups. As I open my journal, I say to Dale, "It seems like forever since we've been at a baseball game." I am taken aback by my own statement and add, "But it's only been four days since the last game." Dale answers, "I know what you mean."

At this very instant, the light is what photographers call "the golden hour" and it always makes me stop whatever I'm doing and breathe it in. I'm happy to be here.

From my seat behind the plate, I count about twenty-five people scattered around the park for this Can-Am Senior League game. Cullen is the home park for both teams, but tonight the Stars will play the part of the visitors. I look around the park while Tyler Jameson takes his last warmup pitches for the Selects, a team made up of players twenty-one and under. I wonder what connections these people have to the players, if there are others like us here who just want to watch a ballgame on a perfect early summer evening.

The game doesn't start out well for Jameson and the Selects. Hit batter, stolen base, wild pitch, walk, and suddenly there are runners at the corners with no one out in the first. Scattered between outs, a sacrifice fly, steal, and single lead to two runs for the Stars. Meanwhile, Dane Little, the starting pitcher for the Stars, cruises through the first in order, pitching to contact for two ground ball outs and a flyout to right field. 2-0 Stars at the end of the first.

The second inning is quick and crisp. It's quiet in the stands but I can hear a chatty, animated rec-league softball game in the distance and a group of little girls amusing themselves with a sing-songy cheer. There's also a kids' soccer game nearby. But the crowd here is attentive, watching the action on the field.

The silence is broken by a mom offering quiet analysis and support to her son, whom she calls "Pook." She's filming his at-bats and offering a running commentary. "Good eye," she says, "Way to work out there. Atta boy." Of his awkward, scrambly base hit, she says, "Ugly. But we'll take it." She doesn't film the other players but she continues to offer support: "Way to work up there, Ty."

They're using wood bats, and I find the sound comforting, unlike the sound of aluminum bats. A solid THOCK instead of a hollow CLANK. A coach paces along the third base side, offering advice, and supplying chatter. "Follow it now. You're alright. Let's go let's go letsgo. Battle it here. Stay tough. Focus now. You're a good hitter. Keep it workin' kid."

Someone in the dugout sends a bystander kid out to find a ball in the neighbouring field and he takes off with a couple of friends to retrieve it. Two dozen Canada geese fly over the outer reaches of left field.

By the time Jameson takes the mound in the fourth inning, he has settled down and his teammates have managed to score two runs to tie the game. He opens the inning with a pair of strikeouts, one swinging and one looking. His pitches are starting to fool the Stars hitters. Just as I think the wildness that got him into so much trouble in the first is gone, however, he walks the next batter.

In front of us sit a father and son, the kid in his ball uniform. Knees dirt-stained, cap askew, it looks like he just finished playing himself. He is intent on the game in front of him, chewing his gum thoughtfully as he watches, occasionally asking his father something. At first base, the runner takes a sizeable lead, dives back in time to beat the throw over from Jameson. I hear the kid ask about the length of the lead at first and the father reply that you need to find a balancing point, neither too reckless nor too safe. Far enough to give the pitcher something to think about, but not so far that you're going to run your team into an out. The kid just nods, his attention never wavering as Jameson sneaks a fastball by the hitter to end the inning.

I count the fans in the stands and realize there are more people in uniforms on the field. There's a group of three older men who look like retired farmers watching attentively, pointing out a good pitch or a strong play discerningly. They're wearing tidy button-down shirts and clean ball caps. Any of them could easily be Dale's dad or my grandfather. It feels comforting to have them in the stands tonight.

When you watch baseball at this level, you pare back. You're not really thinking about things like spin rate or launch angle. Can the pitcher throw strikes is question one. And, if so, is he fooling the hitters with movement or can he throw the ball by them? Is there any deception? What secondary pitches does he have beyond the fastball? Can hitters catch up to a good fastball, especially a high fastball? Can they hit a curve or lay off a slider in the dirt? Do the players make good decisions on the basepaths? Can the infield pick it? Do the outfielders take good routes to balls? Can the catcher block pitches in the dirt? Throw quickly and accurately to second base? Are the teams sound in their fundamentals? At this level—the highest tier of amateur baseball in Canada—the answers are generally positive. Many of the Stars played college baseball at schools like Maine, Central Michigan, Madonna, Saginaw Valley State, Canisius, or Wayne State, and a number of the Selects will go on to play at similar schools, as their alumni have in previous years. A few will play in the minor leagues. It is, undeniably, good baseball and though the players sometimes make difficult plays, like fielding that in-between hop, throwing that lollipop curve, or hitting that fastball up in the zone look easy, those moments come in flashes. But events on the field are sometimes unpredictable, heightening the drama on every play, reinforcing again and again just how hard this game is to play.

Dale just pointed out that the Selects' pitcher has just found his strike zone and has good velocity. I write down what Dale teaches me and try to commit it to memory. Maybe by the end of the summer I'll notice things like this on my own.

I tighten my ponytail and lean in to concentrate on the pitching. More geese fly overhead. The sunlight changes minute by minute. Right now, there's complete silence; no one says a word or takes a breath as they wait for what will happen next. There's no sound, not a bird or a car or a factory. Only silence in the perfect light.

I am woken from my reverie by the THWIP! sound of the ball hitting the glove and the call of "Sttttriiiiiike!" And then people start talking again, cars rumble over roads, factories burble away, and the geese honk atonally over center field.

The score is 4-2 for the Stars as Little walks off the mound at the end of the sixth. The air is still, no hint of a breeze, and the only sounds are the tractor raking the adjacent diamond, the ambient industrial sounds from Prince Metal just to the north of the park, and the occasional ship's horn from the Detroit River. As I sit in the evening's quiet, I think about Roger Angell's idea of the "interior stadium." In *The Summer Game*, he writes, "This inner game—baseball in the mind—had no season, but it is best played in the winter, without the distraction of other baseball news. At first, it is a game of recollections, recapturings, and visions. Figures and occasions return, enormous sounds rise and swell, and the interior stadium fills with light." He means, of course, recapturings and visions of the major leagues, recollections that connect his father's memories of Fred Snodgrass in the 1912 World Series to his own memories of Lou Gehrig in the summer of 1933. That connect the past to the present in one unbroken story of baseball.

I am starting to understand that there is going to a baseball game for the sake of going to an event: to sit in the sun with friends, have a hot dog or a beer, and let the game wash over you like background music. There's going to a game for the sake of a team: to connect with your team, rekindle nostalgia for times and people lost, feel like you're a part of something larger, something everlasting. There's going to a game for the sake of a player: maybe it's your son or your brother or your sister. Or your equivalent of Curtis Granderson. And then, finally, there's what we're doing tonight: going to a game for the sake of nothing more than learning something new about baseball. All are equally valid. All are not mutually exclusive, but the reason you go to the game changes how you watch it and what you see.

As I watch the Selects take the field for the top of the seventh inning, I realize that I carry my own interior stadium, one that links me to Dad and Kurt and Rick and Dave and Heidi. Not through shared memories of what happened in the history of Major League Baseball, but through our shared love of baseball for its own sake, regardless of who is playing on a given day, regardless of who wins. Through the game we all hold in our heads. Through the soul of baseball that lives in every one of the parks we've visited this summer.

Final Score: 9-2 Stars

Saturday, June 30, 2018

St. Clair Green Giants
vs
Lake Erie Monarchs

Lacasse Park, Tecumseh ON
Game Time Temperature: 33°C

There's an Environment Canada "extreme heat event" today, described as "the most significant heat event in the past few years." I'm grateful that we're in the shaded grandstand at Lacasse Park. My brown sundress is picking up the slight breeze. This is the kind of weekend I kept

summoning in April and May, when I envisioned classic summer baseball weather.

I'm watching them chalk the baselines and the batter's box. There
are a few Lake Erie players lounging in the shade of the grandstand,
eating bananas, and imbibing Gatorade. Three have clipboards, each
with a different looking form and a pencil. One has a radar gun. There
are probably thirty people here tonight and the announcer seems committed to creating a baseball mood and ambience by emulating the
kinds of announcers you hear in baseball movies. Announcing the
starting lineups, he says "Batting eighth. . . ! Kevin. Diiiii-onnnnnnn."
About six people, scattered across the stands, clap for Kevin. Other
players get no applause.

It's our first game after getting back from vacation, a trip that
took us out of the country and away from baseball. I wondered if
it would be an adjustment to get back into the project, but by the
time I've settled myself, cracked my first sunflower seeds of the evening, and scanned the players getting ready for the game, the feeling
of being back at the park has already begun to wash over me. The
sights and sounds of the game clear my mind and everything outside Lacasse drops away.

We're here to see a seven-inning Great Lakes Summer Collegiate
League (GLSCL) game. The teams are comprised of college players from universities and community colleges throughout North
America—Toledo, Michigan, Nebraska, Rice, Middle Tennessee
State, Wayne State, Wabash Valley College, Palomar College, Garden City Community College, and St. Clair Community College,
to name only a few. Players are able to keep their NCAA eligibility
because they are not paid for the two-month season that runs from
the beginning of June to the end of July, staying with billet families as they concentrate on baseball. This league, like other summer
collegiate leagues such as the Cape Cod League, immerses players
in baseball played with wood bats. This iteration of baseball is sub-
stantially different—especially for hitters—than what they have
played in college with aluminum bats. For pitchers, it's a chance to
hone their craft by pitching against quality collegiate competition.

Some players from this league go on to play in the minor leagues. Some—such as Nick Swisher, Chad Cordero, and Paul Quantrill— even make it to the majors. Whatever the eventual outcome, for all, playing in the league is both a transition and a trial.

Every announcement seems to be punctuated by an exclamation point. The announcer warns us, "Pay attention to the play on the field! Getting hit by a baseball or a bat could be hazardous to your health!" They play both anthems, which sound like they're on old vinyl LPs. I can tell there are twelve Americans here because there are twelve people holding their ball caps over their hearts during the anthem. I don't see anyone singing, but someone behind me is humming along with the American anthem until the high notes required of "And the rocket's red glare." Four of the standing twelve keep their hats over their hearts for the Canadian anthem. Are they dual citizens? Or just polite guests in our country?

On the mound for the Green Giants is Garrett Nicholson, a lefty who attends Central Michigan, but hails from Sydney Mines, Nova Scotia. He starts out well, with a ground ball to short and a fly to center field to get the first two outs of the first, but then gives up two runs on a walk, an error to the second baseman, a hit batter, and two more walks before getting a ground ball to end the inning. No hits allowed, but two runs cross the plate for the Monarchs. I wonder if Jonathan Fincher, the Louisiana Tech left-hander pitching for the Monarchs, will be able to throw strikes. If he can't, it's going to be a long night.

And he does come out throwing strikes, but unfortunately for him, Carter Mossey is able to use his speed to stretch a bloop hit into a leadoff double. Before Fincher can even collect himself, Mossey steals third with no throw, scoring later in the inning on a ball hit to the right side of the infield. Two more score on a bases-loaded single. 3-2 St. Clair at the end of the first. By all indications, tonight is not going to be a pitchers' duel.

I find the broadcast booth kind of endearing: two guys in the top corner of the bleachers with a desk and a laptop. Like many of the players we've seen, they too seem to be trying to hit their stride. Sometimes they sound like they're emulating pros, but mostly they just sound like likable characters in a baseball movie. "A good battle on our hands here!" one says. "And he's walked in another run!" says the other. A bit later one says, "It's getting to the point where things are a little out of control. This is the eighth batter up this inning!" Sometimes they sound like their unique selves, which is, I imagine, what they're trying to hone.

They're not so loud that you can't tune them out, but they're loud enough that they're always kind of there, especially when silence settles over the sparse crowd. After just such a quiet moment, I lean over to Dale and say, "It's the weirdest thing. I've watched so much baseball lately that I can actually hear a play-by-play guy and a commentator in my head, describing everything on the field!" He does a double-take and then laughs when he sees my impish smile. "That's actually funny," he says.

Five of the Monarchs are sitting behind home plate, just a few rows ahead of us. One uses his radar gun to track pitch speed, another charts pitches as Nicholson induces ground balls to the second baseman from the first two Monarchs hitters. It looks like he's been able to find the strike zone again. I want to ask the Monarchs pitchers if they see any difference in his motion or in the pitch selection, but I stay quiet. Maybe later I'll ask about his velocity.

That brings up the right-handed hitter Jordan Nwogu, an outfielder we saw play for Michigan earlier in the season, in their game against Eastern Michigan. As he does at Michigan, Nwogu wears #42. Nwogu doesn't just tap the plate. Before every pitch, he slams the bat on its outer edge, the bat quaking in his hand before he cocks it over his right shoulder. His swing is smooth, left leg rising and moving back towards the right as he strides into the ball. But on this occasion, the bat never leaves his shoulder. A walk on four pitches. Nicholson seems to have lost the strike zone again.

A couple of rows behind us, at the top of the grandstand, sit the announcers, narrating the action on the field for those watching the web telecast of the game. The soundtrack is distracting and I'd really rather not have the constant commentary. But every time I'm annoyed by what seem like obvious observations on the game, I try to remind myself that these fledgling broadcasters are young, still learning their craft, just like the players on the field. As Nwogu steals second base on an 0-2 pitch, an excited "in with the steal" echoes behind me, followed quickly by "Ground ball to third base. Duluc fields, throws, to get Mazur easily at first." You don't become Ernie Harwell or Dick Enberg without a lot of practice.

I'm noticing something about this level of play but having trouble finding the words to describe it. It's not quite confidence. More like trust? Tonight, I see players with a whole array of trusts. They have trust in their ability to throw from third to first and they have trust in the first baseman's ability to catch it. This trust is rarely absent in MLB. I'd just never noticed the importance of trust before this summer, when I saw players not trusting themselves or their teammates to execute the plays the pros make us think are routine. Baseball at all these different levels is showing me what I never saw in the big leagues. I'm starting to see baseball anew.

With one out in the bottom of the second, Mossey reaches first on an error as the first baseman tries to hurry his toss to the covering pitcher. That brings up Rodrigo Duluc, a player who attends Rice, but comes from New York. As he settles in to the batter's box, I wonder what he thinks of living in a small town like Tecumseh, Ontario. What he thinks of playing in this league.

On the second pitch of Duluc's at-bat, Mossey takes off for second, almost before Fincher even sets himself to throw home. Before coming to the plate again, Fincher tries to pick Mossey off second, but throws the ball into center field, allowing him to reach third, before scoring on a very shallow sacrifice fly to center field. Mossey manufactured that run with his legs and it's 4-2 St. Clair.

There's been a raffle tonight for a gift certificate for Frenchie's Poutinerie, a putting contest, a kids' footrace, some musical chairs, but mostly people are here to watch the game in relative silence.

I add "time called because third baseman noticed an extra ball sitting in the outfield" to my list of things I've never seen before in a

baseball game. Given the nature of the league, there aren't a lot of players' families or friends here—it's mostly just local people interested in
watching some good baseball. For once, we're really not unusual in
how we're watching the game. No one has asked "who's your kid?"
and it's refreshing.

It's the third inning and though Nicholson has only given up
two runs, he's thrown a lot of pitches. I wonder how much longer
he'll be left in the game. Just at that moment, as if there's some kind
of echo, I hear from the top row of the grandstand, "The pitch count
continues to rise and rise and rise."

A pre-recorded "Let's make some Noiiiise!!!"" sound bite comes
over the PA and there's not a peep from anyone. Silence envelopes the
stands like the heat and humidity that blanket the field, which the sun
has cast in a gorgeous golden hue.

Top of the seventh inning and Steven Butts, a lefty from Arizona
Christian, is in to try to close out the game for the Green Giants.
When he throws, his arm comes across his body as he falls violently
towards the first base line. You can almost hear him grunt on every
pitch. There's some intimidation to the violence and funkiness of his
delivery.

A single and a double bring the tying run to the plate and St.
Clair's three-run cushion looks a lot less secure than it did a few
minutes ago. But when Lambeau's fly ball to center isn't deep enough
to score a run and Weyler strikes out swinging, it once again appears
that Butts will be able to preserve the victory. Until, that is, Andrew
Dyke steps to the plate. His three-run home run rolls to a stop in the
grass beyond the outfield fence.

People clap, not because they're cheering for any team or player,
but because it was a pretty home run. As the announcers say to whoever is listening to their broadcast, "Well, guys, settle in. We have
a tied game. It was slated for seven innings, but we're going into
extra innings!" I look at my watch. I'm tired. I try to concentrate. The
announcers fill time. "It's cooling off considerably now that the sun has

gone down," they note. Librarian that I am, I fact check their claim with my weather app. It's still 30°C, even with no sun.

Butts takes the mound again for the top of the eighth, the Green Giants having failed to score in their half of the seventh. An error puts the leadoff hitter on base, but Butts, funky delivery and all, comes back to strike out Nwogu. As Nwogu swings, words seem to float down from the rafters: "He almost grazes the ground with his knuckles as he delivers the pitch."

Just when I think he's back on track, Butts walks Griffin Mazur and hits Casey Slattery to load the bases. At this point, he's either going to keep missing the strike zone or he's going to be so determined to throw a strike that he grooves a hittable pitch down the middle of the plate. But then he doesn't, once again confounding my expectations by setting Bell up with pitches low in the zone before climbing the ladder with fastballs. The third strike is at the letters with a lot of speed, a pitch that Bell has no chance to handle. "All of a sudden" a voice intones from above, "Butts has some confidence."

I think we're all a little drained by this heat and not overly joyful about going into extra innings. The game lags a bit. As one batter steps up to the plate, the man behind me shouts what I'm thinking, "Hit the crap out of the ball and score a run!" Dale, on the other hand, seemingly unfazed by the heat or the late hour, observes, "If he trusts his catcher, and I think he does, he'll throw a breaking ball in the dirt." The batter strikes out with three men left on base. And we go into another inning.

Kyle Bischoff, from the University of Toledo, strikes out the first Green Giants batter he faces to open the bottom of the eighth inning, but then walks the second, Windsor's own Kevin Dion, who attends St. Clair College. A wild pitch moves Dion to second base. A subsequent wild pitch moves him to third. Things aren't looking good for Bischoff and the Monarchs. As if on cue, the announcer behind us says, "Again, we are having some technical difficulties with our center field camera."

Mossey walks to put runners on the corners, but perhaps giving the Monarchs at least some hope that they might turn a double play to get out of the inning. But if Butts found his confidence last half inning, Bischoff has run up against doubt right now. He needs to slow down, forget about the walks and the wild pitches. Easy for me to think, sitting up here in the stands. Much more difficult to execute in the heat of the moment. Doubt builds and it's hard to shake.

Duluc up. Swings at the first pitch, then takes a ball. Swings at the third pitch. A strikeout here is Bischoff's best chance to escape. Fastball that Duluc manages to just foul off. Still 1-2. Still a chance.

But the fifth pitch seems to slip from Bischoff's hand, sailing past the catcher so there's no play on Dion. Walk-off wild pitch.

Final Score: 9-8 St Clair

Sunday, July 1, 2018

London Majors
vs
Barrie Baycats

Labatt Park, London ON
Game Time Temperature: 30°C

With a 6 pm start, there was really no reason for us to have been late to this game. But we were. Dale wanted to stop in Chatham to watch the Croatia World Cup game at a Boston Pizza and our calculation suggested we could make it to London in time. In theory, we should have been able to make it to London in time.

While Dale watched the World Cup, I read a book and kept one eye on the Tigers/Blue Jays game. I was grateful to have seen Kevin Pillar rob Nick Castellanos of a home run. It wasn't that a Blue Jay robbed one of my Tigers of a home run but that the catch was so spectacular that Castellanos gave Pillar a wave and a salute. In previous years, my Tigers fandom would not have allowed me to see the true beauty of that play.

Our initial calculations did not take into account the possibility that the Croatia game could go into overtime. And we didn't consider that there would be penalty kicks. Then, when we got to London, we couldn't find parking anywhere. We'd somehow forgotten it was Canada Day and we had to park a fifteen-minute walk away.

Being late for a baseball game has always bothered me and this summer it's something that we've almost completely managed to avoid. By the time we make our way into Labatt Park, it's the bottom of the second inning and the score is 2-0 for Barrie. As the teams switch places, I'm at first confused by the "Pontiacs" script across the chests of the London players, but then I see that it's throwback night and they're wearing the jerseys of the London Pontiacs, who won the Intercounty Baseball League championship in 1969.

From the earliest beginnings of this project, we were looking forward to visiting this ballpark, which has claims to being the world's oldest baseball grounds, established in 1877.[1] There is a newish grandstand, some tightly packed bleacher seats with backs, and some without. We sit in a few different places, realizing each time why certain seats were available in a nearly full ballpark: obstructed views. Finally, we secure spots on the third base side in the middle of the row.

On paper, going to game twenty-five out of fifty on Canada Day at the world's oldest ballpark on a hot, sunny summer afternoon should be the pivotal point of this project. A week ago, I imagined how this game might pull things together and set the tone for the remaining chapters of the book. I imagined that merely sitting in this storied park would help me summon metaphors and insights about baseball that would somehow replicate the feeling we all had at Comerica Park when Magglio Ordoñez's hit the home run in 2006. In reality, though, I'm truly, utterly, and completely miserable. I just want to go home, sit in my cold basement, eat a popsicle, and watch *Masterpiece Theatre*.

Between the fifth and sixth innings, there's a "Dizzy Bat" contest for the kids, a race that involves spinning around a bat and then attempting to run to first base. Other kids' promotions have thus far included a water-balloon toss and, just after the third, the running of the bases—an activity almost universally reserved for after the conclusion of the game—that felt more like the running of the bulls. I'm surprised no one got trampled.

We're a long way from the plate, but I can clearly hear the fans seated in the grandstand jawing with the ump, unhappy about the three Majors strikeouts in the fifth inning. "Some of those pitches weren't even close, Blue." I know they're just cheering for their team, wanting them to come out of the evening with a win. I watched the Tigers that way for years, but after this summer, that kind of cheering seems odd in ways I never would have predicted.

I've become accustomed this summer to moving around, to seeing the game from different angles. We're fairly close here, but stationary, trapped in the middle of a row, the seats ahead of us tight up against our knees. I can't seem to get comfortable and I'm having trouble paying attention to the game in ways that I haven't all year. Maybe it's the angle and narrowness of the seats. Maybe it's being on the third base side. Maybe it's not being able to take a walk. Last night I was able to settle into the game immediately, to sink back into baseball like we hadn't been away at all. Tonight all I can think about is that my back hurts, it's hot, and I feel hemmed in.

The people between us and the aisle have several coolers and grocery bags each. They made a distinct effort to show us how much we were inconveniencing them by selecting those two remaining seats. Perhaps in retaliation, the woman next to me keeps pushing her elbow into my side, and inching her cooler closer and closer into my foot space. Dale, too tall to sit comfortably in these seats, is giving me some of his space. The man in front and to the left of me has his arm across the back of his son's seat. His elbow is nearly on my knee. The man behind me has trapped my hair between his foot and my seat back a few times. Tucking my hair into my ball cap seems to have done the trick.

Three little boys sitting directly in front of me and to the right are hummingbird-like in their movements and energy, darting about, sitting and standing, changing seats, demanding and sharing snacks. Endearingly, they offer some pretty cute baseball chatter. But it's muggy and still 30°C in the early evening. And I'm tired. I think I could concentrate on the ballgame if there were just one of these factors; having all of them is proving a bit much for me right now.

Ahead and to our left, a middle-aged woman in a red cap and ponytail, red shirt, and green shorts holds forth to her companions on how this game compares to other levels of baseball. "In real baseball," she says, "the situation room has video screens." Is she talking about video reviews of close plays? What does she mean by "the situation room"? I have so many questions, but mostly I want to tell her that this *is* real baseball and that the major leagues aren't everything. I want to tell her and her friends to enjoy it. Savour it. Watch it for its own sake and don't compare it to whatever she thinks of as "real baseball."

In front of us sits a kid, maybe ten years old, Jays cap, black Canada t-shirt, red shorts. He's narrating what would happen if you were up at the plate with three down and the bases loaded. He hasn't stopped talking since we sat down, his friend offering only the occasional word to interrupt his monologue. One of the fathers leans over, says, "Hey, you guys watching the game?" Despite the constant stream of talk, it's clear that all of them are. And not just the third kid, the one on the end in the black baseball cap whose eyes have never left the field, but the talker as well. They see the game past all the distractions, even the ones they've created themselves. They're enjoying this night of baseball on its own terms, in ways I can't seem to access tonight.

I feel guilty and inadequate for being so irritable and cranky at what is really quite a remarkable and lovely way to spend our nation's special day. The heavily coolered and grocery-bagged family next to me have made it abundantly clear that getting out of my seat and going for a walk isn't an option, so I settle in, re-tucking my hair in my cap for safety, and focus on the game. I can do this, I tell myself.

I rouse my hopeful optimism and summon a better mood. I take a deep breath, relax, and watch a batter. I clap for a smart fielding play. It's all good. I can do this. But then the man behind me crosses his legs and dislodges my ball cap with his foot and leans his knee on the back of my seat, trapping my hair yet again. Because my hair is trapped, I cannot turn my head to ask him to move, so I just sit patiently, hoping he'll shift soon. And that the game will end soon. This is not at all what I thought this game would be.

The score is now 11-0 for Barrie. The ringleader hummingbird boy, points out that Barrie has eleven runs on eleven hits, no errors and no stranded runners on base. I have no idea how he can both carry on his wide-ranging conversations while paying meticulous attention to the game. London is getting shelled but the din of chatter hasn't lessened at all. People are just happy to be here.

Today's players look a little older than ones we've seen before, a little tougher, too. Some look like players who would run you down on the basepaths and never look back. It's easy to think about baseball as a gentlemanly sport, and indeed, it can be. But today, remembering the stories about what players from the 1934 Chatham Coloured All-Stars endured, I know baseball has a tough side.

In the 1940s, Earl "Flat" Chase played in this park for the London Majors and he's been on my mind today.[2] Driving here, we took Highway 2 and passed towns whose names I know from reading the newspaper coverage of the All-Stars' 1934 season: Thamesville, Kent Bridge, and West Lorne. Today I imagined the All-Stars travelling these same roads in borrowed cars, not knowing who or what they would encounter at the ballpark upon arrival, especially in those predominantly white towns.

The dad of one of the hummingbird kids has to ask his son not to bang an empty water bottle on his head and adds his now familiar refrain: "Are you kids even watching the game?" The dad doesn't notice that the boy, who has scarcely taken his eyes off the field, just said, "Wild pitch." Nor did the dad notice that the ringleader hummingbird boy is somehow able to simultaneously compare the size of his chewed-up bubblegum wad to his brother's and still accurately call a fielding error against London before it hits the scoreboard. His incisive call is followed up with, "Let's use our bubbles as airbags!"

It's the top of the eighth and Barrie are now up 13-0. If there were a mercy rule, this game would be over. I look around the stadium, survey the crowd, and, when I look back, the bases are loaded yet again. To our right, someone says, "You need to write a poem about this." Does he mean the game? Ode to a blowout? Hardly anyone has left. This is partly because there will be fireworks after the game, but also because the crowd seem happy to be with friends in this old park on a muggy July night. For most, the constant chatter and continuous contests and activities on the field between innings are all part of a good night of family entertainment, as much a part of the backdrop to their evening as the baseball on the field. For others, baseball is still the main focus, despite all the other distractions, like it was for me at the USPBL game. But tonight, for me, there is too much interference, too many obstacles to finding a way into a full experience of this game. I just want to immerse myself in it like I've been doing all summer. Tonight, despite all my anticipation for this game, despite all the ways this is the kind of "real baseball" I've come to appreciate this summer, I'm not feeling it. I just want to hit reset.

I like that the London fans are still cheering for strikes. The four-teenth run gets walked in and the bases are still loaded, but this hasn't cast a pall on the crowd in the least: they're cheering and chattering and clapping every opportunity they get. The announcers are trying to make this fun for everyone and their efforts seem to be paying off. When a fly ball gets London out of a brutal inning, the ringleader hum-mingbird boy says, "Rally caps!" and the other boys follow his exam-ple and turn their caps inside out.

In a lovely moment of baseball karma, London rewards these boys for their hopefulness by scoring two runs, which makes it a 14-2 ballgame. The quiet hummingbird boy, who still hasn't taken his eyes off the game except to offer tie-breaking judgments on whose wad of gum is bigger and to turn his ball cap inside out, stands up, looks around the stands and the field thoughtfully. "We're only down by twelve now," he says, "I thought we were going to lose 14-0. This is okay." And suddenly everything that has irritated me this evening—the heat, my fatigue, the elbow in my ribs, the cooler on my feet, the surly sneers from the family next to us, the kicks to the head, and the pulling on my hair—they all disappear. The little boys cheer for everything for the rest of the final inning. They cheer for balls, strikes, flyouts, tags—everything. "This is okay," the little hummingbird boy said. And he's right. This is okay.

As the crowd settles in for the coming fireworks, Heidi and I are among the few who head for the exit. Anxious to start the two-hour drive back to Windsor, we intend to simply retrace our steps, walking back over the same bridge we did several hours ago. But when we get out to the street, we see that the police have it cordoned off. No one is getting onto that bridge until the fireworks are over.

We walk south to Stanley, turn back east towards the next bridge over the Thames. It's a long walk and we have time to talk. We're both disappointed in our experience of this, our twenty-fifth game, and I wonder how much that has to do with all the other games this summer. I had seen the trip to Labatt Park as a centerpiece game, but it isn't, at least not in the way I imagined. Would we have felt the same disappointment with this game five years ago? Last year? At the beginning of this season?

Earlier this summer, a friend at work said to me, "I don't listen to my favourite album very often because I don't want to get sick of it. Don't you get sick of baseball?" But, of course, every game is different, like its own album, while baseball is like music. But sometimes there is an album that feels wrong to your ears, maybe because you've built it up too much. Maybe because of the other albums you'd been listening to before you put it on. Or maybe because you've started to listen in a different way, attuned to different sounds, different rhythms than you were previously.

Final Score: 14-2 Barrie

Ten
IF YOU BUILD IT . . .
July 4, 2018

Sarnia Braves
vs
Exeter Express

Wednesday, July 4, 2018

Sarnia Braves
vs
Exeter Express

Errol Russell Park, Sarnia ON
Game Time Temperature: 29°C

Neither of us want to get in the car after work today. Neither of us want to make the long drive to Sarnia, to sit out in the heat on a Wednesday night, only to return to Windsor after midnight, tomorrow's morning routine looming all too soon. Neither of us want another experience like the one a few days ago at the Majors game. But as we drive, the blandness of the 401 yielding to the rolling, lush fields north of Chatham, I sense a loosening, our talk drifting back to earlier trips this summer, to the way the landscape and cityscape change, and finally, as always, to baseball. I know that without this project we wouldn't be here, driving through Wallaceburg, talking about baseball and family and the hawks that swoop across the tops of the trees. As we talk, my reluctance about tonight drops away. There is, I realize, no place I would rather be than with Heidi, in this car, on a Wednesday night after work, driving towards Sarnia for a Southwestern Senior Baseball League game.

Work today was non-stop and I dashed out, drove home, kissed the cats, changed my shoes, grabbed my game notebook, and was back in the car within five minutes. The 401 is teeming with trucks, and even though I'm going 20 over the speed limit, I'm getting passed like a Sunday driver. I notice my speed inching up, and my tension, too. Dale is talking and I admit I'm not really paying attention. All I can think about is what exactly I signed up for and how long it will be before I can go home. This is game twenty-six. I have to watch as much baseball as I've already watched. I'm struggling to stay on top of work and stay alert for the games. My garden is a mess and our house is clean because I'm never home to scatter shoes in various rooms. And I realize I'm still a little cranky about baseball from the London game.

Something happens, though, when we turn off the 401, and head north. The trucks and tailgaters vanish and are replaced by open fields of golden grain and warm, cloudless summer-evening skies. I tilt my head a few times and feel the kinks loosen. The open spaces always hit me like a kind of relief. Even though it's been dry and hot, the fields still manage to boast some tall, vibrant corn. I feel at home in these fields and I know Dale responds the same way. It's like the world whispering, "Welcome back. Things are going to be okay."

There are about a dozen people at Errol Russell Park when we arrive, leaning on the fence watching infield practice or lounging in pairs in lawn chairs they've brought from home. Behind home plate lies an expanse of gravel, but no grandstand.[1] Likewise, there is no seating along either baseline, just a couple of picnic tables near the fence to either side of the plate. Past the outfield fences—315 down the lines, 345 to the power alleys, and 365 to straightaway center field—stands of trees partially obscure the small bungalows that lie just beyond the light standards from left to left center. The brown of the diamond has been meticulously carved out of the field's perfect green, an expanse that extends to an abundance of foul territory down both lines. A cool breeze accompanies the evening's quiet.

We take the picnic table on the first base side of home, unpack notebooks, water, sunscreen, and sunflower seeds. In front of us, the Exeter players stretch, take a few swings, joke with each other as Sarnia take the last ground balls before the start of the game. Rather than player names, the backs of the Exeter jerseys display the names of local businesses that sponsor the team. Hay Communications.

Federated Insurance. Delta Power Equipment. Hayter's Farm. Dairy Lane Systems. Holtzman's Foodland. There is no announcer, no program to consult to see who is batting or playing in the field.

By the time we sit down at one of two picnic tables, the day has vanished and I have become fully present here. We're sitting about three feet from the visitors' dugout and players are milling about. Players easily outnumber spectators. We're probably the youngest fans here by about twenty years. Collectively, the Exeter players' jerseys, each with the name of a local business, form a snapshot of life in Exeter. It's like reading the ads in the back of a small-town newspaper.

An Exeter coach and a player wander anxiously between the dugout and the edge of the field, scanning the road up and down. "What does he drive?" the coach says. "Dunno," shrugs the player. Dale is exploring the park from various angles, as he does. I'm enjoying my picnic table.

There's a small speaker mounted to a light standard, facing the street. REM's "Losing My Religion" spills forth into the street, muffled, I imagine, by the summer heat. Aside from the music, the sound of cleats on the warning track gravel, and the distant chatter of the umpires, the field is silent. While pre-emptively moving the car out of foul-ball territory, I saw the umpires suiting up in the parking lot and pulling out their gear from the trunk of a Buick.

Suddenly, the music on the speaker stops mid-song and the game commences with no fanfare or ceremony other than the sound of the first pitch hitting the catcher's glove. None of the things that irked me at the London game are here tonight. No announcer, no inter-inning contests, no crowds, no hot dogs, no vendors. Our presence, and that of the other dozen people, seems not to make a whit of difference— this game isn't being played to entertain us, or to provide a backdrop to a fun night out. As fans, we are inconsequential. An afterthought, at best. This is a game of baseball played for the sake of playing baseball. And as I realize this, I feel like we've stumbled onto something quite magical and rare.

An oldies station comes and goes as the soundtrack for the game, turned up between innings and back down when the game is on. Snatches of Foreigner, Cheap Trick, Rush. As we wait for Exeter, up 1-0, to bat in the top of the third inning, David Bowie wafts across the park. There are no promotions, no announcements, no careful calibration of the fan experience. Nothing except Rock 105 between innings, if someone remembers.

When the game is being played, there's a bit of chatter from the players, but not much. There's none of the raucous excitement of the college players. There are no high school coaches pushing the players to get into the game. There are just players focused on the rhythm of what's happening on the field. Maybe they're clearing their heads, the rituals of baseball replacing the stresses of their daily lives. Maybe they're savouring the chance to still be playing competitive baseball. Maybe they're trying to prove to themselves that they still can. It's a game played only for each other and for themselves, a private contest I don't want to interrupt. It's almost silent, except when the traffic noise intrudes.

A foul ball flies over the fence and lands where our car was. I give myself a little high five for moving it. As I watch a player retrieve it, I see the missing Exeter player jogging toward the park, dressed in his uniform, and carrying his glove and cap. The coach nods and as he puts on his ball cap and takes his position on the bench as if he's been here the whole time.

The only sounds I hear are someone's distant radio, a dog barking, a delivery truck backing up, and the sound of a ball hitting a glove as the Sarnia pitcher warms up. The inning commences. I hear birds in nearby trees, the infield umpire spitting sunflower seeds, balls hitting wood bats, and only the most minimal dugout chatter. Atta boy. Good eye. Keep it goin'. You got it. I deliberately punctuate my transcription with periods, not commas or exclamation points. The solemnity of the game makes me feel like I'm sitting in church.

Top of the fifth and the score is still 1-0 Exeter. For Exeter, #34 has six strikeouts, while for Sarnia, #31, who took over for #7 after the first inning, has four strikeouts. I don't know their names, but I do know that both of them have decent fastballs, work quickly, and throw strikes, and that both have good defensive teams behind them. I know that #31, the right-hander for Sarnia, starts with his feet square to home, glove cupped below his chin, facing the batter. His motion begins as he rotates his hips towards third base and taps his left foot before raising his leg, his body a compressed spring ready to uncoil. Just as his left leg has corkscrewed around to third, he pushes off with his right leg, his arm coming over the top and the ball hurtling towards the plate. The dust explodes from the catcher's mitt every time he throws a fastball. A lazy fly ball to center field is all the first batter of the inning can manage off him.

The second batter of the inning, #12, settles into the box, watches a couple of pitches go by before jumping on a fastball that catches too much of the strike zone. He scorches the ball, a line shot to center field, but he's unlucky with the location. The center fielder doesn't even have to move. As he trots back to the Exeter bench, he says to his teammates, in a voice that is completely deadpan, "Well, that couldn't have been any more fuckin' right at him." I notice that his jersey reads "J&M Drywall."

Earlier today it was screamingly hot but now a cool breeze is settling into the park. The reprieve I feel from the heat seems to mirror the relief I feel at being at a game with no gimmicks, no distractions. Tonight, there's nothing between me the game.

There are maybe twenty-five people here now, but I haven't heard a peep from anyone. A dad and his young daughter just rode up on their bikes and they too are silent, absorbed in the game. There's an ethereal quality about the way the field lights and the humid air blend together. I'm close enough to see a faint cloud of dust slowly rise from the catcher's glove when he catches a fastball.

The PA system comes to life for the first time between the sixth and seventh innings, a jarring intrusion as the announcer reminds us that the score is now tied 1-1. In the bottom of the sixth, Sarnia's leadoff hitter reached first on an infield single. A sacrifice bunt moved him to second and he stole third base on a strikeout pitch that produced the second out. Exeter seemed to be out of the inning on a ground ball to the second baseman, but the throw pulled the first baseman just off the bag, allowing the runner to score the tying run. An unfortunate mistake in a very well-played game. As the teams get ready for the seventh inning, Rock 105 plays AC/DC's "Back in Black."

I hear birds and a bit of traffic from Devine Street, but still very little chatter, only a few words of encouragement for each batter from the Sarnia players and coaches. It's just past 9 pm and the lights have come on, evening turning to twilight, the outfielders haloed in the soft glow of the sunlight's last rays. It's a tableau of what baseball looks like in my imagination. The batter hits a sharp ground ball to the shortstop, who glides to his right, fields the ball, stops himself, and throws as he's falling away, his momentum carrying him towards third base. The throw is wide, but the first baseman is able to scoop the ball out of the dirt for the second out. A strikeout ends the inning. I look around the park: there are now fewer than a dozen people here. It feels like they're playing the game just for us.

Earlier this afternoon, driving to Sarnia to watch yet another baseball game was the last thing I wanted to do. Now, sitting in this ballpark, there is nowhere else I'd rather be. Will this game—the one I most resisted going to—be one of my favourites of this project? Am I loving this game because I saw its opposite on Sunday in London? If I hadn't been so distracted, would I have clung to this silence? If the London game hadn't been such a blowout, would I have noticed the beauty of a 1-1 game? Maybe each baseball game is informed by the sum of all the baseball games you've ever seen.

It's still 1-1 and I know there are some who would say, "Nothing has happened." But so much has happened. My notes on the game are sparse, not because I have nothing to say, but because my mind is occupied only with the sheer beauty and perfection of everything about tonight.

I have seen games this season that I just wanted to end, but this isn't one of them. Tonight, I understand that I've been paying attention over the past games, even though I didn't think I was. I see that I have learned new things about the game, that I have been pushed out of my comfort zone, and my baseball-watching lethargy. I feel gratitude forming a lump in my throat.

It's unclear who these players are playing for. For us? For themselves? For the game? It seems as if they'd play this game this beautifully and this consciously even if no one were here to watch. This evening has a preternatural quality to it, making me wonder if mere mortals like us should even be here.

As the seventh turns to the eighth, I think about how tonight feels like the scene in *Field of Dreams* when it's just Ray, his family, and Terrence Mann watching, the lights illuminating the perfect field in front of them. And it feels like the nameless players on the field are here just for us and will fade away or walk out into the trees when the game is finished. I can, of course, see the houses past left field, but the trees that ring the outfield, the last sunlight of the day, the glow from the light poles, and the silent beauty of the play on the field make it feel like this place was carved out for us, for this perfect night of baseball.

As we head into the final half-inning, I start imagining the conversations I'll have tomorrow. "You drove two hours there and back to watch baseball?" I have struggled to articulate precisely why we're doing what we're doing just as I'm still struggling to find a response to "You must really like baseball." Just now, sitting under these lights with a dozen other people scattered around the field, I am starting to feel an answer forming.

The score is still 1-1 in the bottom of the ninth. The leadoff batter for Sarnia strikes out looking and I wonder if we're headed for extra innings. It's full dark now and I can hear the Fourth of July fireworks in the distance from Port Huron. Dull pops—an echo of the celebration and a reminder that the United States is just across the river. On the field, the batter hits a ball straight up behind second base, but no one is able to pick it up in the night sky. Single. The next batter chops the ball into the dirt in front of home plate, the ball rising straight up, hanging in the air as if on a string. By the time it comes down, the runner is able to beat out the throw to first to put two runners on base with only one out. The ground ball hit to third base is too soft for the third baseman to try to turn the double play and in his hurry to get the ball to first for an out, he throws in the dirt. This time, though, the first baseman can't get his glove on it and the lead runner comes around to score the game-winning run.

When the game ends, I overhear one of the umpires say, "Wow, what an ending." I agree. But it also seems like a new beginning.

As we pack up and ready ourselves for the two-hour drive back home, I glance at the field just to be sure the players aren't fading away.

Final Score: 2-1 Sarnia

Eleven

OHIO SWING

July 6 – 8, 2018

Five Tool
vs
Illinois A's

Lake Erie Crushers
vs
Florence Freedom

Cleveland Indians
vs
Oakland A's

Lake County Captains
vs
West Michigan Whitecaps

Friday, July 6, 2018

Five Tool
vs
Illinois A's

The Pipe Yard, Lorain OH
Game Time Temperature: 72°F

Today we drove to Lorain, Ohio, which calls itself the International City. I was able to find a route that avoided the interstates and instead had us driving along the lake, crossing on a causeway, driving past farmhouses, nature refuges, fields of corn, alternating stands of tiger lilies and cornflowers beside the road. The roads are awful in Michigan but instantly get better once you cross into Ohio.

You don't need to go very far in our one hundred miles for things to change. Today, I noticed how many bait shops there are: we passed Bait Barn, the Happy Hooker Bait Shop, and George's Hook-Gun-Bait and Carry-out, which is next door to Jack and Diane's Lounge. On a pickup truck, I saw a sticker shaped like the state of Michigan, where the Upper Peninsula was a firearm. We passed signs for the Jackie Mayer Miss America Highway going into Sandusky and a Simpsons-like nuclear power plant that dominated the landscape.

We decided to get off 280 just past Toledo and take the scenic route, foregoing the speed of I-80 for a more relaxed drive near Lake Erie. The road to the lake took us past fields of corn and wheat, past fallow fields, through Williston with its flags still lining the

road from the Fourth of July. As we neared the lake, we could see
the Davis-Besse nuclear plant in the distance before we turned onto
Highway 2, the Lake Erie Coastal Trail. It was, for a few miles, an
idyllic drive in the morning sun before the road became a divided
highway just before Sandusky. Efficient but nondescript, except
for the beautiful causeway over the water. Now we're at a ballpark
called the Pipe Yard, a dry, dusty diamond in the industrial section
of Lorain, as the 11:15 am game comes to an end.

We expected to see the Windsor Selects in the Continental Amateur Baseball Association U18 Aluminum Bat World Series at 1:30,
but because of the rainouts yesterday, they played this morning at
another diamond. As we sit in the grandstand behind home plate,
we try to figure out exactly who we'll be seeing in the next game,
but it isn't easy—there's little information at the park, and the tournament website doesn't appear to have been updated. The thinking
is clearly that the people who need to know—players, coaches, parents—will find out anyway; people like us are not part of the equa-
tion. While it would have been fun to see the Selects, to be honest it
doesn't really matter to me who plays. It's a sunny day and there will
be baseball on the field.

Right now there are grown-ups, not players, raking the infield and
running a tractor around the outfield. It's a lovely day but surprisingly
chilly in the shade of this new, spacious grandstand. We're about to
watch the Illinois A's take on the local team, Five Tool, which, pardon my
ignorance, sounds like a last-minute Father's Day gift you'd order late at
night on the Home Shopping Network. There are maybe thirty people in
the crowd. Some are sitting in the sun. There's a crisp, bright Canadian
flag snapping in the lake breeze beside a more seasoned American flag.

Heidi leans over, asks, "What's a Five Tool?" I explain that scouts
look for five "tools": speed, arm strength, fielding ability, the ability
to hit for average, and the ability to hit for power. It's a clever name,
especially for a travel team designed to showcase players to college
coaches. I wonder if other teams ever call them a bunch of tools.

The A's are this afternoon's home team and send a tall left-hander
to the mound. The A's wear the traditional Oakland colours: white

pants, yellow jerseys, green caps with a yellow bill. Unlike most of his teammates, #21, the starter, sports green, yellow, and white striped stirrups, the kind I remember wearing as a kid on summer evenings when Charlie tried to teach us about the game. Old school. The Five Tool players wear white uniforms, their tops ringed in blue and white. Some of them wear stirrups, too.

The Five Tool fans—parents, presumably—are louder than their numbers would suggest. The first Five Tool batter is getting more advice than anyone could possibly hope to process: "You got it. Move 'em forward. Watch the ball. Swing that bat. Be smart. You got it, you got it. Be smarter. Okay, next time." It's 4-0 for Five Tool with one out in the first. Despite the lead, the parents pepper the field with advice on all five tools of baseball: "On top. Location, location. Right there, boy. Heads up, guys. Defense . . . defense. Gotta play hard, now. A little poke's all you need." The A's parents are quiet but engaged. I haven't counted the A's out yet and neither have they. When an A's player steals a base, I join their parents and applaud. "When did you become partisan?" Dale asks. "Early on," I reply.

This summer I've been reading histories of Negro Leagues baseball and annotating stories from the newspapers about the 1934 Chatham Coloured All-Stars. I can't help but notice that the A's are a nearly all-Black team and that Five Tool are a nearly all-white team. Having recreated the 1934 season on paper and in my mind so many times before, it's hard not to conflate this game with others I've read about.

Since there are no lineups available, I don't know the name of the A's starter, but he throws hard for a lefty. Through the first inning, though, he has trouble locating the strike zone and the catcher has to block a lot of balls in the dirt. In the inning, he hits a batter, walks a batter, throws two wild pitches, and gives up three singles as Five Tool score four runs. Fortunately for the A's, four singles, a walk, three stolen bases, and a double in their half of the inning also lead to four runs and a 4-4 tie at the end of the first inning.

As the first inning turns to the second, I walk around the ballpark, chat a bit with some of the spectators. Everyone except us is a parent of one of the boys. I ask the moms from both teams where the players are from, but they have trouble pinning it down very specifically. These are all-star teams that draw from a wide geographic area. The Chicago suburbs. The towns in and around this part of Ohio. The best players, yes, but also the players whose parents have the resources to allow them to play travel ball.

Dale says, "You're funny when you get partisan."

"You're really not cheering for anybody?"

"I'm just cheering for good baseball."

Now it's 8-4 for Five Tool. And now 8-7 at the bottom of the second. After the second inning I try to explain my sudden partisanship. "I can't help myself," I say. Although I know we're not in 1934, watching this nearly all-white team playing a nearly all-Black team helps me imagine what it must have been like to watch the Chatham Coloured All-Stars. Maybe I'm not really cheering for the A's. Maybe I'm cheering for the All-Stars eighty-four years too late.

We watch as two Five Tool players trip over each other between second and third base. It's only the third inning, and already it's a long game.

By the time the fifth inning is over, the score is 12-10 A's. I've lost count of the number of errors and wild pitches on both sides. The A's have run at will and, no matter who has pitched, Five Tool has had no answer. The A's #42 has four steals himself. These may be all-star teams, but they're also just kids and the coaches are still teaching them how to play the game. When the Five Tool coach yells to his outfielders, "It's easier to come in than go back. Give 'em a step," he's trying to teach them how to internalize their decisions on the field so that everything becomes automatic. When the players chatter in the infield, they're reminding each other, and themselves, of what they're supposed to be doing in each situation. The stillness of the Sarnia game is replaced with teaching, with encouragement, with kids being kids.

I get up to wander around the park. Lured by the smell of fresh popcorn, I find myself at the concession stand. The man behind the counter says, "What would you like?"

"Could I please have a Coke and a popcorn. Thanks."

"You talk funny."

"Well, I'm Canadian."

"Figures. How's your team doing?"

"We don't have a team. We're just here to watch baseball."

"You drove all this way to watch baseball? Y'all are crazy. Did you see the flag?" He points to the crisp red maple leaf I'd noticed earlier, the folds still visible. "We thought we might get Canadian fans so we bought it last night. Hung it upside down at first but it's fine now. We're playing their anthem too. The Canadians sure seem to appreciate that."

"We do. Thank you."

As I make my way back to the stands, it strikes me that we're just at the southern edge of our hundred miles and people think I talk funny. For two countries so close, there is a lot of distance between them.

The A's have #88 now on the mound for the top of the sixth, but he starts the inning with a walk and a hit batter to put runners on first and second with no outs. The A's coach walks to the mound, signals to #42 at third base to come in to pitch. He immediately gives up a single that scores a run and still leaves runners at first and second with no outs. But early in the count he's able to induce a perfect ground ball to the third baseman, who's playing close to the line. He steps on the base for the force and throws to first base to complete the double play. #42 is now one out away from getting out of the inning with the lead. It really looks like he's going to do it when he gets another ground ball to third, but a throw in the dirt that the first baseman can't corral yields the tying run. A strikeout ends the inning, but the third out should have come on that ground ball.

Just as Dale says, "This seventh inning is going to be interesting," the game gets called for time. There are a lot of games in this tournament and a complicated schedule to keep, especially with last night's rain. The game ends in a 12-12 draw. Neither Dale nor I got what we were cheering for.

After the game we are at our car, packing everything up for the drive to Avon for our second game of the day. Five Tool parents mill around the truck next to us and I ask them if they play in the next game here, against Top Tier. They confirm that they do, ask us who we have in the tournament.

As always, we say, "No one. We just came to watch some baseball."

One of the moms asks if we are scouts. I reply, "No, but we get asked that sometimes because we're always writing." I tell them about what we're doing this summer, hand them a card with the project's Instagram and Twitter handles.

She offers us a couple of bottles of water for the road, says, "Remember #11. Ford. It's an easy name to remember."

Final Score: 12-12

Friday, July 6, 2018, evening

Lake Erie Crushers
vs
Florence Freedom

Sprenger Stadium, Avon OH
Game Time Temperature: 72°F

Sprenger Stadium is a typical minor league park, charming in its simplicity, the expanse of green yielding to low outfield walls covered with advertisements for local businesses. Mercy Health. Northwest Bank. Drees Homes. Behind the box seats that stretch from foul pole to foul pole sits a small concourse with concession stands, a small press box, a few skyboxes. The infield is artificial, as it is at PAL in Detroit or at Adrian College, and looks much more playable than the sun-blasted dirt of the Pipe Yard we saw earlier today. For $11 each, our seats are directly behind home plate. We settle in for the first inning, but I'm distracted by the constant hum of traffic from I-90, which runs right beside the park. It looks like baseball, but sounds more like NASCAR.

This is the Frontier League, an independent professional league unaffiliated with Major League Baseball, and founded in 1993, with teams located in Ohio, Illinois, Indiana, Pennsylvania, Kentucky, Missouri, and Michigan.[1] Each club must have a minimum of twelve rookies—with no professional experience—and can only carry a maximum of eight players with unlimited professional experience on their twenty-four-player roster. The salary cap for the entire roster is $75,000; the average salary is $725 per month and no player makes more than $2,000 per month. During the season, most players live with host families. As with the United Shores Professional Baseball League, players here—a mix of undrafted college players and veterans attempting a comeback—are looking to catch on with a major league organization, to continue the dream of playing baseball at the next level.

Over the PA comes the announcement that it's Military Appreciation Night, followed by a list of the numbers of POW/MIA from all wars since World War I. Before the anthem, members of the local VFW walk on to the field with full colour guard, congregating around home plate as the Lake Erie players stand, a sea of purple jerseys, each with his right hand over his heart. Stomper, the Lake Erie mascot, stands incongruously alongside the veterans and their flags. In the crowd, there are as almost as many hats indicating military service branches as there are caps showing team allegiance.

As the first inning unfolds, I can tell that Heidi is charmed by Stomper. He walks through the crowd, eyes agog, high fiving children, posing for photos. He stalks the sidelines, clapping his oversize hands, trying to get the crowd to cheer. Like the players, he's decked out in a purple jersey, but, unlike the players, he's not wearing pants. Mascots, it seems, never do.

The Lake Erie Crushers staff have purple t-shirts that say "Fun Bunch," and the mascot is named Stomper. In spite of the grape theme, there are no overt references to wine, which is, presumably, why the grapes are getting crushed. It's also unclear whether Stomper is a rodent or a bear. I'm thinking he's a bear because I can't imagine rodents stomping on grapes effectively. Moreover, would anyone want wine made by grapes stomped on by a rodent? Would wine made of grapes stomped on by a bear be much better?

I spend a full inning trying to process the logic of this team's theme and find none. I consider consulting Dale on the topic, but I think he'd just say, "Watch the game." Just as I'm about to put my musings on hold, I become deeply enthralled by Stomper's giant purple feet and his infectious joie-de-vivre.

As I lean in to ask Heidi if she would like a picture with Stomper, the PA announcer comes on to say that the first hitter for the Crushers in the first inning will be the Labatt Leadoff Player of the Game and that if he gets a hit, Labatt beer will be half price for the next twenty minutes. It's a promotion I can't even imagine at a Tigers game, but from what I've read about Cleveland's 1974 ten-cent beer-night fiasco, it's one I probably never want to see at a major league park. But I don't think things will get too out of hand in this small, suburban Ohio crowd. Besides, I'm thirsty and willing to drink Labatt if it's half price.

So it is with some expectation from the crowd that Aaron Hill, a rookie who played college ball at the University of Connecticut, comes to the plate. And lo and behold, Hill doubles. A loud cheer goes up from the crowd, partly for the man in scoring position for the home team, but mainly for the half-price beer. There's a notice-able exodus to the concession stands as Dane Hutcheon enters the batter's box. As the lines for beer swell, Hutcheon lays down a bunt, moving Hill to third base with one out. Despite the odds being in favour of scoring him, Hill is stranded at third. No runs in the first for the Crushers, but half-price beer for the fans.

We're three rows behind home plate. In front of us are grandparents and their twin granddaughters, who look to be about eight years old. Freeway sounds fill whatever silences the game occasions but there aren't many lulls. There's a large scoreboard with the players' names and pictures, pitch speed, and all the various stats that make up baseball. I realize that watching baseball with a scoreboard like this is sort of like reading a nineteenth-century novel with scholarly annotations and footnotes—things are pointed out that you might not know, or have noticed on your own. The annotations shape how you read the book and what you see. Having been "raised" on MLB, it took a while for me to learn how to watch baseball without all these scoreboard annotations and find what's useful or interesting to me on my own. Tonight I find this information distracting, the way footnotes stop the momentum of a novel's plot.

This is a busy game, like the one in London, with lots of activities and gimmicks. There's a bouncy castle behind the right field fence. The leadoff hitter, Hill, doubles, making Labatt Blue half price. The grandmother says, "Yep. There they all go," with more than just a hint of judgment toward the beer-drinking fans. Just as the crowd settles down, the Fun Bunch launch another activity, Battle Ball, where two girls run at each other inside what look like giant inflatable hamster balls. The grandmother and the twins watch in silence. When it's over, the grandmother says, "You girls should get those." One twin says, "Yeah. But Mom would never buy them for us." The other twin nods.

Midway through the third inning and there's no score. Former and active military have just been asked to stand as Lee Greenwood's "I'm Proud to Be an American" begins to play over the PA. Behind me, a couple of guys discuss how reasonable it is to come to a game here as opposed to seeing an Indians game in Cleveland. It's not only the tickets, but parking, concessions, all of it. Who can afford to take a family? They're in full agreement. I look around the park, see all the families sitting together, laughing, passing around bags of peanuts, taking in the evening's last slanting rays. Friday night in the American Midwest.

The Crushers are down 1-0 as they come to bat in the bottom of the fourth inning. The Florence starter, right-hander Jordan Krauss, has given up a few hits, but still hasn't yielded a run. His delivery is uncomplicated, an easy motion that makes his low-90s fastball look effortless. Tonight he's throwing a lot of offspeed stuff—sliders and either a changeup or slow curve—that sometimes dips down into the 70s and that must make his fastball look even harder.

But he doesn't fool Lake Erie's leadoff batter who hits a hard ground ball between first and second. It looks like a sure hit, but the first baseman, Kewby Meyer, dives to his right, the ball snowconed in his glove, rises to his knees, and tosses it to Krauss, who sprints from the pitcher's mound to cover first. It's a beautifully executed play and seems to give Krauss a shot of adrenaline. The next two batters are easy strikeouts.

This is a better-played game than the one we saw earlier today, illustrating again how hard what these players do is, regardless of how easy they make it look. I just witnessed a double play that a year ago I would have simply added 6-4, 6-4-3 to my scorecard but that tonight I admire and applaud its execution and precision.

There are more inter-inning activities. A little girl dressed in a tooth fairy costume comes out to brush off home plate with a toothbrush twice as tall as she is. This segment ends with a reminder from a local dentist about the importance of regular dental care. Then Brady, Brody, Shane, and Kyle race down the first base side in cardboard ambulances. Shane wins convincingly. I say, "Please don't let this event be sponsored by personal-injury lawyers." Next they announce that the Buffalo Wild Wings Enemy of the Game is #18 from the Florence Freedom. They play the Darth Vader theme as his walk-up music. I wonder how #18 feels about this and whether his teammates envy or mock him for this designation. #18 strikes out, so one lucky row has just received Buffalo Wild Wing coupons. I wonder what it's like to show up at work and have a stadium full of people hoping you'll fail so they can get free wings.

After six innings, the score is still 1-0 Florence. As I watch the "Lucky Lady of the Game" promotion—two women running around the infield collecting oversize necklaces, bracelets, and rings—I think about the contrast between the quality of baseball from this afternoon to tonight, about the difference between kids learning to play and young professionals honing their craft. About the difference between playing in a park with thirty spectators, almost all of whom are family, and playing in a park with 2,800 spectators, almost all of whom are currently clapping for the woman who has just captured the final giant ring.

The players here are older, of course, in their early- to mid-twenties instead of seventeen or eighteen, and much more polished. And these are professional baseball players—perhaps not in the MLB pipeline, but professional nonetheless—who all understand the fundamentals of the game, who know where they're supposed to be, who don't have to think about every move they make. Fielders who make the plays they're expected to make and some they probably shouldn't be able to make. Pitchers who throw strikes and don't get rattled when they give up a hit. Catchers who are able to throw out a runner at second, as Mason Brown does now for the first out of the seventh.

When the twin granddaughters aren't playing a game only they seem to understand (and being told by their grandfather to "Knock it off' when it gets unruly), they're being coached on the finer points of the game by their grandmother. I notice that she's said, "We'll play baseball tomorrow in our yard" twice. And that she's following the Oakland/Cleveland game on her phone. Her husband seems mildly bored.

By the time we see the race between the Grapes and the Dinosaurs in the middle of the eighth inning, the score is 4-0 Florence. I turn to Heidi to check if she's seeing what I'm seeing just as I hear the PA announcer exclaim, "The Dinosaurs are chasing the Grapes." In a night of strange promotions, this is the oddest.

In the middle of the eighth the announcer reports that it's rally time, and in center field a giant green grape is being chased by two brown dinosaurs with their little T-Rex arms flapping. Crusher is out there too, but it's not clear where his allegiances lie. People seem to take it all in stride, but I sit in stunned silence trying to simultaneously triangulate the relationship between a green grape, two dinosaurs, and a purple bear as they lurch around the outfield. My mind is blown. Dale's laughing. He knows exactly what's going through my head.

I return my focus to the game with some difficulty. The grandmother is explaining balls and strikes to the twin girls, and then, moments later, she breaks down a complicated play at first. They listen politely. When she stops talking, they finalize the details on how they'll put a hex on a player they've selected from the field. The grandmother points out they're inadvertently hexing the home team pitcher. They rejig the hex and launch it at the unsuspecting Florence batter, who is walked. The grandmother asks, "Do you know another name for a walk? Base on balls." The girls nod and attempt to hex the next batter, who becomes the final out of the inning. The grandmother says, matter of factly, "You girls did a good job of hexing the hitter," and they concur.

The twins dance to Harry Belafonte singing "Jump in the Line." When the song is over, the grandmother says, "Another pointer: you can't run on a foul ball." They shrug and start hexing the Florence pitcher.

Things are looking bleak for the Lake Erie Crushers, and one of the twins asks, "Is there any way they can win?"

"Sure," the grandmother says, "A home run here would give us two runs—but you wouldn't call it a grand slam because there's only one man on base."

I'm not sure if these little girls will remember much about tonight's game, but I'm pretty certain that, when they're adults, they'll know what a base on balls is, how to deconstruct a complicated play at first, and that there's always hope at the bottom of the ninth inning, even if things look bleak. Also that they're excellent hexers of players.

Final Score: 4-0 Florence

Saturday, July 7, 2018

Cleveland Indians
vs
Oakland A's

Progressive Field, Cleveland OH
Game Time Temperature: 75°F

We meet our friends Greg Paziuk and Claire Ferris for lunch at Butcher and the Brewer, a few blocks from Progressive Field. They've driven down from Toronto for the weekend to hang out and see a couple of games with us. While a Blue Jays fan, Greg is also, for some inexplicable reason, a Browns fan, making the trip down at least once a year to see them play. Greg and Claire will be our guides for the weekend in Cleveland.

The last time we were in Cleveland for a game, the stadium was called Jacobs Field and we were here to see the Tigers. The Indians weren't very good that year, so it was easy to get tickets. We sat in box seats, field level on the first base side. Around us were a lot of empty seats. No one in town was talking baseball at all; bartenders and waitstaff seemed not to know they were even playing that weekend. Today, as we walk along the avenue that leads to the ballpark and slide into the queue for tickets, it's apparent how things have changed and what a difference a winning team makes.

The game is not sold out, but there's a strong crowd on this hot, cloudless summer day, including a lot of walk-ups. Realizing our options are limited, when we get to the ticket window, we opt for $55 seats in the upper deck on the third base side. I wince inwardly as I hand over my credit card—it's the most we've paid for tickets all summer. I've grown used to paying little, if anything, to watch baseball, and to sitting much nearer the action on the field.

As we squeeze through the crowd, the serenity of Sarnia is in the back of my mind. I hold Dale's hand so I don't get separated from him. It's remarkable to think that both these games are the same sport. It's like the day I saw a Clydesdale and a Shetland pony side by side at a county fair and marvelled that they were the same species.

We have been to Comerica Park so many times that it feels like my local park, so I rarely feel disoriented by its vastness. But coming here today, I find the scale of everything bewildering. I'm tossed like a cork between taller, larger fans, and try desperately not to tread upon meandering children, while simultaneously avoiding a roving barbershop quartet. I fear acapella gangs the way some people fear clowns. Walking to our seats, I check the concessions for vegetarian options and find very few.

As is the case with Comerica, there are displays, banners, and pennants outlining the team's long history. I am struck by the way in which memory and tradition are so present in baseball at this level. If one were cynical, one might read all of this as manufactured nostalgia, but I don't think it's that—at least not fully. MLB has done a great job of capitalizing on our emotions, making us feel like our small lives are part of a much larger narrative. MLB encourages us to believe that the story of our team is also the story of ourselves and our families. In this way, connecting with a Major League team is a means of reconnecting with our pasts and embracing all the possibilities baseball offers for the future, especially when they're having a winning season.

As Greg and I wander the concourse in search of local beer before making the long trek up to our seats, I notice how crowded and festive the ballpark is today. Three men in red-and-white-striped suit jackets and Indians caps play old-time jazz for the crowd on accordion, trumpet, and clarinet. Almost everyone sports Indians paraphernalia and in the murmur of the crowd I can feel the excitement. The fans here are catching on that this is a good team, that they should expect to see a win when they come to the ballpark.[2] Most of the community is behind them, sharing an emotional attachment to the team that represents them to the rest of the country. Civic pride through athletics, a way to feel good about their city. As I watch the swirl of the crowd, it's not exactly jealousy I feel at this shared euphoria. I feel detached, as if the feeling in the park today were no longer part of the pleasure baseball gives me. It's no better or worse. Just different.

We're sitting on the third base side, which is unusual for us, and it makes me feel oddly unsettled. I scan the park and see that the team's history is quite literally built into the park. Retired player numbers are painted on the wall: Feller, Boudreau, Averill, Harder, Doby, and, of course the unnamed but unforgettable #42. My recent reading about Negro Leagues baseball makes me pause over Larry Doby's name.[3]

I note to Greg and Claire that the last time we were here, it was called Jacobs Field and I called it "our field." I wonder aloud if Dale and I should change our surname to Progressive. Greg and Claire know we're here for this book, and they seem reluctant to disturb our "data collection." The silence between us feels unnatural. I wish I were chatting with them instead of scribbling notes to myself. It's another way in which this project is making strange the act of watching baseball.

Today it's Cleveland's ace, Corey Kluber, pitching against former Tiger (and National and Oriole and Padre and Marlin and ...) Edwin Jackson.[4] The video board shows not only the pitch count and speed, but also the breakdown of balls and strikes and what type of pitch was just thrown. The scoreboard is certainly helpful if you're seated where we are, since it's impossible to really gauge the finer points of pitching from this distance. Kluber has given up a few hits through seven innings, but no runs, and his teammates have staked him to a 3-0 lead. It's an interesting angle, but from here Kluber is little more than a tiny figure in the distance, all detail bleached from his pitching motion.

Behind me, a young kid says to his mother, "I don't understand baseball at all." As his mother attempts to explain it to him and his sister, I want to turn around and say that you can't really understand it from out here. But I don't.

The last time we were here, we'd taken a road trip to see the Tigers, and seeing my team play in another city filled me with awe and loyalty. I remember being jovially jeered by Cleveland fans after the game. The Tigers lost that game badly, if I recall correctly. But still, I wore my Granderson jersey with pride. I also remember falling into the rhythms of that game effortlessly and unquestioningly, whereas today, I'm fighting to stay on task. I should care about this game, but I do not. Throughout this project I've tried to occupy a space of non-partisanship or impartiality. But there's a difference between being impartial or non-partisan and not caring. If I don't care about this game, does it mean that I'm—I can't even say it, let alone think it—but that I'm bored?

I know, of course, that the way I've been watching baseball this summer is not how most people watch baseball or any other sport. Most people aren't drawn to baseball as baseball, but to a specific team, a specific reason to watch. As my friend Tim Girard says, there are many avenues into fandom, many ways that people are drawn to cheer for a team. It could be anything from proximity—like many of the Cleveland fans here today to support the local team—to a player—like Heidi with Curtis Granderson—to a family allegiance—like all the parents and grandparents we've met this summer. It could even be something as small as the design of a hat or the fact that your friend likes that team. Whatever it is that starts fandom for a specific team, it often strengthens over time, getting caught up in family and friendships and feelings of belonging. Like Heidi and me and Detroit and Windsor and the Tigers. Like me and Dad and the Expos.

I tell myself I'm bored because I'm not paying attention. On the field are great plays, great athleticism, great skill. I tell myself, "It doesn't get much better than this." We're sitting in the equivalent of the 300-level seats in Comerica, my gateway vantage point. I like seeing the expanse of the whole field, and realize this is also a great spot to watch pitching. I can see a curveball curve, I can see a sinker sink. I mentally call balls and strikes and test the accuracy of my calls against the calls on the scoreboard. I'm pretty accurate. "Well done, Heidi," I tell myself, and mentally pat myself on the back.

It's been great catching up with Greg and Claire as we sit in our upper-deck seats, the green stripes of the field laid out in front of us, the city providing the backdrop. Sitting in the sun, drinking a beer, chatting with friends, eating a hot dog. There's pleasure in all of these things and, in so many ways, today is a perfect day at the ballpark. But even as I'm watching the terrific play on the field, I find myself wishing we were at a game like the one in Sarnia. Or last night's Crushers game in Avon. I feel too removed out here, the distance from the field and the presence of the crowd interfering with my connection to the game. This project has altered my fandom, my relationship with baseball itself. And in that process, I can feel my relationship with Major League Baseball changing. I'm not sure it will ever be the same again.

An error at second base gets the crowd booing. A player, they think, should have got the out: he has made a mistake, and players at this level aren't supposed to make mistakes. In much of the baseball we've seen, errors are part of the game, they happen. This is how players learn and there's nothing really to get angry about.

It's easy to forget how hard this all is and how skilled the players are. It's easy, at this distance, to look at players as fine, finished objects who have always been this perfect. The baseball we've seen over the past few months has shown me a bit of what their journey looks like. Not a single player on the field got here accidentally or without slogging through some really tough stuff.

There's a belligerent, angry fan yelling "Throw strikes, goddammit!" as if the pitcher were intentionally not using his stuff today just to piss off this one man in the upper deck on the third base side. It breaks my heart that there's no Davenport Mom shouting down to the field: "You got this, kid. Fire it in there."

With a 3-0 lead, Neil Ramirez comes in to pitch the top of the eighth for Cleveland. He starts out well, completely fools Dustin Fowler with what the scoreboard says is an 86-mph slider on a 2-2 count. He has Mark Canha in that same 2-2 count, but decides to throw him a fastball, hoping to blow it by him. But the ball is straight down the middle and seems to have almost no movement on it. Canha doesn't miss, driving the ball into left field for a single.

Likely the wrong pitch and certainly the wrong location, but that single still only means that there is one on and one out for the left-handed-hitting Jed Lowrie. On another 2-2 pitch, though, Ramirez comes with a slider that doesn't break and Lowrie deposits it just inside the right field foul pole. After Khris Davis slams another fat fastball into the stands in center, a guy with a Reggie Jackson A's jersey near the front of our section jumps up, cheering giddily as the tying run crosses the plate. The crowd around us chants, "Down in front!" while Terry Francona, the Cleveland manager, walks to the mound. Ramirez's day is done.

A section over, mid-inning, people stand up to sing happy birthday to a man who just turned sixty-two. In so doing, they, and all those around them, miss seeing the A's score a two-run home run, turning a 3-0 game for the Indians into a 3-2 game. Another home run makes it 3-3. The birthday party missed most of this but it doesn't seem to really matter to them.

The omnipresent scoreboard makes it easy to be a passive fan. You don't need to mentally keep track of balls, strikes, errors, pitches thrown. If you're hungry, like I am, you can also watch the game on TV while standing in long lines for the concession. If you miss a great play, they'll show it again on the screen and you can watch it again later online. On the other hand, if you miss a great play in a game like the one in Sarnia, you've missed it for life. This is why you need to pay attention in the small parks—you never know what you might miss. Maybe this is why it's easy not to pay attention in games like these; if you miss something important, they'll replay it.[5]

It's still tied in the top of the eighth. Stephen Piscotty hits the ball back to Zach McAllister and the Indians are out of the inning. The crowd goes wild for the play and I realize how here—and with most stadiums—the great plays only matter when they help your team out. Greg points out that when the A's are hitting, the aisles are packed with people leaving to get snacks or wander around: "Fans only want to see their team hit, not pitch," he observes. And he's right.

In the top of the ninth, the A's are once again threatening, with a man on second base, two outs, and Dustin Fowler at the plate. Cody Allen, just in to pitch for Cleveland, starts Fowler with a fastball, but misses inside. His next pitch is on the outside black to even the count 1-1. Curveball for a called strike. Fowler waits on a 2-2 curve and lines what seems like a sure hit between short and third. But Lindor dives to his right, his body fully extended, and picks the ball just before it hits the grass. It's the kind of play we never would have seen in Sarnia or Adrian, at the game last night or at almost all the games we'll see this summer. This is the reason to go to a major league game.

I keep pushing away the question that troubles me: Am I bored by MLB? I don't know if I'm troubled by being bored or by not loving something I thought I loved. This question too big to make sense of right now. All I know is that it's a tie game, I'm really hungry, and the threat of extra innings looms ominously. Right now, I'm cheering for someone—anyone—to win so we can go.

Top of the eleventh and the score is still tied 3-3. Heidi turns to us, says, "Somebody's got to get a home run so we can have supper." We've been here four hours and it's hard to disagree.

Olson singles to lead off the A's half of the inning, bringing Piscotty to the plate. With a 2-2 count, Allen throws a pitch that's called a ball inside. The fans in our section berate the home plate umpire, yelling loudly that there's no way that was a ball. How they can see balls and strikes from here is beyond me. All I could see was Piscotty backing away. The next pitch is, according to the scoreboard, a cutter that Piscotty lifts to left field for a home run. Before the sixth run crosses the plate, the fans are streaming out of the park. We stay for the bottom of the eleventh, an uneventful three-up and three-down inning, before catching a cab to Market Garden for supper and a much-needed beer.

Final Score: 6-3 Oakland

Sunday, July 8, 2018

Lake County Captains
vs
West Michigan Whitecaps

Classic Park, Eastlake OH
Game Time Temperature: 79°F

Driving here this morning, we didn't say a lot but yesterday's Indians game seems to have deflated us. At the onset of this project, I'd hoped that going to all these games would rekindle my love for MLB. I fear it has done the opposite. I'm feeling something that feels like grief over a faltering relationship. I don't know if it's me or MLB, but something feels different. I wonder if Dale is thinking the same thing. I don't ask because then I'd have to articulate that baseball has changed for me. We drive into the parking lot quietly. We both have a lot on our minds.

Something at this ballpark, though, is different right away. The parking attendant, noticing our Ontario plates, welcomes us and gives us a half-off drink coupon for coming all this way. It's sunny and blue-skied as we enter the park, and we are greeted by many ushers and ticket takers. Greg and Claire are here, too. Attending all these base-ball games this summer has meant we haven't seen our friends very often. It's good to spend time with them.

The Lake County mascot, Skipper, wanders the mezzanine. He's a large, green, furry Muppety thing. Greg and I get our picture taken together with a giant yellow chicken from a local restaurant. They have veggie burgers here. Things seem to be looking up.

Fifteen miles from Progressive Field sits Classic Park, home of the Lake County Captains, the A affiliate of the Cleveland Indians. The Lake County players have become part of a Major League organization—the next step for the Freedom and Crushers players we saw Friday night—but it's still a long way from their final goal. Fifteen miles in a straight line from Cleveland, but just the begin-ning of a winding road to the Show, a journey that most of them will never complete.

Today the Captains are playing the West Michigan Whitecaps, the A affiliate of the Detroit Tigers. It's an unexpected chance to check in on the rebuild, a fluke of the schedule that the Whitecaps happen to be in town this weekend. I'm most intrigued to see Brock Deatherage, an outfielder from North Carolina State University drafted last month by the Tigers. As a tenth-round pick, the odds of him making it to the majors are slim, but in his debut game with the Gulf Coast League Tigers three weeks ago, he hit three home runs. He hit another in his next game and was promoted to West Michi-gan. Maybe the Tigers have caught lightning in a bottle.

The other player I'm interested in seeing is Kody Clemens, the Tigers' third-round pick from this year's draft, a second baseman from the University of Texas. He is, by all accounts, a gritty player, in the mold of someone like Ian Kinsler, who can hit for both aver-age and power. He's also the son of Roger Clemens, a dominant pitcher in the majors for over twenty years who also played at the University of Texas. Like his brothers Koby, Kory, and Kacy, Kody's name begins with a "K" in honour of his father's strikeouts. I wonder how much coming from that kind of baseball family helps and how much it hinders.

We splurge for the best possible seats—$12 each, three rows behind home plate. It's in the high 70s, warm, but not yet the kind of summer heat that leaves you a puddle in your seat. Like yesterday, there's not a cloud in the sky. We walk around the small concourse for a few minutes just to get our bearings and then down the few steps to our seats. No escalators up to the hinterlands today.

Today the players come from all over, not just the region: Dominican Republic, Venezuela, Australia. On the scoreboard, they provide the players' Instagram and Twitter handles so you can follow them on their baseball journeys.

On the mound for the Whitecaps is Wilkel Hernandez, a young right-hander from Venezuela who came over from the Angels in the Ian Kinsler trade. Signed by the Angels in 2015, at seventeen he played in the Dominican Summer League and, at eighteen, in the rookie-level Arizona and Pioneer leagues. He's nineteen now and already in his third season of professional baseball.

Neither of the first two Lake County hitters can catch up to Hernandez's fastball as he opens the bottom of the first inning with two strikeouts on six pitches. There's a slight hesitation in Hernandez's motion, a pause before he raises his left knee just above his belt and pushes off towards the plate. It's a streamlined approach that generates good power on the fastball. After a first-pitch single, we start to see his other stuff as Hernandez begins to mix in some offspeed pitches, dropping in two curveballs to get the final out on a strikeout looking.

As we move to the second inning, Kody Clemens is announced as the Beer Batter—if he strikes out, there will be half-price beer for the inning. The crowd cheers good naturedly, but it isn't to be this time as Clemens flies out to center field. F8. A foul ball and the sound of breaking glass plays over the PA. A second flyout to center and Neil McCoy's "Basic Goodbye" starts up. F8. Double. 5-3 to end the inning. But that simple notation masks a great play, the kind you

star in your scorecard, the kind that reminds me that these are legit-
imate prospects, some of the best players we've seen this summer
outside of the major leagues. The play starts with a hard-hit ground
ball that Nolan Jones is able to pick off the dirt at third base. He sets
himself, but his throw is wide, nearly pulling Jose Vicente off the bag
at first. But Vicente is able to fully extend his body, catching the ball
while maintaining contact with the base. By the end of the play, he is
prone on the ground, the tip of his toe just barely touching the bag.
5-3, but with a star.

There is the obligatory t-shirt toss, a trivia contest, a "Skipper's
Birthday Bash" segment where Skipper sings Happy Birthday to Alex,
who just turned eleven. When the Captains score, they show a man
called Captain Kenny dancing on the big screen. This park seems to
have struck a nice balance between intimacy, great baseball, and a
few non-distracting distractions. Mostly though, this experience is
about baseball. It strikes me as odd to have to say that.

That said, there are 2,700 fans here versus 33,100 at the Cleveland
game last night. This is a beautiful place to watch baseball and I wonder—creatively, not judgmentally—why 33,100 people chose to pay
an average of $30 for not-great seats to see MLB players at a vast dis-
tance instead of $12 for this intimate experience. What is it about MLB
that makes it the presumed option for watching baseball? If anything,
this project is making me rethink the primacy of MLB for baseball fandom. So many people I've talked to over the years have assumed that,
because the best players are in MLB, that it must be the best baseball
experience. But is it?

Walking into the park earlier this afternoon, I was feeling like I'd
broken up with baseball, when really I was just questioning my relationship with MLB. Lately when I think about baseball and what I love
about it, my mind wanders back to that evening game in Sarnia rather
than to Comerica Park.

It's the bottom of the sixth and Greg, Claire, and Heidi are all
up getting food. It's 5-1 Lake County as I sit in the sun with a cold
Yuengling in hand, close enough to the action to see exactly what

the hitter is seeing on every pitch. Around me sit several scouts with their clipboards, stopwatches, and radar guns, all business, the ballpark their collective office. Behind are some West Michigan pitchers, charting pitches and working their own radar gun. I can hear one of them saying, "Bender?" on a pitch that goes for a called strike. Captain Kenny dances on the video board as Lake County scores the go-ahead run on a home run by Elvis Perez, the second solo shot that Hernandez has given up. All my tiredness from the driving and late nights melts away as the sun caresses my arms.

Behind us are players from both teams. In our section, they outnumber the fans. Watching the players fascinates me as it shows how much there is to learn about baseball, how many analytical tools are needed to notice its nuances. In seeing this, I cut myself some slack for not knowing as much as I feel I should about baseball. These players are studious, but also young and having fun. Moments of great concentration are punctuated by what can only be described as goofiness.

I like that these players are called "prospects," a word that conjures anticipation, potential, and, perhaps most importantly, hope. Nothing is taken for granted here: every at-bat, every pitch works toward making possibility into reality. The prospects infuse the park with a special kind of energy.

Today we've seen an Emoji Pictionary contest and a promotion in which rubber chickens were flung from a slingshot before being caught in a fryer basket. We've also seen some of the Tigers prospects. Deatherage went 1 for 3 with a walk, singling in the sixth only to be called out on the bases when he overran second base on a fly ball to center field. Clemens went 1 for 4, but made a nice play on a hard ground ball in the fourth. Hernandez pitched six strong innings, a nice mix of fastballs, hard sliders, and offspeed pitches thrown for strikes that kept the hitters mostly off balance. He only gave up two hits, but both were solo home runs and he is saddled with the loss. Who knows where the next few years will take these three young men, but today we've definitely seen players who will be in The Show in a few years. We just can't predict who they will be. Or how long they'll stay.

Final Score: 7-1 Lake County

Twelve

THE GOLDEN RULE
OF BASEBALL

July 14, 2018

Walker Tavern Historic Site
Vintage Baseball Tournament

Saginaw Old Golds
vs
Detroit Early Risers

Canton Union Base Ball Club
vs
Detroit Early Risers

Saturday, July 14, 2018

Saginaw Old Golds
vs
Detroit Early Risers

Walker Tavern Historic Site, Brooklyn MI
Game Time Temperature: 84°F

This morning, we drive south and west and I am struck yet again by the diversity within our hundred miles. We're only eighty-five miles away from the flat, treeless farmland of Essex County and seventy miles from downtown Detroit. Within a short distance, flat, urban terrain has become hilly, lake-filled, lush, shady, and treed. We pass the Rustic Glen Golf Club and I think about putting a character named Rustic Glen in my next novel. I spend the rest of the car ride imagining who this Rustic Glen might be. How does he earn this nickname? What makes Rustic Glen so rustic? As we speed along the road, I plot this scintillating novel I'm sure I'll never write.

We pull in to the Walker Tavern Historic Site just outside Brooklyn, Michigan at the same time as our friends Tim and Suzanne. We're here to see baseball as it might have been played in the nineteenth century. Part historical re-enactment, part athletic contest, these games use rules from the 1860s, with players and umpire in period costume. It's only the second time I've seen baseball played this way, the first just a few years ago with Tim and Suzanne at the World Tournament of Historic Base Ball at Greenfield Village in

Dearborn, Michigan. Today is a much smaller affair, with teams drawn from around Michigan.[1]

There is no permanent field here, just a makeshift diamond carved out of the grounds of the historic site. As would have been the case in the 1860s, the game occurs where there is enough space for it to be played. The ground of the infield is fairly flat, grass freshly cut though not cropped close as it would be in a regular ballpark. In center field there is a hill, its rise not insubstantial, dotted by four large trees, all of which are in play. Not far beyond first base is a dense copse of trees. There is no fence between the spectators and the field of play, and there are no seats beyond a couple of picnic tables. Like the other thirty people in attendance, we unfurl our lawn chairs and settle in along what would be, if there were markings on the field, the first base line.

Suzanne and I examine the goldenrod-coloured handout we were given with our tickets, providing us with an overview of 1865 rules and a glossary of terms. An "ace," for example, means crossing the bases, a "striker" is a batter, a pitcher a "hurler." This is recognizable baseball but the rules take some getting used to. We read that a ball that goes into the weeds and bushes is still in play until it's found and returned to the hurler. Also, there is only one ball, so they need to find it.

The ball field is on a gentle slope with several tall trees in what functions as the outfield. Low shrubs and dense green surround the playing field, and there are historic buildings and a barn on the top of the field. Along the first base line, a man paces. He is wearing black pants, a gold satin-backed vest, a long-sleeved white shirt with a Colonel Sanders tie. He has a wide, flat-brimmed felt hat on his head. His attentions are so fully on the game, he seems not to notice that it's much too muggy for such an outfit. At the end of the first inning he proclaims, "Tally one ace for the Golds!" and a woman in period costume—the "Tally Queen"—changes the score on the wooden scoreboard across the field. He appears to be a combination scorekeeper, umpire, colour commentator, and historical interpreter. The two teams are both in thick, rough cotton uniforms in a flour-sack-white colour. You can tell the teams apart because one has black socks and the other black-and-white striped socks. It takes me a while to realize which team is which.

As the first batter for the Early Risers comes to the plate, the umpire turns to the crowd, explains why the pitcher is throwing the ball underhand. "The hurler has to toss the ball. The wrist may not be snapped when he tosses the ball to the striker." In tossing the ball, the hurler is not aiming to fool the striker, but rather to give him the best chance of putting the ball in play. In fact, the striker can tell the hurler exactly where he wants the ball to be thrown. One ball— slightly softer than a regular baseball—is used for an entire game and, as it is used, deadens and softens over the course of the game. The fielders wear no gloves. All of the players wear baggy, period uniforms: socks high, caps with short bills tight to their heads. Games are a full nine innings, whatever the score or weather.

This game is a blend of sport and anachronism and these players seem to buy into it fully. Indeed, if I block out the fifty or so spectators in lawn chairs wearing sunglasses, flip-flops, and cut-off shorts, the overhead powerlines and the occasional sound of a car, I really could be in 1865 watching baseball. One player is expelled from the game for "expectorating," which makes sense after I read on the handout that this is baseball from the "gentlemanly era."

Far from the flat, manicured, treeless ballparks of today, the trees and slope to the field offer a few challenges. One overthrown ball to first rolls down the hill toward home plate and players stumble on the sloping and uneven ground as they try to chase it down. A ball goes into the thicket past first base, and you can hear a player growling in frustration as he whacks the tall grass looking for the game's sole ball. Occasionally we hear the sound of branches breaking. Someone behind me says something about poison ivy and people chuckle nervously. The players on base have long scored and the teams wait as the fielder, now frantic, hunts for the ball so the game can continue.

As we watch the game unfold, it's quickly apparent that not only does it look different than the modern game, it also sounds different, an archaic translation of a baseball game. Our guide to this terminology is the umpire, who also acts as master of ceremonies. When the Old Golds load the bases, he tells us, "The sacks are gold." When the second out of the inning occurs for the Golds, he says, "Ball trapped by the longfielder. Man lost. Two hands dead." The second baseman turns to the outfield, yells, "Well held! Well held!" The final out occurs when the striker hits a pop fly down the third base line. It goes foul and the third baseman grabs it on one bounce. That's it for the inning, since fouls caught on one bounce count as outs under these rules. As the Early Risers walk off the field at the end of the inning, the umpire turns to the crowd, refers to his notebook, and recaps, "At the conclusion of three innings of play, the tally count is 3 for the Early Risers of Detroit and 9 for the Saginaw Old Golds."

The score is 11-4 when the Old Golds come to bat in the bottom of the fifth. The hurler tosses the first ball to the striker, who lets it go by. The hurler says to the striker, "Too high?" to which he replies, "No, that was a good one." On the next pitch he hits a hard ground ball between second and third base. The shortstop moves laterally into the path of the ball, goes down on one knee, cups his hands together to receive the ball, sets himself, and throws across the diamond to get the runner at first base. A nice baseball play no matter what era, made more impressive by the absence of gloves.

The next batter singles to shallow left field. It's a harmless look-ing play, but instead of simply throwing the ball in to the second baseman, the outfielder throws the ball past first base and into the trees. The runner advances to second as he would in modern base-ball. When the first baseman can't find the ball in the trees, the Old Golds bench yell at the runner to keep going, one of many times the players have to remind each other of the rules. He doesn't stop, rounding the bases all the way to score. Unlike modern baseball, there is no out of bounds in this game and the baseball remains live at all times. It's the only baseball I've ever seen where losing the ball in the trees is a real possibility.

In the top of the seventh inning, the first striker in the Early Risers hits a long fly ball to center field. The longfielder gauges it and begins to run towards the spot where he thinks it will land, up the incline and towards the two massive pine trees that grow next to each other at the crest of the hill. He turns, realizes that the ball is going to be in the branches, and, no longer having a chance to catch it, stops to see where it will ricochet. Single, with an assist to the trees. Single to put runners at first and second. When a hobbled striker gets another single but cannot run the bases, the umpire turns to us, says, "Courtesy runner in play. Sacks loaded with Risers. No hands."

Somehow the next batter strikes out, unable to connect even with pitches thrown exactly where he asks for them. One hand dead. The Risers score on a fielder's choice to second base, announced by the umpire as "One hand lost and tally one ace for the Risers. Two hands." The final out is recorded on a hard-hit ball to the second baseman that is effortlessly fielded and flipped to first.

"Ladies and gentlemen, at the conclusion of seven innings of play, the tally count is 7 for the Early Risers, 12 for the Old Golds."

At the end of the game, the two teams line up and the team captains take a few minutes to thank the other team, the umpire, and to offer a range of other thank yous. When the speeches are done, one team waves their hats and says "HiphipHuzzah!," then the other team waves their hats and undertake their own unique variation on the cheer: "Hip. Hip. Huzzah!" All of this makes me positively gleeful as I love the word "huzzah." In case spectators are confused about the word "huzzah!" the glossary sheet translates it into modern parlance as "hooray!"

Final Score: 12-7 Early Risers

Saturday, July 14, 2018, later

Canton Union Base Ball Club
vs
Detroit Early Risers

Walker Tavern Historic Site, Brooklyn MI
Game Time Temperature: 84°F

As we stretch our legs between games, I think about what we've just seen. I'm not surprised by the way the players and umpire inhabit their roles in this baseball cosplay of an earlier era. But what does strike me is the level of skill the players exhibit on the field, their years of playing modern baseball translated into a bygone era. Why do people decide to play vintage baseball? Nostalgia for a game they've never seen? Interest in the history of the sport? The challenge of fielding without gloves? The desire to be involved in something different? The players take it all very seriously, both the spirit of re-enactment and the way they carefully play within the rules they have all agreed to use. This is play in all senses of the word.

Between the first and second games, Suzanne and I run into the gold-vested man and his wife, who are, like us, seeking a bit of respite from the heat. He tells us his character is named Golden Rule. He's a retired teacher, and answers our questions about the game and the league in a teacherly way. He is clearly passionate about history and about historic baseball. He tells us he won't be calling the next game so he can take a break. I smile at his wife and ask her about her connection with historic baseball. She sweetly deflects the question in a way that feels familiar to me. I learn that there is no mercy rule, or stoppages for rain or weather. I say to Mrs Golden Rule, "I bet you've seen some long, unpleasant games." She laughs and tells me about one game where a team was up forty runs but still had to play the full nine innings. "And sometimes it's raining. And cold." I smile, think of sitting with Dale at the Henry Ford game a few months ago. Perhaps I'm projecting, but I expect it's love of her husband more than 1865-rules baseball that brings her here. They're likely intertwined.

After a short break, the second game begins. Since the umpire is supplied by the home team, our guide from the first game is not present. Instead, one of the members of the Early Risers acts as the umpire and, if he remembers, announces what is happening on the field.

By the fourth inning, I'm not even sure what the score is, so infrequently have there been any announcements from the various umpires. It makes me realize how much more enjoyable the first game was, with the umpire there to make announcements and help the crowd understand the game play. His language and demeanor, his very presence leant an historic air to the first game. He was, as

Suzanne puts it, "a contextual narrator," and without him it's much more like watching a baseball game with slightly modified rules and players in period costumes. That umpire, and the entire Saginaw team, seemed to have a much greater sense of historical integrity, which seemed to bleed over to the Early Risers in the first game. That's much less the case now, the players being far more intent on the game than on the trappings surrounding the game.

Without Golden Rule, this game seems a little less anachronistic and genteel. It's also not quite as engaging, but I'm happy to see him and his wife relaxing under the shade of a tree, still watching the play. I start to think less about the game and more about why these players are here. Are the older players needing a less strenuous league? Are the younger ones hungry for any opportunity to play, or are they the kind of guys who engage in Civil War weekends in the off-season?

I'm getting sleepy in the afternoon heat, and my game notes itemize the things that make me smile: a dog who desperately wants to chase the baseball but is foiled by his leash; a ball called foul because it's "on the other side of the tree"; a player taunted for being a "muffin" (which the glossary tells me is "an enthusiastic but unskilled player"); a player getting a triple running slightly uphill from first to second and then slightly downhill to get to third; a mother coaching her five-year-old to say "We still love you, Dad" after a botched play.

I have been reminded today that sitting in a lawn chair on the grass on a summer day, watching baseball with people you love, is a blessing of an afternoon.

In spite of what Golden Rule told us about the full nine innings, they appear to be calling the game after another ten minutes due to tournament time restraints. Detroit wins and there are the same speeches and cheers. Detroit repeat their cheer, but Canton has their own variant: "HiphipHuzzah! HiphipHuzzah! HiphipHuzzah! Aw shucks!"

After seven innings the game ends, time rather than weather calling a halt to the proceedings. The Early Risers win, but no one seems to really care.

Final Score: 15-12 Early Risers

Thirteen
BEET, BEET, SUGAR BEET

July 22, 2018

Saginaw Sugar Beets
vs
Lake Erie Monarchs (Doubleheader)

Sunday, July 22, 2018

Just at the northern edge of our hundred miles lies Saginaw, Michigan, where we are now for a Great Lakes Summer Collegiate League doubleheader. As we crossed over at the Windsor-Detroit Tunnel, the border guard asked why we were going all the way up to Saginaw to watch baseball. I said something about college players, wood bats, and seeing some good baseball. He looked a bit dubious, as if he couldn't understand why anyone would want to make that drive, especially in this rain—heavy at times—which lasted the whole drive up. Now the sky is overcast with an occasional bit of drizzle. Still, it doesn't look great and I wonder how much ball we will see today.

This is probably the farthest northwest we'll be in our hundred miles. I fill my notebook with details about what I see out the window. I note that we're passed by a sleek black car with "Come to Jesus" written on the trunk, going at least 140 kilometres an hour. I record that, according to a billboard "333,116 babies were born here since 1886." I give up counting the homemade signs advertising $10 firewood and weekend gun sales. A giant Jesus on a billboard asks, "Are you on the right road?"

We're sitting in Culver's, a Wisconsin chain I've never seen before, which is apparently known for its custard. A poster on the wall across from our table reads, "Milkshakes and Bacon. Better together." We're trying the deep-fried cheese curds and I'm having the Butter Burger, a basic grill burger simply dressed with cheese, pickles, onions, ketchup, and mustard. It takes me back to the burgers we would get at baseball tournaments at the concession stand at Czar Lake.

Saturday morning I was grateful for the rain and for Saginaw tweeting that the game had been cancelled. It would have been a long drive to find a cancelled game at the end. I got a weekend day off at home, which I really needed.

But it's Sunday now and I have successfully navigated us to a Culver's in Saginaw where we, and some Sugar Beets, are getting a pregame lunch. The players look a little tired and bored, sort of like people waiting for a delayed plane, eating airport food. I'm enjoying frozen custard and "Mmm . . . curds"—which are basically deep-fried cheese. I'm glad I snuck in a run this morning before we left. Today is supposed to be a doubleheader so, quite literally, "If God be willin' and the creeks don't rise," we'll get two games in today and still be on pace for fifty. I'm feeling smug about screen-capturing the route to Cardinal Field so I don't need to pay roaming fees in America to find the park. I take my time with my custard and savour the last curd. Cardinal Field is only eight minutes away.

Aside from baseball, one thing that's interesting with this project is what changes and what stays the same within our hundred miles. Obviously, the geography changes—from the lush fields of Essex county to the rolling Irish Hills to the shores of Lake Erie— but so too do the towns and architecture. People and accents change. Food and restaurants. And some things, though very different from Windsor, are familiar from the time we've spent in Detroit. Things like Vernors ginger ale, Michigan left-hand turns, and using your left hand palm-side down as a map when you try to explain Michigan geography. Most of these details are in the background for me as I watch baseball, but today they force their way to the forefront.

Until today, the only thing I really knew about Saginaw came from that old Lefty Frizzell song. But here we are. We're both tired and we won't get back to Windsor until sometime tonight. Work will come too early tomorrow. I know that, but as I look over at Heidi finishing her custard, I know I wouldn't want to be anywhere else. That's the real answer to the border guard's question.

We pull up at a very small ballpark, not unlike the one where we saw Henry Ford Community College play, and there's a little league game underway. Clearly I've got us to the wrong place. I give in, pay for roaming, and discover after a lot of Google searches that the Saginaw Valley Cardinals play at the Baseball Complex, another twelve or so minutes away. So much for my navigational skills and my librarianship. We'll miss the first pitch for sure. Bother. In retrospect, I should have paid attention to the giant Jesus: we were not on the right road.

Sunday, July 22, 2018

Saginaw Sugar Beets
vs
Lake Erie Monarchs (Game One)

Cardinal Field, Saginaw MI
Game Time Temperature: 66°F

We get to Cardinal Field just as the top of the first inning is ending. That is, we get to the correct Cardinal Field after first going to the one located at the Michigan Lutheran Seminary. We're now at the ballpark at Saginaw Valley State University, home of the NCAA Division II Cardinals and home to about half the Saginaw Sugar Beets home games.

This is a small but lovely ballpark, quite new and reminiscent of so many other American college ballparks we've seen of similar size. There's a comfortable grandstand and an electronic scoreboard. I have yet to see whether they need to chase down foul balls. Like the rest of the college ballparks we've visited in the United States, with the exception of Papp Park, this is far more established and outfitted than any field we've seen in Canada. Surrounding this facility are countless other sports fields and complexes supporting collegiate athletics.

I'm in a great mood: how could you not be watching a team with a Sugar Beet logo on their uniforms? This is the first time on this journey that I've been really tempted to get a t-shirt. I love the fact they're named after a root vegetable and that their logo is a baseball with sugar beet greens. And it's fun to say "Saginaw Sugar Beets."

There are about fifty people here, mostly in the bleachers behind home plate or scattered in lawn chairs along the third base line. As we walk to our seats, Lake Erie—grey uniforms with black sleeves, hats in blue, green, and white—take the field for the bottom of the first. Ryan Robinette, the leadoff hitter for the Sugar Beets—classic home whites, hats blue and white—doubles, moves to third on a long fly ball to center field, and scores on Max Trucks' single later in the inning. 1-0 Saginaw.

From across the diamond I hear an excited voice yelling, "Go, go, Sugar Beets! Yeah! Yeah! Yeah!" over and over again. I hone in on the voice and see that it's a woman in a wheelchair, hair in a ponytail, eyes hidden by sunglasses, sitting under a blue and pink umbrella. "Go, go, Max!" Beside her sits her companion, a big man in shorts and a Tigers jersey. His cheering is less constant, but no less intense.

In front of me are some of the players we saw in Culver's, this time looking more focused and alert, armed with clipboards, stopwatches, and radar guns. I love how being a baseball player is also being an observer, documenter, and, ultimately, a student of the game. Still, though, they seem tired.

With the Sugar Beets still up 1-0, the PA announcer introduces the leadoff hitter for the Saginaw half of the second. Adam Proctor. St. Johns, Michigan. Michigan State University. Exactly as he had for every other hitter on both teams, he lists name, hometown, and school. As I'm listening, thinking about all the different roads that led to this game in Saginaw, Michigan, I hear, "State sucks! Go Blue!"

from that now-familiar voice across the diamond. It doesn't matter that she's been cheering wildly for the Sugar Beets throughout the game. Proctor goes to State and the Michigan-Michigan State rivalry trumps everything.

Because it's a doubleheader, I've been told this will be a seven-inning game. Normally, I imagine, one might feel ripped off but I'm relieved to have just fourteen innings of baseball to watch this afternoon instead of eighteen. Even so, we'll get home late tonight and I have an early day tomorrow.

During the third inning, I walk towards the gate to buy a program. On the way back, I stop to watch near the small bleachers in the outfield down the third base line. The Saginaw shortstop makes a pretty backhanded play on a ground ball to end the top half of the inning. Without really thinking, I say, "Nice play." It's not directed at anyone, or at least not anyone there.

As I say it, I realize it's a reflex, an understatement that acknowledges something beautiful on the field, something I wish Dad could see. On the bleacher just to my right, an older woman turns to me, says, "That's my grandson, Cooper. Coop. We call him Coop."

They're down from Traverse City to watch their grandson play ball. Try to see him whenever they can. We have a nice chat about the summer league, about Coop and what it was like to watch him over the years. We talk about the super fans across the diamond. But mostly we just talk about baseball. I appreciate that they never ask me who I'm here for today.

A Sugar Beet super fan near home plate is cheering for every single player in the Saginaw lineup using their first names. She makes me reflect on baseball fandom. How does one become an avid Saginaw Sugar Beet fan? Or, how does one become such a dedicated follower of a team that's only been in existence for six weeks?[1] Maybe you just decide you're a fan of the home team and then you're a dedicated Sugar Beet fan. People pick their teams for all sorts of reasons. Look at me: I'm cheering for this team simply because they are named after a root vegetable with edible greens. And they're fun to watch. Perhaps in that order. The super fan chants: "Sugar Beets Sugar Beets Rah Rah Rah!" Or, given that they're a vegetable, maybe it's "Raw Raw Raw!"

Robinette is on third base, Connor Charping on first, and Noah Marcoux at the plate with one out in the Sugar Beets half of the fifth inning. Marcoux fouls off the first pitch then takes a ball to even the count at 1-1. From the third base side, I hear a man's voice yell, "Get out your whuppin' stick!" On the next pitch, Charping takes off for second and, just as the catcher releases the throw to second, Robinette bolts from third. The second baseman doesn't attempt a tag, but instead ships the ball immediately back to the catcher to try to get the out at the plate. The throw home and the runner arrive simultaneously and the runner seems to slide into the tag. It looks to be an out, but the home plate umpire calls him safe. The pitcher, Jack Huisman, catches the ball, glares at the umpire, and stalks back to the mound. The Lake Erie pitchers who sit ahead of us with their radar gun and pitch chart are seething. When Cooper Marshall doubles on a 2-1 pitch, the pitcher looks at the ump, says, "That's on you, Blue." He's echoing what the players in front of us have been saying for the past five minutes. The umpire replies, "Did you say something?" as he walks towards the mound. Huisman just shakes his head, picks up the rosin bag, and sets himself for the next batter. A pop fly out to right field ends the inning with the score tied at 3.

The announcer alerts us to an upcoming Sugar Beets game. He says it's at La Cayse Park in Tecum-suh Ontario. We're at the outer edges of our one hundred miles and Ontario's particular pronunciations of "La Cass" and "Tecum-see" haven't travelled this far. But, at game thirty-three, we're starting to see players we've seen before. We saw the Monarchs play in Tecumseh and also saw some of the Sugar Beets playing for Adrian College. In this way, our one hundred miles doesn't seem that vast.

The score is still 3-3 when the Sugar Beets come to bat in the bottom of the ninth. Alex Theis, who came in to pitch for the Monarchs at the beginning of the sixth inning, is still on the mound. On his first pitch of the inning, Brady Wood singles, bringing up the pinch hitter Sean O'Keefe. Standish, Michigan. Adrian College. The first pitch is a called strike, but the second is in the dirt, blocked by the catcher but just enough out of his reach to allow Wood to get to second base. Smart baserunning. But a strikeout and a fly ball to right field leave him at second with two outs. That brings up the number nine hitter. Ryan Missal. Kalamazoo, Michigan. Western Michigan University. On the first pitch from Theis, Missal squares around to bunt, pushing the ball past the pitcher and cleanly down the third base line. Safe all around and it looks like they might be able to manufacture the winning run. The bunt with two outs is completely unexpected and, for that reason, perfectly timed. When Robinette flies out to right field, Heidi turns to me and says, "They're killin' me." I don't know if she's hungry or cold. Probably both.

I'm enjoying myself, but I do make a mental note that the seven-inning game I was promised is tied and going into the tenth inning. I mutter "They're killing me!" Dale laughs a bit and then says "Just enjoy the game." And he's right. Baseball is not a sport in which to watch the clock. And this is a good game. I settle into my seat and turn off all the chatter in my head about what I need to do for work tomorrow. And how I'm getting hungry. Instead, I focus on what's happening on the field.

It's the bottom of the tenth and there are runners in scoring position and two outs. I mentally list all the things that could happen right here, right now. It occurs to me that this long list of possibilities is precisely what I love about baseball. Not only can anything happen, there's time in the play to sit back and itemize all the things that could happen.

As I was watching all the small and big movements on the field, I observed the pitcher's windup. I said "sac bunt" quietly, but out loud. And it was a sac bunt. I didn't trust myself so I confirmed with Dale and he nodded. As I write this down, I am fully aware of how simplistic my observation was. A sac bunt isn't hard to predict or recognize. But fourteen years ago, or even four months ago, I wouldn't have seen a play evolving and said "sac bunt." Over the past four months, I've felt like I know comparatively little about this game, lamented that I will never be as thoughtful or skillful a watcher of baseball as Dale or many other people I know. But saying "sac bunt" out loud changed things for me. I need to trust myself. I know this game. With a little faith I can see more than I ever thought I would.

Both teams have chances in the tenth—the Monarchs with a runner on third and no outs, the Sugar Beets with the bases loaded—but neither can score. Andrew Dyke leads off the top of the eleventh with a walk and then reaches second on Griffin Mazur's sacrifice bunt down the first base line. Jake Goodreau's single puts runners on the corners with one out. "Now climbing into the batter's box, Zach Schwartzenberger. Saline, Michigan. University of Toledo." The first base coach claps his hands, looks at the hitter, says, "Pick that run up. Find a way. Come on, Zach." The count goes to 2-2. Schwartzenberger chops at the next pitch, a swinging bunt to the first base side of the mound. Blair, the pitcher, fields the ball, realizes he has no play on Dyke at home and throws to first for the sure out. The final out comes on another ground ball to the pitcher, but the damage has been done. 4-3 Monarchs.

In the bottom of the eleventh, the Beets have a runner on third and an older fan nearby utters, again, what seems like his signature line, "Come on. Bring out your whuppin' stick." The little boys behind me giggle and repeat it with bravery and incredulity: "Whuppin' stick." Their mother firmly says, "We don't say that word," and the boys stifle their giggles. The sky is growing darker, clouds and misty rain are settling in. The skies could open up at any minute. A Sugar Beet is walked, putting runners on first and third. One of the kids behind me whispers "Whuppin' stick" and they snicker until their mother shushes them.

"Come on, Sugar Beets! Let's go! Bring your whuppin' sticks!" Maybe Sean Fannon hears him as he doubles on the next pitch. Or maybe if you say it every pitch it has to apply at some point. Either way, with the sacrifice bunt from the next hitter, Saginaw have a man at third with only one out. Brenden Lovell, just in to pitch for the Monarchs, looks to third before throwing to Robinette at the plate. Ball. Foul. Ball. Ball. Foul. Full count. Mazur, the catcher, sets up low and outside. Lovell brings the ball up to his glove, glances at Fannon, and comes with a nasty curve in the dirt, right where Mazur had stationed himself. Even a whuppin' stick can't hit a ball out there.

I think again about all the possible things that could happen at this very moment. Then there's a crack of the bat and the fly ball goes looping into the glove of the Monarch's first baseman. The Monarchs win the eleven-inning, four-hour game. We have one more game to watch tonight and a two-hour drive home, both of which, it seems, will happen in the rain. But I'm smiling. Sac bunt, I say to myself. Sac bunt.

Final Score: 4-3 Lake Erie

Sunday, July 22, 2018

Saginaw Sugar Beets
vs
Lake Erie Monarchs (Game Two)

Cardinal Field, Saginaw MI
Game Time Temperature: 66°F

We had a short amount of time between games so we got a Rice Krispie square and a coffee at Starbucks. As we walked through the concourse area of the park, it was filled with players, parents, girlfriends, and grandparents. The batting cages were all in use and players in uniform were loading into cars and trucks to dash out for a break, and maybe lunch. Our car was surrounded by players' cars and we walked among them. This is something that never happens in MLB (for good reason). It's a different experience to see players up front and present.

Back at Cardinal Field, the Monarchs score two runs in the top of the first inning on a walk and a Jake Goodreau home run. The Sugar Beets answer in the bottom of the fourth, scoring a pair of runs on a single, double, and fielder's choice. Between those runs, there are some beautiful defensive plays, as there have been all day. Fannon, in the top of the second, sprinting full out from right field to make a running catch in foul ground. Slattery, in the bottom of the second, diving to his right from first base to stop a sharp grounder off the bat of Noah Marcoux, getting to his feet, and stepping on the bag for the third out. Marcoux with a long running catch in left field in the top of the third. Caleb Balgaard with two pretty picks in the bottom of the third. Nice play. I hear the echo of Dad's voice in my head, say it under my breath into the evening's now perfect silence. Nice play.

The score is now 2-2 and the runner advances to second on a passed ball. Dale says, "Well, this is setting up to be another eleven-inning game." And somehow, this doesn't worry me as much as it might have a few hours ago. The threat of rain has thinned the crowd and only the faithful have returned. It's a much quieter park now.

I can hear the secret sounds of baseball. The gravel shifting under the catcher's feet, an actual cardinal in the trees behind the outfield, the pounding of a runner's feet as he hustles toward first, the scramble of the first baseman's feet as he stretches for—and gets—the out, the way the whole ballpark holds its breath for the exact amount of time it takes the ball to leave the pitcher's hand and hit the catcher's glove with a snap, the melodious "Dok!" of a wooden bat, the metallic jingle of the rings attaching the protective netting to the poles around home plate, which reminds me of the sound of the metal clips on the flagpole at my elementary school when I waited for my mum to pick me up.

I close my eyes and just listen to the game. There's the thud of the bat on home plate, and the scuffling of shoes. There's the slight echo of the umpire's calls bouncing off the trees, the faint sound of cars in the background. I identify six different kinds of footsteps, each of which tell a story about the action on the field. This could never happen in a vast, noisy ballpark.

Brady Wood is hit by a pitch to open the bottom of the fifth inning for the Sugar Beets and then advances to second on a ball in the dirt. On the next pitch, Fannon hits a deep fly ball to left center field. Schwartzenberger tracks the path of the ball, settles under it to make the catch, and then fires a strike to third base to get Wood, who has tagged up and tried to advance. 7-5 double play. You don't see that every day.

Robinette, the next batter for the Sugar Beets, doubles and around me I hear some murmurings about how that should have scored a run. Fans like to do that. What would have been. If only. But that's not how the game works. There are no crystal balls, no second sight that will tell a baserunner what the next batter will do. The game is close and Wood took a calculated gamble that Schwartzenberger wouldn't be able to make a perfect throw to third. It's a gamble he would only take with one out, since you're taught from a young age to never make the first or third out at third base. That's good baserunning, the smart decision given all the information he had at that moment. Unfortunately for him and for the Sugar Beets, it was an even better throw.

Robinette advances to third on a pitch in the dirt that doesn't get far from the catcher. It's an excellent read, anticipating what's possible, another calculated gamble to try to score the go-ahead run. More good baserunning. And this time there's no perfect throw to make the fans grumble.

Man on third, two outs, and Daniel Page is still at the plate with a 2-2 count. Another pitch in the dirt that Goodreau blocks, keeping the ball directly in front of him. He jumps out, cocks his arm, looks Robinette back to third base. From the Lake Erie bench, one of the coaches yells, "Way to be a wall there, kid." Four pitches later, Page strikes out swinging. Game still tied 2-2. No rain in sight.

Seeing two games in the same park on the same day with the same two teams is a good reminder that no two baseball games are ever the same.

Increasingly, I find myself both loving and resisting the notion of baseball as a silent sport. There's a part of me that feels guilty that, more and more, this is how I like to watch the game: alone in my thoughts and able to concentrate and think. But I also recognize that baseball is a social sport: it's the way people connect with the game and with each other. Baseball shouldn't be like going to the symphony where the crackling of a candy wrapper can get you a stern shushing. And some of my favourite moments this summer have happened when overhearing people's comments, watching them get really engaged or enraged by this sport that I've somehow devoted a great chunk of my life to historicizing and experiencing.

It occurs to me—at game thirty-four—that maybe it's useful to think about baseball not as a monolithic, homogenous entity, but as a spectrum ranging from Henry Ford Community College to Sarnia to MLB, with infinite variations along the way. It's not MLB or bust, where every team's worth is considered in relation to its distance to or from MLB.

A nicely turned double play by the Sugar Beets in the top of the sixth. A fly ball to each Monarch outfielder in the bottom of the sixth. Strikeouts to end threats for both teams in the seventh. Extra innings. Still no rain, but it's beginning to get dark.

The top of the eighth opens with Goodreau drawing a walk. Mazur, the pinch runner, advances to second on Casey O'Laughlin's sacrifice bunt. Bell pinch hits for Dyke, drawing a walk on a 3-2 pitch. Runners at first and second with one out and Watson up to bat. One of the Saginaw fans yells, "Twist it!," a call for the double play that will get the Sugar Beets out of the inning. Instead, Keegan Watson singles to load the bases and bring Slattery to the plate with only one out. With so many ways to push the run across, it's going to be difficult for Saginaw to keep the score tied.

Jack Tagget looks for the sign, comes set, and throws to Slattery. Ball. Strike. The third pitch is in the dirt, a swinging strike that gets past Houle. All three runners burst into motion. Houle leaps back to retrieve the ball, grabs it, and flings it to Tagget, sprinting towards home on a collision course with Goodreau. It's extremely close, but the call is out at the plate. The crowd cheers madly. The Lake Erie coaches are livid. After a minute, the home plate umpire takes off his mask, raises his arms, yells, "Time! We got a warning on the dugout." The noise from the Lake Erie bench subsides as the inning fizzles out on a fly ball to center field. Still 2-2, but darkness and rain are threatening.

"There's no extra charge for extra innings!" the announcer proclaims cheerfully. I realize most of the people are rooting for players, not a team. And this is important. It changes the way you think about baseball. Some of the people, like Coop's grandparents, are cheering for a player they love or, in the case of one young woman behind home plate, perhaps think they might love. Others, like Dale, are cheering for a good game and for the love of a sport. I am very soggy but it doesn't seem to matter. This is great baseball and I'm happy to be here.

By the time the Monarchs bat again in the top of the ninth, the rain is steady and it's hard to see the ball. They once again load the bases and this time are able to cash in the runs, the score 5-2 by the time the end of their half inning. In the bottom of the ninth, the Sugar Beets score a run and have two more men on base. The rain is even heavier now and we're soaked to the bone. The mound has become slippery and the area around home plate has standing water. Time is called so that the Saginaw players can try Quick Dry on the mound in hopes of getting the rest of the game in. O'Keefe takes the mound again for Lake Erie and throws four pitches before the game is called because of rain, field conditions, and the coming darkness. Game suspended after eight innings of play. In the scorebooks, it's as if the ninth inning never happened.

Final Score: 2-2

Fourteen

HOMESTEAD

July 27 – 29, 2018

Premier Baseball League of Ontario
U18 Championship Tournament

Windsor Selects
vs
London Badgers

Terriers U17 (Mississauga)
vs
Ontario Royals (Oakville)

Terriers U17 (Mississauga)
vs
London Badgers

Friday, July 27, 2018

Windsor Selects
vs
London Badgers

Cullen Field, Windsor ON
Game Time Temperature: 25°C

I left the office mid-morning to come to the game. Thinking I can both watch and deal with work email, I've balanced my phone on my notebook. I've tried this enough times already this summer to know it won't work well. Still, I think I can. There are about thirty people here and the crowd is mostly parents. The moms are out in force. There are few more loyal attendees of this level of baseball than the moms. "Hustle 2-5. C'mon, Richie."

I'm sitting in one of our folding chairs, which we've just left in the trunk for the past month. A tiny concession behind the backstop is open, offering Gatorade, an assortment of canned pop, freezies, hot dogs, and sunflower seeds. The staples. The flags here and across the city are at half-mast for Sergio Marchionne, the chairman of Fiat Chrysler, who died last week. It's a reminder of what kind of town Windsor is.

The leadoff hitter for the Selects—the away team today as per tournament draw—works his cleats into the dirt and cocks his bat as he awaits the first pitch. When he hits the ball—a soft single to right—it's the kiss of wood on leather rather than the ting of aluminum, a sound we'll be hearing all tournament weekend. The teams are all members of the Premier Baseball League of Ontario, a league that includes the London Badgers, Ontario Royals (Oakville), Ontario Yankees (East Toronto), Ottawa-Nepean Canadians, Terriers Baseball (Mississauga), and the Windsor Selects. As it states on their website, "PBLO member franchises provide amateur players with the resources required to live out their collegiate and professional dreams. The PBLO member franchises have produced more than 500 college baseball players, highlighting the emphasis placed on academic success and degree fulfillment. The PBLO has also seen over fifty players selected in the MLB Draft, with notable alumni like Dalton Pompey (Toronto Blue Jays) and Jamie Romak (L.A. Dodgers)." It's a league that grooms players and showcases them for advancement to the next level, which, in most cases, means a scholarship to an American university or college. The young men we will see this weekend are among the elite players in their age groups, drawn from extensive geographic areas around the host cities. Players like #19 standing on first base or #25, now walking to the plate.

As he digs in to the left-handed batter's box, I recognize him. Noah Richardson. Off to Northern Kentucky University, he's soon to be added to the list of PBLO alumni who have gone on to play college baseball. He's already well over six foot, and my guess is that if we see him play in a couple of years, his frame will be much more filled out. As I think about how he looks like a full-grown man on a field of teenagers, he strokes a solid single up the middle. He has a sweet swing and it's easy to see why Northern Kentucky recruited him.

Trying to keep one eye on email and another on the game is proving difficult, as predicted. I keep feeling my mind wander and, as if I'm nodding off, I keep trying to pull myself back into the game by watching pitches carefully. I'm not bored, I just can't concentrate. Dale says—and I see this—that when he gets to a ballpark, his mind slips into the game and he doesn't think about other things. My mind is half on work and half on the game, and I know this isn't an ideal frame of mind for watching baseball.

London has what you might call a soft tosser on the hill. The kind of pitcher who needs to keep hitters off balance with a mix of movement and pinpoint control. He manages to get the third batter to fly out to left field, but then walks the bases loaded. He's either catching too much of the plate or missing way out of the strike zone. Until he gets a weak fly ball to the second baseman for the second out, none of the batters seemed at all uncomfortable. The bases are still loaded, but with two outs it looks like he might be able to get out of the inning without giving up a run.

With the bases loaded and no threat of a steal, he's pitching out of the full windup, trying to entice a weak grounder or pop-up. The Selects third base coach looks in at #10 at the plate, cups his hands to his mouth, says, "Be smart now." #10 doesn't bite on the first couple of pitches, letting them go by, waiting on a pitch that he can drive. The catcher rises from his crouch, throws the ball back to the pitcher, as he has so many times already this game. But this time the throw is a bit errant, ticking off the pitcher's glove, just off the mound towards first base. It doesn't roll far, but enough to allow Richardson to advance to third base and #19 to score ahead of the hurried throw back to the catcher. On the next pitch, #4 breaks for second on the steal attempt. Instead of throwing through to second and risking the run scoring from third, the catcher throws to third, but the ball sails over the third baseman's head and the run scores anyway. Two runs scored on smart baserunning. Or poor fielding.

The inning ends on a tough grounder to third base, but by that time the Badgers coach is apoplectic. As the London players jog in from the field to take their first turn at bat, a steady stream of profanity issues from the dugout. "Time to wake up! Time to fucking wake up!" He's as livid as I've seen anyone in a long time and he won't stop shouting at these teenagers. I want to walk over to the dugout to tell him to stop, but I don't. Instead, I sit pinned to my chair, angry at the coach on behalf of the players, angry at the parents for putting up with it. I don't know whether it's that I don't think it will do any good or just that I'm a coward, but I don't move. I think about Charlie Chapman and remember that part of the reason we didn't listen to him was because every so often he would become unhinged, like the coach here today, yelling at us for making a mistake on the field. I can't move. All I can do is watch and write down what I see.

Dale points out that the London coach "just lost his shit" after a single inning. I see it, but I'm blocking it out. The moms' talk is much more compelling. I'm learning many things. One says her son is a PO, and when I look at Dale, he passes me a note that says, "Pitcher only." A Windsor player just got a single and his mom shouts, "That one was for Grandma." She seems a little teary.

The Selects players are already unhappy with the home plate umpire in the top of the second inning, griping constantly about the strike zone when they are hitting. After #3 strikes out with a man on base, he walks back to the dugout, says to the bench, "That's so fucked up."

One of the coaches replies, "How many strikes did you actually see?" The sarcasm of the question is abundantly clear.

It's not a tirade like the London coach threw, but it bothers me more than I care to admit. I realize this isn't house league. It's high-level, competitive baseball, but these are teenagers who are still learning. What is that question teaching them? I think about coaches like the Sarnia Midget Major coach saying, "Not necessary, not necessary," teaching their players with every play in the field, every at-bat, not only about the game, but about how to be in the world. All the things that sports are supposed to teach.

There's a lot of banter between the benches. A Selects player shouts to the Badger on first: "White pants look better with dirt on them!" His teammates laugh, which seems to inspire the Selects player to say, "They make laundry machines, you know." His teammates don't laugh as much, but I hear someone in the Badger dugout shout over the infield, "Laundry machine? They're called washing machines, man."

While most of the parents and moms are focused on the game, I cannot seem to block out the two moms further down the baseline talking loudly about everything except baseball: they've covered spas and varicose-vein procedures, whether McDonald's fries have too much salt or just the right amount, whether the salmon in sushi is cooked or raw, how to make a good taco, why it's good to freeze chives, all the things you can clean with lemon juice, finally finishing with a long yet inconclusive debate about mayonnaise vs ranch dressing. I realize a whole inning has gone by and I have no idea what happened. I also realize I am blaming the chatty moms for my inability to concentrate when, really, it's that I am mentally writing emails, updating my to-do list, processing a work interaction that did not go well and still stings, regretting ordering pens instead of pencils for our conference, feeling guilty about the state of my garden, feeling ill from the amount of take-out food we've been eating because we're never home long enough to cook or grocery shop. And, perhaps most acutely, fighting tears about news of the death of a kind, gentle man in my Scottish dance community. I shake my head and focus on the game.

I think I'm concentrating, but then Dale starts clapping and I realize I've somehow missed a great play. As a consolation, I have learned from the moms that you can use peppermint spray to get rid of ants in your kitchen. And that peppermint is a useful household disinfectant.

The score is tied 2-2 as we move towards the Badgers' half of the sixth inning. Despite a bit of a shaky first inning for the London starter, both pitchers have had good control, always right around the strike zone, and the defenses have played well, other than a fielding error allowing London to score two in the bottom of the third. As the game has progressed, there's been a bit more complaining about balls and strikes, especially by the Windsor bench, but no more meltdowns. It's settled into the kind of well-played game I find myself constantly chasing.

I notice Dale has become unusually partisan in this game. I'm not sure if he's cheering for Windsor or against London or, more specifically, the London coach. There's a really bad error by a Windsor infielder, which gets a London player on base. My heart breaks as the London bench taunts him. I imagine how hard it will be to shake off those words when he takes his cleats off after the game. Up close, you see how hurtful baseball can be. In my head, I've been summoning the

Sarnia coach's words: "Not necessary, not necessary." I find myself becoming fully engaged in this game now, as if cheering for Windsor can somehow quell some of the hurt that player might have felt. Maybe wanting justice, a sense that wrongs can be righted, is my way in to today's game.

The Selects pitcher seems to briefly lose command and walks the first London batter of the sixth, who gives way to a pinch runner. The third baseman can't come up with the ball on the sacrifice bunt attempt and everyone is safe. Runners at first and second with no one out.

The pitcher goes into the stretch, looks in to the catcher, back to second, spins, and throws the ball. Into center field. Neither the shortstop nor the second baseman is there to receive the throw. Runners on second and third, still no one out.

THWOCK. Ball hit to the shortstop. He centers himself, looks the ball into his glove, and looks the runner back to third base before throwing to first base for the out.

That brings up #19, prompting the Windsor coach to call for the intentional walk. No one seems to know if they have to throw the pitches or not. The umpires confer, ask the advice of an older man sitting behind home plate, watching intently, arm folded across the cane in front of him. It's decided that they do have to throw the pitches. Bases loaded, one out.

The pinch hitter grounds to the pitcher, but he can't quite field the ball as it caroms off his glove to the second baseman, whose throw is in time to get the out at first. As the play on the field unfolds, the runner comes in to score. At the end of the inning, the Badgers are up 3-2, the go-ahead run scoring without a hit.

London wins but a Windsor player applauds his team, saying, "Still a lot of baseball left. Still a lot of baseball!" I know he's talking to his teammates, but I take his words to heart. We have fifteen more games this summer. The prospect both emboldens and overwhelms me.

Final Score: 3-2 London

Saturday, July 28, 2018

Terriers U17 (Mississauga)
vs
Ontario Royals (Oakville)

Soulliere Field, Windsor ON
Game Time Temperature: 25°C

I'm really starting to wonder if gardening and baseball can coexist in my life this summer. I was excited to finally have a morning where I could do some work in my garden. Perhaps as a conciliatory gesture, Dale agreed to help pull some tall weeds from around the garage. After about fifteen minutes, his eyes began to burn. I dashed to the drugstore and bought a bottle of eye wash, and while it helped momentarily, his pain grew more intense. I was able to get him to our eye doctor before they closed, but the wait was long. I can't begin to describe how I horrified I felt watching Dale in agony of my causing. I should have just let him read his book on the porch this morning.

The doctor flushed out Dale's eyes for about twenty minutes and then gave him some drops. He rested for much of the afternoon and is on the mend, I think. I am totally gutted by guilt. There are no drops for that.

At first, we weren't going to go to a game tonight, but at 5:15, we decided to dash across town to the 5:30 game. We missed only the first two batters. Then we realized we'd both forgotten our phones and that, without them, we couldn't take photos of this game. I drove home and then back to the park. By the time I returned, I'd missed two innings.

I'm having trouble seeing, my field of vision narrowed by the squint to which I've been reduced. The field is hazy, as if a thin film of gauze had been draped across my eyes. A dream version of a baseball game.

I probably shouldn't be here, should instead be home resting my eyes. But it's July 28 and we're only thirty-five games in. When will I ever have this chance again? I want to be here. I feel compelled to be here, the game unfolding on the cloudy field in front of us.

The Royals come to bat in the bottom of the second down 2-0 and start the inning off with a single and a walk. #78 tries to bunt them over, but pops to the pitcher for the first out. A wild pitch moves them over anyway. One of the Terriers dads yells, "Shake it off! Shake it off!" while a Royals mom hollers, "Two ducks! Two ducks!" A double to the wall in right center scores the tying runs and the Royals bench erupts in sound.

Man on second, one out. Called strike to the hitter. The man I've started to call Royals Dad in my head says to the hitter, "Not you. Not you." The man is middle-aged, maybe late forties by the grey in his hair. He's wearing a green t-shirt, checked brown shorts, Nationals hat, diver's watch, sunglasses, and white flip-flops, dressed for comfort rather than style. Dressed like a dad. Dressed like a baseball dad.

Foul ball. Royals Dad: "Way to protect."

Another foul ball. Royals Dad: "Way to spoil."

Yet another foul. Royals Dad: "Good battle, Nick. Now win it."

Yet one more foul, on the eighth pitch of the at-bat. Royals Dad: "Do a job. Protect."

Weak ground ball to the second baseman. Royals Dad: "Next time. Next time."

A single scores the runner on second. The Terriers bench, trying to pick their pitcher up, scream, "Way to go 2-1!" No blame. They're in it together.

The parents have all travelled to the game. Looking around, I see they have it down to an art, with complicated chairs and enough accoutrements to prepare them for any kind of weather or contingency. It's evident they've been baseball parents for the long haul.

In the third, it's a 4-2 game and there are maybe thirty or forty people here. It's a warm, sunny evening typical of July in Windsor. There are picnickers just past the Terriers' dugout and a playground further behind it. Not everyone is here to watch the ballgame—for some it's a backdrop, ambient noise contributing to a lovely night deep in mid-summer. I watch the parents watching their nearly adult sons play a game they've loved their whole lives. I think about the miles they must have driven, the things they've put on hold, the interests they've put off so they could take their sons to baseball games and watch them play. The parents I've seen here tonight are fully present, like there's nowhere else they'd rather be. No one is talking about how to make a taco.

The Terriers are able to score a pair of runs in the top of the fourth to tie the game back up. As the Royals walk off the field, one of the parents shouts, "Come on, boys. Get 'em back." Royals Dad claps his hands, yells, "Get back on the sticks." The Royals bench huddle, scream in unison, "1-2-3 team!" Everyone in the park is as into the game as any I've seen all season. There's so much going on—constant chatter from the players, yells of encouragement from the parents—that it almost feels like I'm listening to the game, taking it in with my ears rather than my narrowed vision.

The teams are evenly matched, though most of the Terriers players are younger by a year. Between innings, I use my phone to look at the team website and see that they field four teams for ages fifteen to eighteen rather than the standard two (16U and 18U). As I scan the page, their mission statement leaps out: "To be the defining force in developing student athletes who become successful young men both on and off the playing field." I have a feeling that if the Terriers play London in the final game, my efforts to remain impartial will go by the wayside.

This summer has given me a small glimpse into what living a baseball life must be like, the way a season shapes your weeks and how game time and weather conditions determine your days. I've been trying to sort out the place that baseball occupies in my life. The question remains: how much room will baseball occupy next year?

People ask, "Will you do one hundred games in a two-hundred-mile radius next year?" I notice that while I'm quick to say "No!" Dale pauses non-committedly and does not answer. This is a once-in-a-lifetime summer—and not just because I can't see doing this again—but because it has given us something we could never recreate.

Each team scores a run in the fifth, though it's only a perfect throw to the plate from the Terriers left fielder that prevents the Royals from scoring the go-ahead run in the bottom of the inning. A home run in the top of the sixth once again breaks the tie. Then, with runners on the corners, the Terriers send the runner from first. On the throw to second, the lead runner breaks for home and is safe when the catcher drops the ball on the throw back from the second baseman. Seven runs on just five hits for the Terriers.

This is a more aggressive game than others we've seen in terms of fielding and running. The teams are accruing a lot of errors and I'm not sure if it's because they're not skilled or because they're taking chances on plays they can't quite make. But when they do make those plays, they are beautiful—like the breathtaking catch and throw I just saw by the Royals shortstop to get an out at first. What made that catch so remarkable is that I'd seen the same play tried and botched so many times these past few weeks. I've come recognize how difficult a play that is.

As the Royals walk onto the field to take their warmups in the top of the seventh, it's nearly silent. I can hear cheers from Cullen behind us—something must have just happened in the other tournament game—but other than that brief intrusion, it's just an occasional clang of steel from the Prince Metal factory beyond left field. I close my eyes, savour this moment of calm before the chatter picks back up when the inning starts.

The Royals parents are looking a little disheartened by some of the errors but still hopeful—it's a close and aggressive game. Anything could happen. Raindrops are beginning to fall.

It's the top of the seventh and the score is 8-5 for the Terriers. There are runners on first and third and a fielding error just cost them an out and a double play. I calculate all the possible scenarios on how this inning could shape up. Imagining all the plot possibilities that could happen, the only thing certain is that someone will win this game and someone will lose. Everything else is up for grabs.

"All we need is three!"

Bottom of the seventh. Final inning. Royals Dad paces behind us, says to the leadoff hitter, "Be a leader. Start us off."

Two quick strikes looking. Foul off his foot. Two balls high. Double.

Royals Dad: "Come on. Do a job."

New pitcher. Pinch hitter. From the Royals bench I hear, "Now we work."

Flyout to left field for out number one.

An error puts runners on the corners. The next batter hits a ready-made double play ball, but the second baseman can't handle the flip from the shortstop. The run scores and it's 8-6 Terriers.

Royals bench: "Come on, shooter. Come on, 1-6."

Flyout to left field for out number two.

Terriers coach: "No doubles."

Single. Run scores. Runners on the corners with two out. Royals down by just one.

A ball in the dirt almost gets away, the man on third ready to take off down the line. But the catcher is able to lunge to his left, keep the ball in front of him, and prevent the tying run. The next pitch is hammered just foul down the third base line.

It's 8-7 now and there are two outs. Everyone in the crowd is hollering and so is Dale. He seems to have been able to forget the pain in his eyes while cheering for great baseball. The game ends with a 6-4 play at second and I see Dale smile for the first time today. This is another game we almost didn't go to. If we'd stayed home and watched TV, we would have missed all of this. Like Sarnia, there's a lesson here.

I turn around and look back at the Royals parents as they say goodbye to each other. They probably didn't know each other before the season, but I can imagine the hours they've logged in each other's company. Or at least adjacent to each other as they watched their sons play ball. It's the last game and they won't see each other tomorrow, or possibly ever again.

I begin to put my lawn chair back in its bag, squinting to make sure one of the legs doesn't get caught. Behind me there are handshakes, a few hugs. Hard to believe, but we're already at the point of endings this summer.

"That's it. See you."

Final Score: 8-7 Terriers U17

Sunday, July 29, 2018

Terriers U17 (Mississauga)
vs
London Badgers

Cullen Field, Windsor ON
Game Time Temperature: 24°C

Fluffy clouds float above the trees that ring the outfield, lending depth to the blue of the early afternoon sky. Spectators filter in, stake out their territory. Players stretch, take ground balls. Coaches look over their lineups. The umpires confer in quiet tones. Everyone is preparing for the PBLO championship game.

Over the PA, we hear, "Players and fans are asked to return balls as quickly as possible to help move play along." It's time to play ball.

We're sitting behind the plate in the non-partisan zone in the shade of the press box. We can tell it's going to be hot today and are clinging to the shade for as long as we can. Dale's eye, which had been getting better last night, seems worse this morning. I expect his eye will heal more quickly than my guilty conscience.

We've seen both of these teams before. London we saw Friday afternoon and the Terriers last night. The crowd is small, maybe thirty or forty people, mostly parents you can identify by how quickly they assemble their elaborate system of chairs, umbrellas, coolers, and other gear. Today someone has a red beach umbrella on some sort of tripod. I've not seen anything this elaborate since the man with the portable heater at Wayne State. We're so obviously amateurs at this, bringing only sunscreen and ball caps, slouching into whatever sliver of shade we can find in the bleachers.

There are a few other outliers here just to watch baseball. A woman sitting nearby asks Dale a couple of questions about where the teams are from and how far London and Mississauga are from Toronto. Proximity to Toronto appears to be how she's choosing her rooting interest for today. Odd, I think, but perhaps no odder than my choosing to cheer for the Terriers because my childhood pet was a terrier and one of their players reminds me of Curtis Granderson.

As the game begins, the PA announcer says, "Hot dogs will be coming later, but there are sunflower seeds and Mr Freezies available at the concession now."

As the third inning comes to an end, I notice Noah Richardson, wearing a Northern Kentucky t-shirt, sitting in the bleachers behind home plate with a couple of his teammates from the Selects. They're laughing, relaxed as they watch, but at the same time intent on what's happening, three sets of eyes scanning the field as the Terriers warm up for the fourth inning. One of them points towards the third base dugout and I turn to see what's going on.

The Terriers coach walks towards the mound, says a few words to his starting pitcher, holds out his hand for the ball, and claps him on the shoulder. His day is done, though he's only given up one run. The coach must have seen some hitch to his motion, an indication of a problem or injury. If I had to guess, I'd say it's a precautionary move.

The new pitcher is announced as Karlis Mikelsteins, a right-hander who throws out of the stretch. It's a fairly simple delivery. Facing third but looking home. Pitching hand dangling as he looks for the sign. Both hands coming together near his face, ball hidden in glove. Knee raised slightly before he plants and throws the ball. He's missing pretty badly as he takes his warm-up tosses, but as he works through the inning—ground ball to short, pop-up to second, ground ball to second—he seems to compose himself and find the strike zone.

Both teams are playing well, especially on defense, staying calm and making the plays they should in the field. It helps that the pitchers have been working quickly, helping the fielders stay focused. The Terriers are down by a run, but, like yesterday, the chatter from the bench is upbeat.

While the third base coach gives the shortstop instructions on where to position himself, I watch three little boys freak out over the presence of a great black wasp in the stands. One of the boys sets out on his own and wanders around the bleachers. He's wearing a Blue Jays cap and Blue Jays batting gloves that are a few sizes too big for him. He's holding a white Mr Freezie, his sunglasses perched on his ball cap emulating big league players. My attention is brought back to the field by a man shouting up to correct the announcer, "There's only one out!" And Dale agrees. I don't know how long I've not been paying attention to the play, but I don't recall seeing any outs.

Each game I continue to admire Dale's ability to concentrate on the game and remember each play. Later in the game, it doesn't surprise me that when the official game scorekeeper says, "I looked away for a second and missed that play. Was he safe at home?" It's Dale he's asking. "Nope," says Dale. "Double play." And this is Dale distracted by his injured eye.

My left eye is watering constantly and I still can't open it all the way. It feels like there's grit under the lid, but no matter how many times I flush, the feeling won't go away. The doctor said it would take time, but I admit I'm concerned. It's so sensitive to light that I have to pull my cap as low as possible and squint to see the field. I don't want to leave and, realistically, I'm not sure that being at home would be any better. At least here I have the perfect 12-6 curveball that the Badgers pitcher just threw to distract myself.

The announcer seems pleased to be able to say, "If you've been waiting for them, I believe the hot dogs are now ready." Among those waiting for hot dogs are an older man and a little boy, maybe five or six, seated two rows in front of us. I recognize them from last night, when they walked in off the street and into the stands. It isn't clear if the man is his father or grandfather, uncle or friend, but last night I was struck by how captivated they both were by the game and each other's company. The man takes bills out of his wallet and is counting seven dollars carefully into the boy's hand. He watches the boy go down the stairs and walk toward the concession. His attention turns back to the game only when the boy is out of sight. A few minutes later, the boy returns, climbing the stairs one at a time, balancing two ketchup-loaded hot dogs and a can of Sprite in his little arms. The man takes the hot dogs and opens the Sprite while the boy snuggles in beside him. They eat their hot dogs in silence, together. When they're done, the man wipes ketchup off the boy's fingers: neither shift their eyes from the field.

I take a cue from them and return my attention to the game. The Terriers' bench will need lozenges this afternoon for all the hollering they're doing this morning. They're loud until the pitcher winds up and then there's silence for as long as it takes for the ball to reach the plate. I write down things like, "There's an overthrow at second base on a stolen base" and "The pitcher catches the ball on a hit and there's a half a second pause when he processes—too slowly—where to throw the ball. Without the pause, he would have made the play. When he throws it, he throws it too hard, as if to make up for the moment's hesitation. His throw is too anxious, too desperate to make the play."

Three players from the Selects team come in and take seats behind home plate. They duck down as they pass us, as if they're late taking their seats in a movie theatre and don't want to disturb others' view. I smile at their reverence for the game and their respect for those watching it.

I also smile as I hear the ketchup-hot-dog boy ask his companion, "Do they mow the grass and then put the sand in there?" I can't hear the gentle explanation he's given, but I hear the answer to the boy's next question about baserunning. I feel a lump in my throat thinking about what baseball is giving these two people who walked down the street from their neighbourhood to watch a game, for free, on a summer Sunday. There's no high-priced nostalgia here or fast-paced entertainment: it's simply baseball.

My attention keeps drifting from the action on the field to watching this man and boy watch baseball. Watching them doesn't seem like a digression because they're also teaching me what baseball means and what baseball is. The boy exudes a quiet love for and trust in this man. The way the man holds the boy and answers his questions reveals an incredulous, gentle reverence for him, as if he can't quite believe this little boy exists. This moment will stay with them the rest of their lives. And they have this moment because of baseball.

London scores the tying run in the top of the seventh. As the Badgers take the field, I hear their coach shout, "Defense! Defense!" There's been none of the yelling we saw on Friday, but I find myself waiting for him to blow if something goes wrong. From the Terriers bench someone yells, "I believe! You believe!"

The inning opens with a strikeout followed by a ground ball to the third baseman that looks like it will be the second out. But the throw sails over the first baseman's head and the batter ends up on second base. I glance over at the London bench, but I can't see any change to the coach's demeanor. Neither do I hear any encouragement from him or from any of the other coaches. I don't know if I'm imagining it through my slitted eye, but the players on the field seem to visibly slump, like the loss is a foregone conclusion.

The bloop single to left field that lands just inside the line feels like an inevitability. As the winning run crosses the plate, the Terriers players stream from the dugout, mobbing each other and jumping up and down in unison. Seventeen and on top of the world. The London players look at the ground, never even glancing to home as they walk off the field.

How the game ends, I'm not sure. I was watching the man and the boy and thinking again about baseball and relationships. About my dad. And Dale's dad. I am woken from my reverie by the crowd moving and gathering up their things. As I pack up our bag, the announcer says, "Let's give these boys a hand for an exciting game of baseball. You couldn't ask for anything more!" I smile at the press box in agreement.

We stay in our seats for the medal presentations. After the celebrations have died down, the two teams make their way to the infield, lining up on either side of the trestle table that's been shuffled out for the occasion. On it sit the gold and silver medals and, behind it, presiding over the ceremony, is the man with whom the umpires consulted on Friday about the intentional walk. The PA announcer introduces him as Bernie Soulliere, and it's only now that I realize that the other field at Mic Mac Park—where we saw the Terriers win last night—is named after him. Beside him, ready to assist in handing out the medals, stands Noah Richardson.

Final Score: 3-2 Terriers U17

Fifteen

A BLUR
OF BASEBALL

August 2 – 6, 2018

Great Lakes Summer Collegiate Playoffs/
Ontario Senior Mens' Elimination Tournament

Saginaw Sugar Beets
vs
St. Clair Green Giants

Sarnia Braves
vs
Bolton Brewers

Windsor Stars
vs
Tecumseh Thunder

Windsor Stars
vs
Mississauga Southwest Twins

Saginaw Sugar Beets
vs
St. Clair Green Giants

Brampton Royals
vs
Strathroy Royals

Tecumseh Thunder
vs
Ilderton Red Army

Thursday, August 2, 2018

Saginaw Sugar Beets
vs
St. Clair Green Giants

Lacasse Park, Tecumseh ON
Game Time Temperature: 27°C

At this point in the season the grandstand at Lacasse Park—paint peeling on the ceiling, support posts that partially obstruct the view of home plate—is very familiar. We know where to sit, where we can get the best angle on the game as we walk up the bleachers behind home plate. Seventy-five years of baseball in Tecumseh and people have been watching from this grandstand since 1949. Tonight we're here for the first of the three-game series, Jacob Moskowitz pitching for the Green Giants against Ryan Jungbauer for the Sugar Beets.

I've been following the results of the Great Lakes Summer Collegiate League more closely this past week, hoping St. Clair would host a playoff game. When I saw there was a chance the series might be against Saginaw, I found myself hoping for that result, for what I was sure would be a well-played series.

Lacasse Park is fuller tonight than I've ever seen it—perhaps two hundred people are here. For the first time all summer we've had to park around the corner. It's Thursday tonight and this weekend we have plans to see five more games. Walking into Lacasse, I bought a pop and wandered around. I was struck by a familiar feeling that I didn't immediately recognize, one I finally identified as nostalgia and affection for this little ballpark—something I'd only ever felt walking into Comerica. This project is creeping up on me, affecting me in ways I would not have predicted. I count the games in my notebook index and realize that, after tonight, we only have twelve more games. After this weekend there will be only seven games left.

We stand as instrumental versions of both anthems play over the PA. A few people mouth the words, but most just stand looking across the field, the players lined up down the baselines, the umpires arced around home plate. Tonight there are three of them, one more than in the GLSCL games we saw earlier in the season. As the last notes of "O Canada" trail across the summer night, a young man in shorts walk towards the mound, ball in hand, to throw out the first pitch. He's introduced as Brandon McBride, NCAA 800-metre champion, Canadian Olympian, and Windsor native. Behind us sits Noah Richardson, wearing a Herman Baseball t-shirt.

It's warm tonight but the skirt of my sundress is getting picked up by a gentle, cool breeze. Noting that it's now August, I'm grateful for the sunglasses that hide the hint of tears I feel forming. I climb up a few rows and perch on the bench beside Dale. He's already writing notes, taking it all in. "You okay?" he asks. I wipe away a tear or two. "It's August," is all I need to say. He knows. He gets it. This summer has changed him, as well. I think we're both trying to keep things in present tense, enjoy the game, and let the words and thoughts come later when it's all over. I put my hair in a ponytail and try to focus on the field.

Moskowitz is a tall right-hander who hides the ball well as he twists towards second base, showing the batter his uniform number, before unfurling his body and releasing the pitch to the plate. He's got a live fastball, a good curve, and a nasty cutter that breaks away from right-handed hitters. Through five innings, he's struck out four and only given up an infield single and a double. He's locating his pitches well, moving the ball around the zone and changing speeds, keeping the hitters off balance.

Jungbauer, on the other hand, opens the game with a walk, a strikeout, and another walk. He throws hard and his curve has good break on it, but he's all over the place and doesn't seem to know where his pitches will end up. By the time he leaves the game at the end of the fifth, he's given up four walks and a single, but he's also struck out six. More importantly, he's only given up one run, on a single in the first inning by Harrison Jones. Tonight, Jungbauer is the very definition of effectively wild.

The crowd is so quiet that between the windup and the catch you can hear cicadas. Everyone is here to watch baseball. When people do talk, it's between batters or innings, and it's always about the game in front of us. Unlike many other games we've been to, there aren't many families because most of these players are far from home. We aren't the outliers we usually are.

Not cheering for a specific team or outcome is liberating as we can just focus on the game itself and not the score. But, were I wanting a team to cheer for tonight, I'd be divided. Do I cheer for St. Clair because they're Canadian or do I cheer for the Saginaw Sugar Beets because *they're the Sugar Beets*.

I just witnessed a pretty double play: second base with a perfect flick of the wrist to the shortstop and then a precise snap of a throw to first. It was ballet: instinct and muscle memory, no hesitation, no pause, no second guessing. Glimmers of what we take for granted in MLB are particularly beautiful to see at this level and in this park. Dale points out what a difference a few more years of playing and coaching makes.

The Sugar Beets' catcher seizes the ball and stares down the runner at first, who, in turn, stares back. In other games we've seen, the runner would have run, having, probably correctly, sussed out that he can run faster than the catcher can throw, or that the second baseman can't make the catch. But today there's a bit of a stand-off. I can see both of them triangulating, evaluating, comparing their abilities with those of the other players involved. The stand-off, lasting only a few seconds, ends when the catcher raises the ball menacingly. The runner retreats to first and the game carries on. If you blinked, you'd have missed this moment.

Behind the two pitchers, the defensive play has been stellar. A beautiful flip from the St. Clair second baseman to the shortstop to usher in a double play in the top of the second. An off-balance throw from the Green Giants third baseman on a slow hop down the line to get the batter at first. A smart and gutsy throw home from the Saginaw first baseman on a hard ground ball to prevent the runner from scoring and erasing the leadoff triple. Tough plays that look routine. Smart baseball. A well-played game, the kind Dad and Kurt and Dave would appreciate. The kind I'm happy I can share with Heidi.

Between innings, there's a footrace between players from the Kingston Colts. They look to be about seven or eight, and they're eating up this opportunity to run along the first base foul line to home plate. They run, herd-like, across the plate, all twenty systematically giving each other high fives, holding up the game as they do so. The St. Clair coach comes in to try and clear them out. "Good job boys, but you gotta go. C'mon." The catcher tries to shoo them away but, like the Canada geese in my parking lot at work, they won't move unless they want to move. And while you're bigger than they are, they out number you, so you just need to wait until they decide to move along. Which, eventually, they do.

Once shooed off the field, the little Kingston Colts gather beside the St. Clair dugout. They're working their way through a range of cheers and chants. "Gimme a G! Gimme an I! Gimme a . . . !" There's a pause until someone remembers, "An A!" They're loud and sometimes the players on the bench have to shush them. The two little boys behind me really want to go down and join in, but their parents say no, they're too small, so they come up with their own slightly random Giants cheers. Somehow they've learned to boo players and the youngest boos the Giants and the Sugar Beets equally. He boos batters and pitchers, walks and hits. But he also claps and cheers whenever people around him clap and cheer. This is how baseball fans are born, raised, and nurtured.

The Sugar Beets get a man to third base with two outs in the top of the sixth. That brings up Cooper Marshall. When he's introduced, I hear in my head, looped over the PA announcer, the voice of his grandmother telling me, "We call him Coop." As he rotates his spikes in the dirt, readies himself for the pitch from Moskowitz, I wonder how many games his grandparents saw him play this summer. As he swings and misses a cutter that dives outside, I wonder how many games the families of all the players we saw watched this summer. As he strikes out on another nasty cutter to end the inning, I wonder what the other players' families would tell us about their sons, brothers, and grandsons.

Between the sixth and seventh innings, several children have been selected from the crowd to play musical chairs around the on-deck circle. I recognize one as the boy who'd been sitting a few rows in front of us. A more than slightly pushier older boy "out maneuvered" him and won a gift card for his efforts. When the boy in front of me returns, his disappointment is waylaid by the fact he's been given a cracked bat to take home. He contemplates the two pieces of bat for a good long while. "Is it corked?" he asks his dad between batters.

In the top of the seventh, Adam Proctor hits a no-doubt home run, past the flagpole in right center to tie the game at 1-1, but in the bottom of the inning, the Green Giants retake the lead. Gavin Homer opens the inning with a walk. He then advances all the way to third base on an errant pickoff throw and scores when the next pitch is thrown in the dirt past the catcher. Both teams put a man on in the eighth, but neither is able to score. After eight innings, the score is 2-1 Green Giants.

The broken-bat kid stares at Dale intently, in that way that only seven-year-olds can. He then asks Dale the question he appears to have been formulating for a while, "Are you a Saginaw fan?"

"Nope."

"Green Giants fan?"

"Nope. I just like baseball."

The kid nods and focuses again on the game. I like how easily this boy has managed to get Dale to reveal his quintessence in a four-word précis of this summer: "I just like baseball."

Leading off the ninth for the Sugar Beets, Marshall hits what appears to be a solid single up the middle, but it caroms off the mound and straight to the shortstop, who throws to first for out number one. The next batter, Connor Charping, hits a ground ball to third for what looks to be the second out, but Gibson Krzeminski double clutches, hesitating just long enough for Charping to reach first ahead of the throw. It's a tough play, ruled an error according to the PA announcer, but one that could easily have been scored an infield hit. Either way, that's the end of the game for Moskowitz. Steven Butts, a left-hander, comes into the game for St. Clair.

I glance back at Noah Richardson. Flanked by his parents, he's leaning forward, intent on what's happening on the field. Like all the players we've watched this summer, he's become part of my own baseball landscape, my own interior stadium where games layer over each other, where the past, present, and future exist simultaneously, a matrix of baseball of which I am only one small part.

As Proctor fouls off strike two, I wonder if Richardson imagines himself playing in a game like this one, ready at first to field a ground ball or cover the bag, or ready at the plate to try to move the runner over to second. Is he imagining himself breaking from the batter's box on Proctor's bloop single that lands between the shortstop and left fielder, putting runners on first and second with one out? Does he look the ball into his glove as Homer fields a ground ball and flips it to the shortstop for the fielder's choice at second base? Does his future layer over the game in front of him or am I reading too much into a young man watching baseball with his parents?

Meanwhile, Krzeminski very nearly catches a foul pop near the Green Giants dugout, sliding along the grass, the ball and the third out just beyond his grasp. A curve for a strike puts the count at 0-2, but the next pitch catches too much of the plate and Max Trucks doubles home two runs for Saginaw. 3-2 Sugar Beets heading into the bottom of the ninth.

Jake Tagget, who took over in the top of the eighth for Saginaw, blows a letter-high fastball past Jones for the first out. But when Tagget hits Homer to put the potential tying run on base, I start to wonder if we're going to see another extra-inning game, like the two we saw in Saginaw. Taking no chances, the Saginaw manager walks to the mound, retrieves the ball from Tagget, and waits as Billy Blair trots in to face Matthew Ornelia.

Blair looks in to the plate, but then, after a quick glance over his shoulder, wheels and throws to first base. Homer is safely back. Again, a look to the plate and a throw to first. Homer is safe again, but he's drawing some of Blair's attention. Blair sees the sign from the catcher, quickly looks to first, and this time comes to the plate. Ornelia swings, his bat exploding on contact, shards splaying out towards the field, along the path of the ball. Robinette, the second baseman, calmly fields the ball amidst the chaos of the shattered bat, tosses the ball to the shortstop, who steps on the base, and immediately releases the throw to first. A perfectly executed 4-6-3 double play to end the game. No handshakes. Game two tomorrow in Saginaw.

Final Score: 3-2 Saginaw

Friday, August 3, 2018

Sarnia Braves
vs
Bolton Brewers

Oriole Park, Woodslee ON
Game Time Temperature: 28°C

We're both dragging today, suffering from a night where the carbon monoxide detector kept sounding until 2 am. Add in the trip to Saginaw last Sunday, where we got home after midnight, a full week's work, a game last night, and the summer's accumulation of this routine. I'm tired and I know we have a stretch of five games over the next four days. For the first time in my life, I understand what people mean when they say baseball is a grind—like Earl Weaver once said, "This ain't a football game, we do this every day."

The first game we'll see today is between the Sarnia Braves and the Bolton Brewers. Since it's a double-elimination tournament, the loser goes home, each team having lost their first game. As I watch the Braves in their bright red jerseys and already-stained white pants get ready to bat in the top of the first, I'm momentarily back in Sarnia, a perfect tableau of baseball laid out before me on the field. Then I'm back here, in Woodslee—its emerald grass and manicured dirt cradled by mature trees that ring the entire outfield—on a beautiful mid-summer afternoon, cool breeze blowing across my back. These might be the dog days and I might be exhausted, but this, this afternoon, this diamond in front of me is the only thing that matters right now.

The two umpires are behind home plate with the coaches, explaining the ground rules for this park. What's in play. What happens if a ball rolls under the fence. The Bolton pitcher finishes his warmup pitches, the catcher calls, "Go two," fires the ball to second base, and we're ready for play to begin.

There are maybe thirty people here. The game starts without ceremony: the ump simply says, "C'mon boyce, let's get it going" and they're off. The first batter for Sarnia gets a home run on the third pitch. Then there's a base on balls and a strikeout. Because I put my phone away and have tuned out conversations, I see the Sarnia pitcher reach up and ably catch the ball and throw it to first to get the out.

By the time Bolton comes to bat in the bottom of the third, the score is already 7-0 Sarnia. It's been like batting practice, starting with the home run that #10 hit to lead off the game, a 1-1 pitch smashed over the Plumbing Now sign in right field. Since there is no program and no PA announcer, I don't know his name or the name of the Brewers pitcher. Most of the people watching know at least some players on one of the teams, but to us they are anonymous, generic baseball players that flit across our summer. There's none of the "known-ness" of watching Tommy Parsons or Noah Richardson or Cooper Marshall. Instead, the men are reduced to numbers, perhaps vague remembrances of baseball past if we've seen them before.

The Sarnia starter (#33) throws much harder and with a lot more control. An intimidating presence on the mound, he begins his motion with his glove in front of his face. Only his eyes are visible to the hitter before he explodes towards home with a fastball that's too much for most of the Bolton hitters. Sometimes he mixes in a curve that he throws for strikes. He walks the first hitter of the third (#8), but then spots two fastballs on the outside corner to the next batter for the strikeout looking, his fifth of the game. From across the infield I hear one of his teammates yell, "Way to go, Chucker. Chuck, chuck, chucker!" Flyout to center field before #8 steals second.

With two outs, #44 walks to the batter's box. His name is Hodge, a bit of information I picked up in the first inning when he hit a bloop single down the right field line and his teammates yelled their congratulations. He is what my mother would have called a stout man, compact, but with a quick bat. I don't know what his batting average is for the year, just as I have no idea about the Sarnia starter's ERA. Statistics have melted away for me this summer, become irrelevant to the way I've been watching. I don't know anything about these two players beyond what I've seen today and I really don't want to know. This lack of a statistical past forces me to stay in the moment. To forget about sample sizes and projections and advanced metrics. To pay attention to what's happening on the field, to savour baseball for its own sake. Hodge doubles to score Bolton's first run. He is batting 1.000 for today.

On the bleachers, to my right, are four men in their sixties. One is with his wife, who is also watching the game with interest. The men chat quietly amongst themselves between batters and it's clear they know and understand the game.

Sarnia are hitting the ball hard. It's 7-0 in the bottom of the fourth and there are no outs. Bolton have just changed pitchers. I overhear someone on the Bolton bench say, "S'okay. Just chip away at it, let's just chip away at it." Sometimes I think it's the optimism of baseball that keeps me coming back. A 7-0 deficit is not insurmountable. It's now 7-1 in the top of the fifth.

Players for the next game are showing up. When they arrive in their different shirts and shorts, they're clearly individuals. When they put on their uniforms, especially without their names on the back, they're just guys on the field. And in parks like this without an elaborate score-board, we know nothing—and thus have no preconceived ideas—about who they are or what they're hitting. They just stand at the plate, and, for people like us who don't know them, there are no expectations.

A ball bounced off a Brewer glove, advanced a runner from first to third, and scored a run. It's 8-1. A flyout to right field scores another run and runners are now on first and second.

There have been a lot of foul balls this game, some over the small clubhouse set on the first base side, others back to the road that runs behind the park and along the left field fence. It's been mostly the players getting the balls, as is usually the case in amateur and low-er-level college games, but an older fan from Sarnia, sitting just to our right, has been walking back to pick up a ball here or there for most of the game. I guess it's something to do when the score climbs to 9-1. He'll walk back towards the road, pick up the ball, and amble back to the volunteers' table set up in front of the clubhouse. This time one of the volunteers looks up, says in the most deadpan voice, "You know we don't give quarters, right?" They both smile, a shared joke from years of watching amateur baseball. I smile too, instantly back at Czar Lake, chasing foul balls, hoping for a quarter that will get me a popsicle to eat between innings.

A crack of the bat pulls me back to the game, the ball launched towards the outfield, arcing towards the fence in left center, landing just beyond the 4D Sausage sign to make it 11-1. The Sarnia pitcher ends his day with nine strikeouts. Hodge gets two of Bolton's three hits, the other going to a player called "Loooouuu," as far as I can tell from the reaction of the bench in the bottom of the sixth.

A little boy, about four, is playing with a truck in the dirt by the back-stop fence. He pauses periodically to ask how the blue team are doing. "Yay blue team" he says, whether there are things to cheer for or not. The game is called after six innings for time.

Final Score: 11-1 Sarnia

Friday, August 3, 2018, evening

Windsor Stars
vs
Tecumseh Thunder

Cullen Field, Windsor ON
Game Time Temperature: 26°C

Walking up to the gates of Cullen Field, I expect to see the Stars or the Thunder taking infield. Instead, as we move to seats in the bleachers behind home, I see a beautiful diving catch by the right fielder, full extension in foul ground, ball raised to show he caught it. A swarm of black jerseys exits the field, clapping the right fielder on the back, talking excitedly as they descend upon their dugout. A set of blue jerseys fills the void that's been left on the field. Top of the sixth in a 1-1 game between Martingrove and Oakville, with Martingrove coming to bat.

News of what's happening at other diamonds filters into the park in fits and starts. Who's won and lost. Who's going home. Who will play next. I overhear one of the Thunder players say that the Tecumseh Juniors lost both games—a no-hitter and two-hitter—and are out of their tournament. Meanwhile, the Martingrove pitcher gets the final out of the seventh on three consecutive swinging strikes to strand a runner on third and keep the score 1-1.

The game moves on through the eighth and ninth and the score remains tied. To our right sit most of the Tecumseh players, sprawled across the bleachers. One of them turns to his friends, says, "This is worse than a rain delay." They're focused on their own upcoming game, waiting for their chance on the field. For them this extra time is an annoyance, a delay in their schedule. And in some sense it is for us as well, ensuring another late night before another early baseball morning. And yet, it's compelling baseball. Despite it all, I find myself not wanting it to end, not wanting one of these teams to have to lose. Finally, three singles in the top of the tenth for Martingrove are enough to score two runs and win the game.

Erindale vs East York, which was to have been the late game here, has been moved to Lacasse Park; the Stars and Thunder will play the final game here tonight.

Dale watches the end of the game intently, but I take the opportunity to close my eyes for a few minutes and think about nothing. Left to his own devices, Dale would watch baseball continuously this weekend, but I just cannot watch any more than I have to. These are indeed the dog days of the season.

There are about two hundred people in the park—divided fairly evenly between Tecumseh and Windsor fans—as the Stars infielders take their final tosses from the first baseman before the start of the game. Both teams have won this tournament many times and the rivalry between them goes back more than twenty-five years. I've seen them play before and while there didn't seem to be any real animosity between the players, it was clear the fans didn't much care for each other. Even though it's early in the tournament, this is a big game.

As I wait for the game to begin, I check my phone and see that the Green Giants won today. The deciding game in their series against Saginaw will be tomorrow night at Lacasse Park in Tecumseh. I hope we can fit it in amongst the tournament games.

Unlike the game at Woodslee this afternoon, tonight the players are announced over the PA, names attached to numbers, glimpsed as pitchers stride home, fielders break for balls off the bat, and hitters burst from the batter's box. From the speaker mounted behind us, I hear that today's pitching matchup is Steve Teno for the Stars against Joel Pierce for the Thunder.

Today is the second fourteen-hour day in a row, and I am tired. But these players tough it out and so must I. A coach yells, "Stay aggressive Steve, make 'em hurt." My inner coach says, "Stay focused Heidi, make that pen hurt." As I walk to where Dale is sitting, I overhear one official say, "I hear they're running out of baseballs."

I look around to orient myself to the crowd, the park, and the teams. Because these are local teams, there are a lot of families, wives, girlfriends, children, and grandparents watching. I notice there's a female umpire and I'm thrilled to see the first woman on the field in an official capacity in this project. There's a kid with a "You're killing me, Smalls" t-shirt and I'm reminded how much I love Smalls from *The Sandlot*. The evening light is nearly at the golden hour, making the leaves and grass an ethereally vibrant green, and the sky glow with warmth.

With runners on first and third and one out in the bottom of the third, Steven Adam hits a ground ball to second base. Instead of trying to turn the double play against Adam's speed, the second baseman pivots towards home. The throw is high, but the catcher manages to get the tag down just before Jake Lumley can touch the plate. It's a heads-up play and the Tecumseh fans clearly appreciate it. A few of the Windsor supporters grouse, but from where I'm sitting, it was the right call.

"Now at bat for the Stars, Anthony Dufour." Runners on the corners, two out.

Pierce stands on the mound, glances at Mitch Hudvagner at third, back to Adam at first, raises his left knee, and quickly cocks his arm. As he begins to release the ball to the plate, Adam breaks for second. The catcher throws through and Hudvagner bolts from third. The run scores and when the second baseman can't corral the ball, Adam advances to third. The catcher shouldn't have thrown the ball. Easy enough to say from my seat behind the screen.

The inning ends when the third baseman sprawls to field a hot ground ball, pops up, and makes a desperate throw. The first baseman digs it out of the dirt on one hop, his toe just on the bag before he falls towards second and off first base. The out call is greeted by howls from the Stars fans, part of the general complaint about the umps that both teams and both sets of fans have been nursing the entire game.

Four Canada geese just flew overhead and another dozen followed them. When I lived in the United States, the sight of these birds nearly broke my heart with homesickness. Nowadays flocks of them menace me in the parking lot at work most mornings and swarm me when I ride my bike along the river in the evenings, so I feel much less nostalgic about them.

Tonight's two teams are more equally matched than the teams we saw this afternoon. It's more enjoyable to watch games when one team isn't getting crushed. The fielding is precise. There's good speed and athleticism with these players, and seeing strong plays like these help me keep my head in the game.

Someone in the crowd just yelled, "Make shit happen!" An error gets a runner to third. I'm not sure if the person in the crowd is happy or displeased with this turn of events.

I've been updating Chris Wainscott, who runs the Tecumseh Thunder Twitter account, on the score throughout the game. After four innings, I send him a note that the score is 4-1 and that the Thunder are getting outhit 9-2. He writes back, "Yeah, the Stars are really good this year. Probably the top-ranked amateur team in the country." When I tell him the score is still 4-1 after five innings, he writes, "Wait until you see Bobby St. Pierre pitch. Just got back from the Roswell Invaders last night. Unfortunately, he's on the Stars. But we're all friends."

I text Chris when St. Pierre comes in to pitch in the top of the sixth, relieving Teno after a bases-loaded walk to score the third Tecumseh run. Immediately, I get a text that reads, "If his breaking ball is working, it's disgusting. Slides about a foot and drops off the table. And can hit 93 mph with a four-seamer." I look up to see just how hard St. Pierre is throwing. Andrew Wasyluk can't seem to handle the fastball and strikes out on a slider that's as nasty as Chris said it would be. A couple of those sliders to Jack Zimmerman, the next hitter, just miss the strike zone—though according to the Tecumseh bench and fans they didn't miss—bringing the count to 2-2. Zimmerman manages to foul off the next two pitches, just barely getting a piece of each. When the catcher can't handle a fastball up, Tecumseh score the tying run.

Tecumseh just scored a run on a passed ball and it's a tied game. The sun is nearly setting and there's a light, cool breeze spreading out over the field. There are no races, gimmicks, or giveaways here: just baseball. In spite of my earlier grumblings, life doesn't get much more pleasant than this.

Pierce is still pitching for the Thunder as the Stars come to bat in the bottom of the eighth, the score still tied at 4. He pitched out of a two-on and no-out jam in the top of the seventh, getting strikeouts on a slider away and a changeup before inducing a short pop-up to first base for the final out. I relay the information to Chris, who replies, "Former Milwaukee Brewers farm hand. He'll bounce back and pitch Sunday, too." It's nice to have this insider knowledge, the kind that comes from being part of this baseball community, the kind that we miss in every other town as we traverse our hundred-mile radius. We see who's on the field wherever we go, but we never really know any of their stories. At most, we get their names, maybe see them a couple of times as we weave in and out of their baseball lives.

St. Pierre continues to pitch for the Stars as the game turns to the ninth inning with the score still deadlocked at 4-4. Leading off for Tecumseh is Matt Sykes, who squares around to bunt, deadening the ball down the third base line. The ball seems to be rolling foul, but St. Pierre picks it up just before it crosses the line and tries for the out at first. Safe. He never really had a chance to get Sykes. As St. Pierre walks back to the pitching rubber, the Stars fans make their displeasure known to the ump. One of the Tecumseh fans yells, "You can't get every call!," and there's some general jawing back and forth. No one seems happy, but from where I sit, it's hard to see that either team has really been advantaged in any way. I wonder why any rational person would ever want to be an umpire.

There are Thunder players on first and second and a wild pitch advances them both. There are no outs. A player is hit by a pitch and loads the bases, and then a long single scores two runs. It's 6-4. A sacrifice fly to right scores a run, a double scores a run, and a single scores a run. It's 9-4 now with one more half-inning to go. It's easier to stay focused on skilled, precise baseball.

When the center fielder squeezes the final out, Pierce has pitched a complete game and the Thunder have won 9-4. Though he gave up some early hits, Pierce's performance is one of the better ones I've seen this year, especially the way he got out of the two-on-and-no-out jam in the seventh. I wonder if Chris is right about him bouncing back to pitch on Sunday on only two days' rest.

As we walk back to the car, the air is almost chilly, but it's still humid. I hear a train whistle. And a freighter sounding its horn on the Detroit River. I'm feeling awake and happy. Baseball has worked some magic on me.

Final Score: 9-4 Tecumseh

Saturday, August 4, 2018

Windsor Stars
vs
Mississauga Southwest Twins

Cullen Field, Windsor ON
Game Time Temperature: 23°C

If we're not at work, we're at the park. No matter how good the baseball, we're at the point in the season—game forty-one—where it's starting to catch up to us. At least the weather is cooperating—the sky is pure blue and it's already quite warm.

The Stars are the home team today. Lose and their tournament is over. Lose and they won't be one of the two teams that goes on to Nationals in Victoria. Survive and play another game.

It's only 9:30 in the morning and you can already tell it's going to be hot. A tiny boy clutching a thermos is being gently led by his dad to the bleachers, his head turned toward the field, eyes fixed not on where

he's going, but on the players warming up on the field. He seems surprised. "Lookit," he says to his dad, "They're playing baseball. Lookit."
"I know buddy, come on."

We're sitting in what has become our regular location at Cullen,
in lawn chairs in the area just in front of the grandstand, just to the
third base side of home. Scattered around the park are about fifty
people, though most sit together in pockets near the plate. As the
Stars prepare to bat in the bottom of the first, an older guy to my right
spots Noah Renaud taking swings near the Stars dugout, calls out,
"Hey, Noah! You can knock this guy out of the park." Then laughs.

Around first base there's nothing but mud from the overnight
rain. The grounds crew move to put down some Quick Dry, but the
umpire waves them off, telling them to wait until the first inning is
complete. The mud slowed the Twins leadoff hitter in the top of the
inning—his uniform is slick with grime from his slide into the bog.
It's only fair that the Stars should deal with the same thing in their
half. Two strikeouts and a groundout later, it turns out it wouldn't
have mattered.

Behind us, an older woman complains to the woman sitting
beside her, "He's calling them high." She replies, "As long as he's consistent." I nod to myself as the grounds crew make their way to first
base.

I ask Dale where these players would be in their baseball careers:
on their way up, on their way down, or about where they'll stay, and
he indicates the latter. I realize that where players are determines how
their families cheer for them. Are parents cheering for a college scholarship? A chance at the big leagues? A chance to be publicly proud of
their son? Or, later, are wives cheering that their husbands don't injure
themselves? Today it mostly seems like a public expression of pride in
their sons or grandsons.

There's a pep squad of women behind me. A grandmother yells,
"Double play, guys, double play!" and a mom does a little wolf howl.
Another mom calls out, "C'mon Matt, take him. That's okay. It's only
two. Keep on playin'!" The dads are less vocal, but still watch intently.

A grandmother using a sunflower umbrella as a parasol shouts to the batter, "C'mon Mitch. Pick out a good one. Pick out a good one." I've come to love these women. Anyone who thinks women don't know baseball needs to come and watch a game like this. I wonder again about whether they watch MLB when they're not watching their kids or grandkids. Next year, will I be at a game like this or watching the Tigers? As we near the end of this project, that's the question people keep asking us and it's one neither of us can or wants to answer right now.

This all-female cheering squad looks at home as if there's nowhere else they'd rather be. "Way to watch, Brian. Way to watch." Sunflower Grandma is cheering for the whole team. I like her. "C'mon. Everybody hits, everybody hits. Follow it in. Follow it in. All the way." One of Sunflower Grandma's friends says, "Ump's got a big strike zone, boys." Sunflower Grandma follows with, "Only takes one."

Having seen the Stars play just last night, I have some idea who the players are, can recognize that it's Jake Lumley who comes up with a nice scoop on a ground ball to shortstop for the first out of the second inning. That it's Bryan Dufour at first who nearly snags a hard grounder as he dives to his right. And Mitch Hudvagner flashing the signs behind the plate.

Matt Krutsch catches the ball, walks back to the mound. A left-hander, he faces the batter at first, sees the length of the lead without having to look over his shoulder. When he throws over, the entire Twins bench screams, "Back!" in unison. Behind us the two older women yell, "Double play! Double play!"

Flyout to center field. From behind us, I hear, "AAOOOHH!" like the sound of a coyote baying at the moon. Man on and two outs.

Single. Runners at the corners and two outs.

"Throw him the old dart ball!"

Fastball for a called strike. Curve for a called strike. Ball high.

Then it's a pop fly into very shallow center, a long run but playable for Anthony Dufour, the second baseman. Unfortunately for the Stars, he can't make the catch and two runs score. None of the fans scream their disapproval, no one calls him out for the miscue.

When he comes to bat in the bottom half of the inning, one of the women behind us calls, "Pick out a good one, Anthony."

I'm enjoying the Mississauga dugout—they're into the game but not obnoxious. I love watching them watch their runner at first trying to get a lead while the pitcher and catcher negotiate trying to pick him off. "BACK!" they all yell in unison. For some reason I find it funny.

The score is 2-1 and a player named Dale is up to bat. The bases are loaded and someone's dad says, "Come on, Dale. No pressure here, no pressure." I wonder if the dad is being ironic or if he's trying to keep player Dale calm under pressure.

Another dad comes down behind home plate when his son is at bat and I mentally nickname him Grumpy Dad. "Posture, get your posture right. Get your ass in the game!"

The Stars are down 3-1 when they come to bat in the bottom of the sixth inning, but the two women behind us haven't lost faith.

"Come on, guys. Let's have some hits."

"Pick out a big hole."

Lumley starts the inning with a perfect bunt down the line. The third baseman has no choice but to field it, but Lumley is able to beat it out. It's a smart play at the right time against a pitcher whose fastball has been giving the Stars trouble all game. As I think about kairos, the familiar coyote yowl of approval sounds from behind us.

By the time the inning ends, the Stars have scored four runs to take a 5-3 lead. As Krutsch takes the mound for the top of the seventh, one of the women behind us says, "Hold 'em. Hold 'em. Come on, Matt." Her voice is more muted than it has been, the words said as much to herself as they are to the pitcher, a silent prayer of hope that those runs will be enough. Two runs up and three more outs to go.

But Krutsch gives up a single to the leadoff hitter and a walk to the second hitter. To my right, a disgruntled Stars fan calls to the home plate umpire, "Too late in the game to change your strike zone." Krutsch's day is over—Chris Renaud in to pitch for the Stars.

Early in the count the Twins runners take off. Both get great jumps and there is no throw. The double steal, with the Twins down two and in their final at bat, seems to catch the Stars off guard as much as it did me. That's aggressive baseball.

And it pays off. When Hyslop, in left field, loses a fly ball in the sun, it drops in for a double to score a run. When Wasyluk can't handle a hard liner at third, another run scores to tie the game. When the Twins have runners on second and third with one out, they run a squeeze play that scores the go-ahead run. More aggressive baseball.

I find myself getting caught up in the game in the same way that I lose track of what page I'm on when I'm really enjoying a book. The game washes over me, and I put my pen and notebook down. I say to Dale, "That was kind of low for a strike," and he agrees. Before I know it, it's the bottom of the seventh inning and the score is 7-5 for Mississauga.

After watching games at so many levels, I've come to realize that the final score only tells part of the story. Tonight's game is close, even though the score doesn't suggest it. Sometimes a game is 1-1 because neither team can get anything going offensively. Other times a game is 1-1 because the plays have been skillfully executed.

In the final half-inning, one of the grandmas in the cheering squad tells a man in front of her to put his rally cap on. He mumbles, "I don't really want to wreck my cap." The grandmas, wearing visors, find that statement hard to believe.

A player named Jake gets a walk and then he's out on a fielder's choice. One out with a runner on first. Sunflower Grandma says to the next batter, "Pick yourself a good one." He's out F2. Two outs. It's down to #11. "There's a big hole out there," says Sunflower Grandma to the next batter. "Pick a good one and find that hole."

He hits the ball and it soars toward an infield glove. Before it hits the glove, Grumpy Dad says, "Well, there's our season." One of the cheering-squad moms says, "They played well," to which Grumpy Dad says, "Doesn't matter. They lost." I try not to imagine the conversation Grumpy Dad will have with his son on the car ride home. I'd rather be in Sunflower Grandma's car.

Final Score: 7-5 Mississauga

Saturday, August 4, 2018, evening

Saginaw Sugar Beets
vs
St. Clair Green Giants

Lacasse Park, Tecumseh ON
Game Time Temperature: 29°C

After this afternoon's game, we went home, sat on our shaded front porch, and talked about not going to the Green Giants' game. "What else would we do? Watch TV?" We both silently mulled our options then leapt up, grabbed the baseball bag, and now we're here at Lacasse for game five of the weekend, our eighth game in eleven days. Tonight, I'm sitting with my pen uncapped, wondering what I should watch for. As we near the end of this project, I'm clinging to these final games. I spent much of my summer pining to read a Jane Austen novel on my porch. Now I'm struggling to visualize what a life without baseball is going to look like.

I scan the field, see Harrison Jones skipping ground balls to Gavin Homer at second, Carter Mossey and Matthew Ornelia playing catch in the outfield, Adam Proctor and Connor Charping talking near the Sugar Beets dugout, Ryan Robinette and Cooper Marshall swinging bats as they loosen for the start of the game. We've seen each of these teams only a couple of times, but in our peripatetic summer of baseball, that makes them seem like old friends.

People are still filtering into the park when Marshall, the second batter of the inning, crushes the first pitch he sees from Gage O'Brien. His teammates pour from the dugout to watch as the ball lands beyond the Mr Meat sign in right center. A no-doubter for Coop.

A couple of batters later, Proctor comes to bat with a man on and two outs. He takes the first pitch for a ball, but takes a mighty cut at the next offering. Behind us, the St. Clair play-by-play announcer tells viewers, "Proctor was not swinging for a single on that pitch."

Indeed. Two more enormous swings and the inning is over on the strikeout.

This game is for the Northern Division championship and I can see the trophy waiting a few rows ahead of me. It's a wood plinth with a gold tripod holding what appears to be a baby-sized baseball glove and baseball. The benches are remarkably quiet. All the players are currently sitting, and while there are a few cheers and comments, you'd never guess they were playing for a championship. There are no Sunflower Grandmas here tonight, nor Davenport Moms. If there are Grumpy Dads, they're not saying much.

By the time the Sugar Beets come to bat in the top of the third, the score is 7-1 Green Giants and the outcome of the game appears to be a foregone conclusion. Heidi turns to me, points out that the dugouts are silent, except for when there's a hit or run. There's little of the constant encouragement we saw this morning, no soundtrack of chatter to accompany the action on the field.

I'm wondering if the players are tired, too. For the first time ever, I'm starting to feel how long the baseball season is for players. If I'm this tired after a summer of watching baseball, I can't imagine how the players feel.

From my seat, I can see the radar gun timing all the pitches and feeding them into a monitor. Dale's explaining curveball and fastball speeds to me, and I can see the pitches clearly and the differences in their velocity. At the beginning of the summer I tasked myself with "learning baseball." I realize now that learning baseball is something that takes longer than a summer. There's no end to the learning. And there's no "examinator" to test me.

Jordan Williams, an Adrian College right-hander, comes in to pitch for Saginaw in the bottom of the third inning with the score still 7-1. He's locating the ball well, just as he did when we saw him pitch early in the season against Albion. At this point, though, he's just here to eat innings and get Saginaw to the end of the game.

We're keeping an eye on the other tournament via Twitter as our games for the rest of the weekend will be determined by the results coming in. It strikes me that we aren't following the Tigers game right now. MLB and the Tigers have existed on the periphery of our summer of baseball. I'm still not sure what I think about that.

The crowd is quiet and intentional in its watching of the game. When the pitcher winds up, I quite literally hear crickets. And cicadas. I look around and see a captivated crowd, none of whom, I'm convinced, is seeing this as inferior to the majors. No one is here thinking, "I wish I were watching MLB right now."

The Sugar Beets half of the fourth opens with Proctor being hit by a pitch and Jacob Crum singling up the middle. When the center fielder bobbles the ball momentarily, both runners advance and it looks like Saginaw might be in business. On the mound, O'Brien rubs the baseball as Noah Marcoux walks to the batter's box. From the Saginaw bench I begin to hear a steadier stream of chatter, an incantation for an improbable comeback.

After two quick strikes and a foul ball, Marcoux hits a hard shot straight back at O'Brien, who knocks the ball down and recovers in time to get the out at first base. When Proctor strays too far towards home, the first baseman fires back to the catcher and Proctor is caught in a rundown. Proctor retreats towards third as the ball is tossed over his head to the third baseman, then fired back to the pitcher who is now covering at home. Score the out 1-3-2-5-1.

Even though the Sugar Beets are still down 8-1 when they come to bat in the fifth, the bench is upbeat, the players laughing, trying to get each other up for the last few innings. They've only been together a couple of months, congregating in Saginaw from colleges and universities all over the United States, but they seem to genuinely like each other. Maybe it's the short season, maybe it's the nature of collegiate summer leagues, but the players are about as loose as any I've seen all summer. Their season could end tonight, but there's none of the tense atmosphere we've seen in other elimination games, no sense of an ending.

Missal starts the inning with a single, just beating out Homer's too-casual throw from second.

"Attaway, 4."

"Come on, boys. Let's bring the sticks."

Top of the order for the Sugar Beets. The Green Giants get an out on a ground ball from Robinette, but a single, double, and walk give the Sugar Beets some life. One run in, bases loaded, one out. The Green Giants coach walks to the mound, infielders converge. Still up by six runs, they want to talk it over. Daniel Page is announced as the pinch hitter for Proctor.

A walk on four pitches for a run. Crum's double scores two more. The Sugar Beets are within three runs.

Marcoux is announced as the next hitter. I look at the program and see that he plays for Davenport University, a team we saw twice at the GLIAC tournament in May. At six games, it's a sure bet we've seen him more often than any other player. An inning ago it looked like he probably wouldn't get another meaningful at-bat this season. Now he's up with a chance to get the Beets right back in the game.

He takes the first pitch for a ball, fouls off the next two. 1-2. Protect the plate, but don't chase. Ball. 2-2. Breathe. Tune out the noise from the stands, from your teammates as they urge you on. Set yourself. Focus on the pitch, watch the rotation as it leaves O'Brien's hand. Start your swing. Stride through the ball. Feel the solid contact as the ball hits the bat's sweet spot. Watch as the ball sails just to the left of the light standard and over the wall in left center field. Lean into the mob of your teammates as they greet you at home plate, the game now tied 8-8. I think about the women who sat behind us this morning, hear a chorus of their voices in my head saying, "There's a lot of baseball left, boys."

Saginaw come to bat in the top of the eighth with the score now 9-9. It would be hard to call this a well-played game, but it has been highly engaging, with all the twists and turns of a good summer blockbuster. There's a certain joy in this kind of sloppy, shambolic high-scoring game. There's also a sense that, as the Green Giants broadcaster says while the first hitter of the inning walks to the plate, "Anything, I mean anything, can happen."

The eighth inning opens with Robinette laying a bunt down the third baseline for a single. A strikeout, error, and fly ball to center put runners on the corners with two out and Daniel Page coming to the plate. On an 0-2 pitch, Williams wanders too far off first base and it looks like the Green Giants have him picked off and will get out of the inning. But the throw is wide—Williams makes it to second and Robinette scores the go-ahead run. A walk and another error load the bases, but Saginaw can't score an insurance run. 10-9 midway through the eighth.

Going into the ninth inning, the crowd is getting louder. This is great baseball. I'm tired and my body is sore from sitting on benches, crouched over a notebook all day. I'd like to go home to bed, but I also don't want this moment to end. This is the culmination of the Sugar Beets' season and the beginning of the end of ours. I focus my attention on the field. It's the final inning. The first Green Giants batter strikes out. The second is out on a fly ball to center field. A single gets the third batter to first base. Then there's a 5-4 fielder's choice and the Sugar Beets win. Game forty-two is done.

Williams' final line tonight: seven innings, four hits, two runs, zero earned runs, zero walks, and eight strikeouts.

The final line on tonight's game, in clichés: It's not over 'til it's over. Baseball has no clock. Keep working and good things will happen.

We gather our things and shuffle out with the crowd. I hear the announcer thanking everyone who supported the Green Giants this year, inviting us to join them again next spring. I'm struck by this talk of spring when there's just a dash of chilly air in the thick August humidity. Winter seems unimaginable right now, let alone spring.

As we're getting in the car for the ride back to Windsor, Heidi says, "We're getting to the time of year where seasons are coming to an end." We think of this with Major League Baseball, about how baseball will break your heart, about how seasons begin and end.

But we see the same thing in these games, too, and will continue to see it over the next few weeks as we begin counting down to the end of the season ourselves.

Koppett writes that baseball "is the only sport that has its competitive schedule coincide with the subliminal feelings of a new year." That's the lovely thing about baseball: even before fall starts, there are thoughts of spring. The beginnings of endings are laced with certainties of new beginnings.

Final Score: 10-9 Saginaw

Sunday, August 5, 2018

Brampton Royals
vs
Strathroy Royals

Soulliere Field, Windsor ON
Game Time Temperature: 33°C

By late afternoon on Sunday, there are five teams left in the Senior Elimination tournament: Milton Red Sox, Ilderton Red Army, Brampton Royals, Strathroy Royals, and Tecumseh Thunder. Round six will be Milton vs Ilderton at Cullen; Brampton vs Strathroy at Soulliere; and Tecumseh with the bye.

Royals vs Royals—Brampton, the home team, in powder blue jerseys with white lettering and Strathroy, the visitors, in dark blue jerseys with red lettering. I lapse into Fahrenheit when I think about how hot it is today—in the upper 90s—but there's at least a bit of a breeze to cut the heat. A few fluffy clouds float by, but for the most part it's blue sky and scorching sun.

I'm just going to own this. I am tired. I am cranky. I am hot. I don't want to be watching my forty-third game of baseball this summer right now. Since July 1, I've had just one day where I haven't had to be at work or the ballpark or both. I don't want to be here. I want to be home by myself reading a book. I want to buy milk for breakfast tomorrow. I want to unload the dishwasher and do laundry. I want to pull weeds from my garden. I want to ride my bike through Willistead Park and stop and sit on a bench and not look at the time. But I'm here. And I don't want to watch another inning of baseball. There it is. What do I do about it?

These two teams each played two games on Friday, two games on Saturday, and one game this morning. How exhausted must all of them be? How sore their muscles? This tournament is an absolute beast, a four-day marathon where you have to play six games in three days to even get to day four. Neither team can really have any rested arms left and all the players must be bone tired. It could be a very high-scoring game.

Around us sit the retinues of both teams, some at the picnic tables behind the backstop, a few in the small bleachers down either line, most in lawn chairs scattered near home plate. The players' families look almost as tired as the players, a weekend of baseball immersion beginning to take its toll on everyone. For us, it's the sixth game in four days, with another on the docket for tomorrow. Watching a tournament like this one—GLSCL playoffs aside—entails giving yourself over, letting it wash over you. I'm tired, yes, but to be honest, I could have watched today's morning and early afternoon games as well, just like I would have driven back to Adrian for the final day's games. It's good that Heidi is here to be the voice of reason.

Brampton loads the bases in the bottom of the first, bringing to bat their cleanup hitter, #8, with no one out. Unlike Cullen, there's no PA announcer at this field, so we're back to being unable to attach names to players. I've never seen #8 hit before, but when he connects, there's no doubt that the ball will fly beyond the outfield wall. Grand slam and suddenly the score is 4-0 Brampton. As #8 rounds third base, the three runners who scored ahead of him doff their helmets, stand between the plate and their dugout, and hold their helmets out to the hitter, who taps each in turn before being mobbed by the rest of his teammates. Three fly balls end the inning, but the damage is done. As the Strathroy pitcher walks off the field, he brings his glove to his face and yells, the expletive barely muffled by the leather webbing.

I sit, pen poised over my notebook, trying to watch the game. Do I have anything left to say about baseball? In five minutes I don't see a single play. My page is blank. I make one notation: "Both teams are the Royals. They both have blue uniforms."

In the top of the second, Strathroy's #20 hits a three-run home run. A gauntlet of high fives awaits him as he crosses home plate. A triple (#4) and an infield single (#14) score the tying run. As #4 crosses the plate, I hear one of the Strathroy players call, "Atta fuckin' boy, boy!" *Letterkenny* isn't much of an exaggeration.

I've got nothing, I say to myself. I sit silently for a few minutes.
"I've got nothing," I tell Dale.
"It's okay. Just enjoy the game," he says.

When Brampton come to bat in the bottom of the second, they're down 5-4. A single and a hit batter put runners on the corners with one out. #34 hits a ground ball to the shortstop, but there's no chance at the double play because Brampton have the hit-and-run on. After the run scores, the catcher calls to the bench, "Hey, boys, a little chatter. Let me know if he's going."

I try to talk myself out of my bad mood. I put all my thoughts aside. I focus on the game. I nod when Dale says, "At this point in the tournament, there's no pitching left." There's a part of me that's very interested. That part of me is silenced by the part that wants to go home, close my eyes, and listen to the wind in the maple tree outside our house.

Strathroy score a run in the third and two more in the fourth to take an 8-5 lead, but there's not a single person in the park who thinks the score will end that way. Not in the sixth game in three days.

#44 crosses the plate, picks up the bat discarded on the RBI single, yells to his teammates, "Keep grinding. Never enough. Never enough."

As the inning ends and the Brampton players jog off the field, one of them says, "We need an inning, boys."

I notice an ice cream truck. I tell myself ice cream will help me concentrate. I buy an ice cream. Eat my ice cream. Then I talk to a small dog. I take photos of the game from a different vantage point. I hear a coach yell, "One more! One more!" to his team. I take his words to heart. One more game, Heidi. One more game.

Brampton's #9 reaches first base on an error in the bottom of the fourth. With two outs, he steals second on an 0-1 pitch and third on a 3-2 pitch. How many innings has Strathroy's #13 caught this weekend? How sore must he be? Like most of the players for both teams, his uniform is filthy, pants closer now to brown than to white. He looks at #9, now standing on third base, throws the ball back to the pitcher, and crouches back down behind the plate.

I take my seat by Dale again. I put my hair in a new ponytail. I look at the field. People are cheering for something that I didn't see, even though my gaze was fixed on the field.

Not knowing what to say about this game upsets me. Dale knows I've just about hit my limit today, this weekend, this summer, this project. "It's okay," he says calmly.

This week, for the first time, I referred to going to baseball games as "data collection," which is, I suppose, technically what we're doing. I cast my mind back to my Research Methods for Librarians course, where they talked about data saturation points—the point where adding more data doesn't add more information to the research question. When adding more data adds nothing to the research question, it's time to stop collecting data. I realize what I'm feeling might just be me embodying data saturation. Unlike those hypothetical researchers I learned about, I cannot stop collecting data. We still have seven games to watch to make our fifty.

We hear from someone who was at Cullen that Ilderton beat Milton 17-0 and that the game was called after four innings. Ilderton will play Tecumseh tomorrow morning at 10 am, a game that will likely be our last of the tournament. Meanwhile, #23 fouls off four tough pitches and finally draws a walk to put men on the corners, but the rally ends with a ground ball to second. Another home run for Strathroy puts them up 10-5 by the time Brampton come to bat in the fifth.

"Turn the key, start the engine."

"Everyone hits."

And they do. A couple of singles put runners on the corner with one out. On a pickoff attempt at first base with #12 at the plate, the runner on third breaks for home. The throw from the first baseman comes in high, but the catcher is able to corral the ball and get it down ahead of the runner's foot. On the next pitch, #12 hits a two-run home run. After five innings, 10-7 Strathroy.

I cap my pen and close my notebook, loosen my ponytail and rest against the back of my lawn chair. I do something I haven't done all summer. I watch a game of baseball as if this project doesn't exist. I watch the game, let it all wash over me. It's all okay.

There are a lot more people here now, since the other game was called early—at a guess, more than a hundred scattered around the diamond. Farther back, beneath the shade of the trees, the Ilderton players stand watching, wondering which of these two teams will join them and Tecumseh in the final three. As they watch the bottom of the seventh, the score is 10-8 Strathroy.

#11 walks to the plate.

"Right man, right spot."

"Be the leader you are."

Unfortunately for Brampton, he strikes out on a curve, leaving it all up to #23. The Strathroy coach and the entire infield converge on the mound to ensure everyone knows what's going on.

It's the seventh inning. The tying runners are at first and second and the lead runner just got to third on a wild pitch. A walk loads the bases. A single could tie it. A double could win it. A strike here would end Brampton's season. A strike here, one dad says, will end his son's baseball career at this level.

There are two outs, three balls, and two strikes. So much depends upon this one pitch. As it happens, a fly ball to right brings it all to a close, but it's not really about the final score. It's that beautiful moment when you can outline all the possible and seemingly infinite outcomes of a single pitch and when you realize that there's nothing you can do to change the outcome. All you can do is sit back, watch, and marvel at all the forces at work. This game shows me what I've always loved about baseball—its insistence on the power of possibility and the need to give oneself over to the simple act of watching. A simple lesson but, tonight, a hard-earned one.

Like a couple of prizefighters at the end of a long bout, the two teams of Royals line up to shake hands.

Final Score: 10-8 Strathroy

Monday, August 6, 2018

Tecumseh Thunder
vs
Ilderton Red Army

Cullen Field, Windsor ON
Game Time Temperature: 26°C

Three teams left. Strathroy are on to the final three with the bye since they've played six games and Tecumseh and Ilderton have only played five apiece. Ilderton won against Tecumseh earlier in the weekend—1-0 in extra innings—so I expect a very good game. Jeff Davis for Ilderton, this morning's home team, against Chris Horvath for Tecumseh. If Ilderton win, Tecumseh are eliminated and Ilderton will play Strathroy in the final game, with those two teams going to Nationals. If Tecumseh win, all three teams will have one loss and there will be a draw to see who gets the bye into the final game.

The sun is behind the clouds as the coaches huddle with the home plate umpire to exchange lineup cards. Heidi leans in, asks me if I realize that this is the tenth game we've seen in eleven days. I knew it was a lot, but didn't realize it was quite so many. I've been so immersed that the days have blurred one into the other, the rest of my life becoming the backdrop to baseball instead of the other way around.

The Ilderton coach shakes hands with his counterpart from Tecumseh, claps as he walks back to the bench, says, "Come on, boys. Here we go."

If you asked me a year ago what qualities I would include as part of a perfect day of watching baseball, I would have said, sitting high up in section 325 in Comerica, watching the game spread out below me over the field, a spectacular cityscape surrounding the park. Part of the perfection, I know, was an emotional connection to the Tigers and those players. That affection kept me rapt and attentive and coming back game after game.

The things I'd list now would be vastly different. This summer I've learned to love being close to the dugouts, hearing encouragement, heckles, jokes, and the mundane details of playing inning after inning for an entire season. I like hearing cleats in the dirt and baseballs hitting gloves on a warm summer night.

Tecumseh get a runner on in the top of the second. Davis tries to keep him close, throwing over to first to try to slow down their running game, prevent the steal. The older woman next to us isn't having it and complains bitterly throughout the inning.

"Just play the game."

I know I should keep my mouth shut, but that kind of cheering has always seemed ridiculous to me, a fundamental misunderstanding of the game that grates on me in irrational ways. And a summer of cheering without a rooting interest has heightened those feelings. Before I can stop myself, I turn to her and say, "That's part of the game."

"Thank you for pointing that out." I'm not sure I can convey the level of snark she is able to achieve in that short sentence. It's only the second inning and I think I've made an enemy.

Both starters are pitching well—mostly breaking stuff for Davis and hard fastballs for Horvath—staying around the strike zone and pitching to contact. In the top of the third, Tecumseh manage a run on an error, sacrifice bunt, single, and sacrifice fly to right field. Go to the plate, do your job, hand it off to the next man in the lineup. It's a well-executed string of at-bats to get the run, the kind of small ball you don't often see in major league parks any more.

More than just good baseball, what we're seeing is *interesting* baseball. Unlike the major leagues, where so many at-bats result in either strikeouts or home runs, here the ball is in play most of the time. And, yes, there are more errors and you won't see the kinds of plays we've seen over the years in Detroit or Cleveland or Kansas City. After a summer of watching mostly non-MLB, I think what I like about these games is that they show baseball's seams, its imperfections. I love the continual shifting of possibility, the calculations that change with every pitch. The sense that anything can happen.

The woman I spoke to earlier has had her umbrella up to shade her from the sun for most of the game, even when there's been cloud cover, as there is now. Her family members behind her say they can't see and she doesn't seem to care. They aren't very happy, but after a couple of attempts to say something are abruptly cut off. No one says a word. I, too, keep my mouth shut.

Today was only the second time in nearly thirty years I've seen Dale lose his patience with a fellow spectator at a baseball game. The first was when a woman behind us at a Tigers game kept yelling, "Run! Run!" at Gene Lamont. Finally, around the seventh inning, she said with exasperation, "Why is he not running when he's at third base!?" Dale calmly said, "Because he's the third base coach and he's not supposed to run." "Oh!" she chirped, grateful for the explanation, "Thanks!" Tonight, his feedback was not so well received by She Who Would Not Put Her Umbrella Down Despite Numerous Requests From Her Family And Everyone Else In The Section. I fear he, and by extension me, has made an enemy. She continues to glower at us.

I'm not sure why, but I've been charting Horvath's pitches all game. Maybe it's because I was asked again yesterday if we're scouting. Maybe it's to see if I could do it. Maybe it's just because he's mixing his pitches so well, keeping the Ilderton batters off balance. Since he's only thrown fifty-four pitches through five innings, it hasn't been difficult.

Horvath's sixth inning. Fastball called. Fastball just low. Ground ball to first base for the out. Pop-up to the shortstop for the second out. Foul. Ground ball to the shortstop, who slides to his knees, gets up, spins, and fires a bullet to first base for the third out. Six-pitch inning; sixty pitches in total over six innings.

The most vocal person in the crowd is a boy, about eight or nine, who's hollering at the teams: "C'mon! Let's get some wood on that." I like both teams. I like that they're both showing up, being strong competitors, but not being jerks about it. The Red Army coach is toss-. ing out supportive clichés and he seems to be having the time of his life. Both teams, who have their original pitchers, are pretty equally matched, and this is — I am realizing — a true treat to watch. The cheering boy yells, "Good eye, kid. Good eye!" to a player more than twice his age.

Bottom of the seventh and Ilderton are down to their final three outs. Single. Fouled bunt attempt. Fastball called for a strike as the batter pulls the bat back. Fastball foul. Fastball low and outside. Runner steals second. Ground ball to the second baseman. Runner to third base. Foul straight back. Fastball just low. Sacrifice fly to center field to tie the game. A perfectly executed sequence of at-bats to score the run, including the ball hit to the right side of the infield to move the runner to third. Small ball for the tie.

It's the top of the eighth and it's 1-1. The hits are 4-3 for Tecumseh, and only one error for both teams. Dale just said, "This game might be the best played game of the year."

There's an intentional walk and I ask Dale, "Is that so they can set up a double play?"

"Exactly," he says.

We go to extra innings. Tecumseh put men at second and third with one out in the top of the eighth, but can't score when the runner takes off from third on contact and a perfect throw comes in to the catcher at home. Ilderton put a man on in their half of the inning, but he's doubled off on a liner to second. One of these teams might not make it to Nationals, but these are, all around, two of the best amateur teams we've seen this year.

Neither team scores in the ninth. Horvath is at ninety-three pitches.

Last night I heard a catcher say, "Can you let me know if someone's going to steal?" Today, that doesn't need to be said. As the Thunder pitcher stares down the batter, his dugout yells, "Runner!" and then a ball hurtles toward first and the Red Army dugout yells "Back!" And this carries on for a few minutes. Unfortunately, the runner's lead is so long that he can't make it back in time and is out. Clouds are starting to roll in.

Brandon Gignac opens the Tecumseh tenth with a triple. Matt Sykes then hits a liner to center that just eludes the outstretched glove of the center fielder to score the go-ahead run. There is, appropriately, thunder in the distance as Eric Cunningham settles in to the batter's box. The Tecumseh fans cheer while the umpires signal that, though the rain isn't yet heavy, the game is being suspended. There are reports of lightning in the area.

Just as I think, "No matter who wins, it's going to be a heartbreaker," clouds roll in quickly and emphatically. There are no outs and there's a Tecumseh player on first when they call a rain delay. The crowds disperse under the sudden deluge. Dale and I drive to McDonald's and the wipers can't keep up. We order coffees and muffins and wait for the rain to stop.

After a forty-minute rain delay, we're back at Cullen and it's like a steam bath, not a cloud in the sky, the sun beating down on the humid air. The tarp comes off, Quick Dry is applied to the mound and the areas around the bases, and we're ready to play ball. Ilderton again take the field with a man on first, no outs, and Cunningham up with an 0-2 count.

We change to the third base side of the ballpark and, happily, Dale's nemesis is still on the first base side. The runner is back on base for Tecumseh, and, to our surprise, the Ilderton starter is back out. On the other hand, we're not surprised to see the woman's umbrella still blocking the view of those behind her.

"Finish this!" yells the cheering boy.

"Don't hit the ball! Don't hit the ball!" chants the cheering boy's brother.

A run is scored on a throwing error and the announcer interrupts this high-tension moment to say, "For those of you who have been waiting for a sausage or a hot dog, the buns have just arrived." No one budges: hot dogs can wait. 3-1 Tecumseh going into the bottom of the tenth.

Horvath needs only eleven pitches to get the final three outs, finishing the game at 104 pitches. It's one of the best pitching performances we've seen all summer.

The three teams left have all played six games and have one loss. In order to determine who has the bye into the final, a team name will be drawn from a hat. When the bye is announced, a huge cheer erupts from the Ilderton bench. They will play in the championship game, but, more importantly, they know that they are going to Nationals.

Final Score: 3-1 Tecumseh

Sixteen
EAT
SLEEP
BASEBALL
REPEAT

August 14, 2018

Lansing Lugnuts
vs
Bowling Green Hot Rods

Tuesday, August 14, 2018

Lansing Lugnuts
vs
Bowling Green Hot Rods

Cooley Law School Stadium, Lansing MI
Game Time Temperature: 75°F

It's been just over a week since our last game, but it feels much longer, this disruption in the rhythm of our summer. We needed the break after the stretch of games we had at the beginning of the month, some time at home without baseball, without thinking about the logistics of games. Being at the ballpark has become so ingrained in my routine that, after a few days, I found myself anxious to be back on the road.

I tried watching some baseball on television, but it didn't hold my attention in the same way it did a few months ago, didn't offer the same immediacy as being back in our seats in a little park some-where in Ontario or Michigan or Ohio. As I sat in all those ballparks this summer—from Adrian to Windsor to Sarnia to Avon—the world dropped away and there was just Heidi and me and baseball. Nothing else mattered for those few hours.

Now we're on the road heading to Lansing, Michigan for our for-ty-fifth game this season and, for a few hours tonight, I'll be back in that familiar place. I'm happy to be here, with Heidi in the passenger seat, talk of baseball and writing filling the car. But it's bittersweet,

as I know we only have one of these trips left, to this weekend's U21
Canadian Championships in St. Thomas. Our summer of baseball is
almost at an end.

Crossing into Detroit at the tunnel, the border guard asks, "Why are
you going to Lansing when we've got the Tigers right here?" Thankfully
it was a rhetorical question or we'd still be there, trying to explain the
complexity of his query.

It was a long day followed by a long drive. I dashed home from
work, leaving again within five minutes. We got to Lansing, nearly at
the northwestern edge of our hundred miles, at 6:30 and grabbed the
very last parking spot in the lot. "Your lucky day," said the attendant.

As we stand in line for our tickets, I say, "Doesn't it seem like forever since we went to a baseball game?" Dale nods. It's been eight
days, our longest stretch without baseball since early June.

Tonight we're back to minor league baseball, at Cooley Law
School Stadium for a Midwest League game between the Lansing
Lugnuts and the Bowling Green Hot Rods, Class A affiliates of the
Blue Jays and Rays, respectively. Despite the Jays affiliation, I see lots
of Tigers hats in the crowd tonight.

The park is basically the same as the last time I was here several years ago, though now there are new "Outfield Lofts" ringing
most of the outfield: apartments with bright green, blue, and yellow façades with balconies that face the field. Last year there was a
lot of excitement in Lansing because of Vladimir Guerrero Jr and
Bo Bichette, but there aren't any prospects this year with the same
pedigree or expectations. Maybe that's what accounts for the sparse
crowd tonight.

Dale is walking around the park and I am quietly watching the
Lugnuts pitcher warm up. I'm eating some cheese pizza and a vendor
is making a second round with $2 hot dogs. There's an elderly lady
behind us with a cowbell she's not afraid to use. A cool wind picks
up my hair. I'm pleased to see another female ump—only the second
in this project. Tonight will be the last night where we dash out of the

house and drive nearly a hundred miles to go see baseball. I should feel excited, or relieved, but I'm just feeling sad. Dale comes back from his wanderings. He bought me some Lugnuts pencils.

Like most parks of this size, there are lots of distractions and forms of entertainment. The Lugnuts mascot, Big Lug, dances along to their theme song.

> You got inhibitions? Lose 'em! You got vocal chords? Use 'em! You got the rhythm, you got the beat. You gotta clap your hands, you gotta stomp your feet. You gotta . . . go nuts, go nuts, go nuts, go nuts. Lugnuts. lugnuts, lugnuts, lugnuts. Go Nuts! Lugnuts! This is our town. This is our team. If you're up against us, you're gonna get creamed. Just stick around. See what we mean. Get ready to yell. Get ready to scream. Ready to scream. Ready to scream. Ready to scream. See what we mean. Go nuts, go nuts, go nuts, go nuts. Lugnuts, lugnuts, lugnuts, lugnuts. Go Nuts! Lugnuts!

It sounds like something right out of a Christopher Guest mockumentary.

The game starts with the "Play Ball Kid," Allison, who seems to be about two or three years old. She stares out at us from the giant scoreboard and says, "Pay baaaaaah!" Next there's a video sequence featuring Lugnuts players trying to pronounce Michigan place and street names: Gratiot, Menominee, Charlevoix.

They've swapped out Bowling Green player photos on the big screen with joke photos: Zach Rutherford has been replaced by Rutherford B Hayes, Ronaldo Hernandez becomes Cristiano Ronaldo, Trey Hair is Cousin It.

By the end of the fourth inning, we've seen some great defense, especially by the Lugnuts, including an absolute gem in the top of the second on a ball hit to short. Vinny Capra dove to his right to just snag the ball, popped to his feet, and threw a bullet to first base to get the runner by a half-step. Then in the top of the fourth, Chavez Young made a tough running catch under the 407 sign in right center on a ball that might have gone for a triple if he hadn't caught it.

They may not be prospects like Guerrero or Bichette, but plays like these remind me how skilled minor league players are.

I look up from my notes and notice that there's a guy wearing a hot dog hat riding in a golf cart and shooting something out of an air cannon. T-shirts? Soft baseballs for kids? No, he's firing hot dogs into the crowd from what the video board tells me is the Hot Dog Cannon. He fires again, but the dog doesn't make it over the mesh behind home plate. The crowd boos.

Heidi returns from getting us $1 cans of beer, one of the Lugnuts regular mid-week promotions. She sits down, hands me a beer, and says, "Thank the goddess I missed that."

"What?"

"Hot dogs being shot at me out of an air cannon."

This is fast, precise, well-played baseball and it doesn't take me long to settle into its rhythms. The game is a hybrid of others we've seen: small park with a few non-intrusive entertainment interludes but, at the core, great baseball. I notice things like the barely perceptible signals between players—far subtler than the shouting of "BACK!" and "RUNNER!" that we saw in the dugouts last week. In the bottom of the fifth, there are still no errors. I now notice the absence of errors because I've seen a lot of them.

I am finding that good baseball—like good writing—holds my attention, and that helps me see and remember things. "That was low," I say of a strike. Later, Dale asks me where the error came from and I remember. Things about work that had been occupying my thoughts have faded away. I'm here. I'm watching. I'm seeing. I'm understanding. I note how the Hot Rods' pitcher's delivery throws him off balance, making him unable to field the ball. Noticing these small things seems big to me.

Top of the seventh and the Lugnuts are up 7-3. Moises Gomez leads off with a home run to make it 7-4. When Jim Haley is hit by a pitch, it looks like Bowling Green have something brewing. But Young makes another long running catch, this time to deep right field near the foul line. On a ground ball back to the mound, Rodning slips, loses his glove, but still manages to make the play. A single puts runners on the corners with two out. It looks like the runner will score from third on Trey Hair's soft ground ball, but the second baseman, Samad Taylor, sprints toward first, scoops the ball, and flips it from his glove in one motion without transferring it to his throwing hand. More great defense from the Lugnuts.

I'm not sure if it's the quality of baseball tonight or if a season of trying to figure out how to watch baseball is finally paying off. Or, perhaps, I'm finally lifting the pressure I've been putting on myself all summer to take my knowledge and understanding of the game to new levels. Tonight, baseball is meditative—I am simply here, watching and enjoying the things in baseball that bring me joy.

I am, just tonight, beginning to realize I will never fully watch baseball like Dale, for the simple fact that I am not Dale. I am me. I am the one who didn't notice there were two outs and the tying and go-ahead runs on base at the Tigers game. Instead, I saw a bug bite Curtis Granderson. This is the way I watch baseball. I need to embrace that.

Emerson Jimenez comes in to pitch the eighth. Between innings, we watch contestants trying to catch frisbees in pizza boxes, which is nearly as entertaining as the boxing with giant gloves that happened after the third inning. Maybe it's the great baseball on the field, but tonight the wacky promotions don't bother me, they even add to this very typical minor league experience.

I'm pretty certain Dale has no idea that I've been trying to watch baseball like him all summer. Were I to tell him, I'm certain he'd say "You need to watch baseball like you watch baseball. You see things I don't see." And then I'd probably say, "Like the maize pants?" And he'd say, "Yes, exactly. The maize pants." And I'd say, "I still don't know how you didn't see those maize pants." "I was watching pitching." And then we'd both shrug and shake our heads.

This summer has also confirmed that, for our nearly thirty years together, this is what we've always done. We've looked at the same things but seen them differently. And when we talk about what we both saw, we learn new ways of looking and seeing. I imagine that next summer, when I watch baseball again, I'll go back to watching baseball like Heidi—and that it will be richer for my having stepped out of my Heidi-zone for a summer and for trying to see more like Dale. Maybe next year I'll see more curveballs, and he'll see more maize pants.

Jimenez finishes off the 7-4 Lugnuts win. As the Lugnuts players congratulate each other and walk off the field, we start to pack up and prepare for the long drive back to Windsor. I take one last look across the diamond, at the soft glow that illuminates the players on the field. In many ways, there's nothing that makes this ballpark unique—no Monster or Ivy, no statues to the greats who played here. It's just a park where they play baseball, four bases marked out in the shape of a diamond, fields of green extending out to a wall that marks the terminus to the park. A place where it was just Heidi and me and baseball on a perfect summer night.

For most of the summer, baseball has been our life and I've never been happier. But now the summer is coming to an end, fading like every other season of baseball, and I'm not ready. Baseball is breaking my heart.

As the crowd shuffles toward the exits after the last out, a kid behind me, about fifteen years old, tells his mother, "This is the best game I have ever been to in my life!" It fully hits me that this is the last late-night drive we'll take home this season. I'm sure there will be others in our future, but none quite like this one. No summer will be quite like this one.

As we leave, I take Dale's hand and point to a Lugnuts t-shirt in the closed gift shop window: "Eat Sleep Baseball Repeat." "No need to get the t-shirt," I say, "we've lived it." We find our car easily in the nearly empty lot and head home.

Final Score: 7-4 Lansing

Seventeen

FINAL INNINGS

August 17 – 19, 2018

U21 Canadian Baseball Championship

Manitoba
vs
Oshawa

Windsor
vs
Nova Scotia

Québec
vs
St. Thomas

Mississauga North
vs
New Brunswick

Windsor
vs
Mississauga North

Friday, August 17, 2018

Driving down the 401, the fields of southwest Ontario a blur outside the passenger window, I'm mesmerized by the slow turning of the wind turbines that have risen throughout this part of the country. I'm happy to be riding today, lost in my own thoughts about this last trip of the season. Another tournament, another few days of living in a whirl of baseball, no different from so much of our summer. But it feels different knowing that, when we drive home on Monday morning, the project will be over.

We leave the traffic of the 401 behind at Chatham in favour of the more sedate Highway 2 to London. Neither of us says much as we pass cornfields and little country churches, roll through rural Ontario towns. It's more quiet than usual in the car today, as if neither of us quite knows what to say. Or what to feel. We're both tired and it's time for us to be finished, but I know we'll never have another summer like this one. The endless talks about baseball and writing as we drive through rural Ontario and Michigan. The sense that Heidi and I—just us—are doing something strange and glorious. The chance to fall back in love with baseball together.

All summer I've been thinking of this project as a gift, but I've struggled to articulate or come to terms with how much this summer has meant to me. It took this full immersion to make me realize how much it bothered me that baseball seemed to be slipping away from me these past few years, how much it felt like my connection to Dad was unravelling as baseball receded. I know how that sounds. I do. But the cliché holds and I can't let it go. I've felt closer to my father this summer than I have since he died ten years ago. I feel him next to me every time I take my seat behind home plate, every time I say "Nice play" under my breath, every time there's something about the game I want to tell him. Not because of a certain team we share. Because of baseball.

Friday, August 17, 2018

Manitoba
vs
Oshawa

Emslie Field, St. Thomas
Game Time Temperature: 26°C

We pull into the parking lot at Emslie Field, well ahead of the 2:30 start time listed for the Manitoba-Oshawa game. However, as we approach the ticket table, it's clear that Manitoba are already batting in the top of the first. If the previous game ends early, the law of tournament time preservation means that the next game starts early. As we take our seats, Manitoba score the first run of the game.

The air is heavy and my allergies are in full force. As I'm settling in to watch the first game of our final five, I notice a few people staring at me. One of the men comes over, points at my notebook, and asks if I'm a scout. I say, "No, sorry." Disappointed, he goes back to his friends. Maybe they thought my cornflower-blue sundress and matching shoes with polka-dot bows were some sort of scouting subterfuge.

There are about two hundred people here; most seem to be locals, checking out the game without major rooting interests. There are a few parents from Oshawa, but not many. They cheer on the players by first name.

The game is moving along quickly. In less than forty-five minutes, we're into the fourth inning. Dale and I talk about the mechanics of Manitoba's pitcher. The pitching is fast and well-executed. Mostly this is a three-up, three-down baseball game, with a few men left on base.

We notice that at the end of every inning the Oshawa team comes out of the dugout to high five their teammates. Manitoba don't do that.

A ball goes over the fence on the third base side. Two little kids in the stands, one quite a bit smaller than the other, take off after it. The littlest kid outruns his bigger friend by a lot and holds the ball up victoriously. He sees the sadness on the bigger boy's face and gives him the baseball to assuage his disappointment. They both run back to their families.

I smile, and Dale sees me.

"Are you smiling at that breaking ball?"

"Something like that," I say, shifting my gaze and my mind back to pitching.

A few hours ago, I got news that my mum is in the hospital. She called and said, "Don't come out. Finish your baseball project. I'm okay. Don't worry." I don't believe her. From my bleacher seat I book a plane ticket to Edmonton for next week.

I soon grow distracted by a little girl who has just learned to climb stairs on her own. She's been practicing the entire inning. She's rewarded at the bottom of the stairs by a hug and a snuggle from her mom, and by a hug and a snuggle from her grandmother a few rows up. She has a determined look on her chipmunk-cheeked face and I notice her shirt has little yellow buttons. My mum would have noticed those little buttons too and would have beamed at the little girl, her mother, and grandmother. As I make a note to tell my mum about the buttons, a roar from the crowd brings my attention back to the game. I'm grateful for my allergies, as I think they might disguise my tears.

By the time Oshawa come to bat in the bottom of the sixth, with the score still 1-0 Manitoba, it's just past 3:30, the game clipping along faster than any we've seen all summer. Both pitchers are always around the strike zone and there's little wasted time between pitches. Catch, set, fire. Repeat. No time for the defenses to lose concentration.

But then the left fielder drops a fly ball to open the Oshawa sixth, the batter ending up on second base by the time the ball is thrown in from the outfield. Next to me, an Oshawa fan calls to the hitter, "Nobody better, bud!" just before he hits a sharp ground ball to the second baseman. When he can't handle it, the tying run scores and the hitter is safe at first base. The defensive concentration seems to have disappeared.

Oshawa singles and has the tying run on second. "A single scores a run," I think to myself. And, seconds later, a single scores a run. I focus on the pitching, the fielding, the hitting, the running. We have four more games this summer. I notice that players either don't call the ball or they don't listen; collisions in the field are narrowly avoided.

The score is suddenly 4-1 Oshawa, their first lead of the game. Manitoba can't recover, going in order in the top of the seventh, doomed in the end by two ill-timed errors. It's just past 4 pm when the two starting pitchers are announced as the game's most valuable players.

Final Score: 4-1 Oshawa

Saturday, August 17, 2018

Last night Dale and I ate at the hotel restaurant and sat at the bar. The Blue Jays/Yankees game was on TVs throughout the restaurant without sound. It was too loud in the bar to talk, so we watched the ballgame attentively.

Sitting there, I realized this is where I began watching baseball in earnest in the 1990s, with Dale and the Blue Jays on TV. In lovely circularity, Curtis Granderson, "my gateway player," is batting for Toronto and I'm watching him among the din of diners at this off-the-highway hotel restaurant. While I have definite thoughts about the Blue Jays and the Yankees, I'm not really watching a game, per se, I'm watching eighteen men show me how it can be done. I'm not caring about the score, but I'm watching the graphics showing the strike zone, the speed, movement, and location of the pitches, and the trajectory of hit balls. Tonight, I realize I understand more about baseball than I ever have and, more to the point, I find myself caring about the smaller things, rather than the score.

But I also perk up at the sight of Granderson, knowing this might be his last season. And if it's not his last season, it's close. This project has shown me that MLB is just part of a much larger baseball universe and that there are other parts of that universe just as fun to watch. Still, I have an emotional attachment to the Tigers that I find myself unwilling to surrender.

As this project and this summer come to an end, I find myself wondering what next year will be like for me as a baseball fan. This question, it occurs to me, is different from the one I asked at the beginning of the project: what will next year be like for me as a Tigers fan?

Saturday, August 18, 2018

Windsor
vs
Nova Scotia

Cardinal Field, St. Thomas ON
Game Time Temperature: 21°C

It rained overnight and the ground is sloshy below our feet. One of the Windsor coaches just emptied out a bucket full of baseballs and rainwater onto the concrete, hoping to dry them out. Someone asks Bernie Soulliere the time. He says, "Ten to nine, but make it nine." It's going to be a hot day and everyone is impatient to get the game underway.

The sky is overcast and the breeze a bit cool, but all in all it's a pleasant morning to drink coffee and watch baseball. We've found seats in the bleachers behind home plate, looking directly down the third base line. All around us are faces now familiar to me from high school and midget games in Windsor. The parents are out in full force.

Nova Scotia take the field to open the game. In their home whites and blue caps with the Olde English D, they look, from a distance, like younger versions of the Tigers. It's not until I realize that Nova Scotia are being represented by Dartmouth that the logo begins to make sense.

As the first batter for the Selects walks to the plate, I hear someone yell, "We're up early, we're up often!"

The moms behind me seem surprised that the Selects are up and talking on the bench, surprised that there's clapping and chatter. It's hard not to listen as they talk and I quickly gather that there was a players' meeting last night after they lost both games yesterday. There are only eight teams in the tournament, including the three Ontario teams this year because of the inclusion of the host team, and the format is not double elimination. I get the feeling the parents see this game as a must-win, even though I'm not sure if they're out of the tournament even if they lose. Some are staring down not only the end of the season, but, for those not going on to college, perhaps the end of their baseball careers as well.

I'm having trouble thinking about the baseball on the field, because I'm thinking about the Tigers. About Curtis. About next season. But mostly about my mum. Dale, as always, is fully focused. He just said to me, "He's trying to make him chase the slider, isn't he?" I nod, grateful that he thinks my mind is on the field when it's actually floating like the pink mylar balloon I see bobbing over the treetops in the distance.

In the top of the second the Selects leadoff hitter gets on base with a walk, steals second, and gets to third on a bad throw from the catcher on the steal. He comes in to score on a ground ball to the shortstop. The Windsor crowd around us hoots and hollers, doing everything they can to push their boys on to the win. Even though we're from Windsor, this kind of partisanship now makes me uncomfortable. I'm torn between a desire to sit apart from them and a desire to keep this vantage point. Since there aren't a lot of seats in the park, vantage point wins out.

"Thunderstruck" fades from the PA as the Selects come to bat in the top of the fourth, AC/DC a staple of our summer soundtrack in almost every ballpark. On the field, an error and a single put two men on with one out. Behind me, a woman sings "Louie, Louie," the batter's name in song echoing among the Windsor contingent. A walk loads the bases, but a nicely executed double play—pitcher to catcher to first base—ends the inning. The two women behind us start singing "The Gambler."

I don't think I could watch another five or ten games, but I have to admit I'm a little sad to be starting game forty-seven right now. While Dale and I do spend a lot of time together, this has been incredibly special. I know this project has meant things to Dale that he hasn't fully articulated to me. I know it's offered him joy, solace, and connections to people he misses. Driving home from Lansing last week he said, "Thank you for doing this project with me." It was dark and I might have seen a tear. I gulped down a tear myself. True to his stoic Norwegian ways, Dale doesn't always say a lot, but when he does, the words are weighty.

The sixth inning ends with a pop foul dropping into the glove of the Selects third baseman. One of the women behind us calls to the pitcher, "Good job, Seth. Having a day." One more inning to go and the Selects are up 1-0.

As Dartmouth take the field for the top of the seventh, "Don't Stop Believin'" starts to play over an iPhone. The two women behind us sing about South Detroit. One of the men asks, "Rally music?" They nod in unison, continue to sing along with Steve Perry. Later in the inning, when a Windsor triple scores a run, one of the women says, "It was our singing." The two start again with the chorus.

"We're good. We could take this on the road."

"Mobile inspiration."

One of the other fans yells, "Pick the one you want, Pook!" Pook's mother stands by the fence, filming his at-bat, just as she has every other time we've seen him this summer. Someone else says, "Sit on one, Pook." Pook connects, but it's a fly ball to the right fielder. The runner holds at third.

The Dartmouth coach walks to the mound for a pitching change and Journey is back on the iPhone, the two women harmonizing the entire song. At least they both have good voices. The Dartmouth pitcher finishes warming up just as "Don't Stop Believin'" starts to play over the PA. The Windsor crowd cheers.

What Dale and I have done this summer is what we've always done: we explore, we observe, we think about stuff, we compare ideas, and we learn from each other. But this summer has also been different. It's not really just the two of us. Dale's brought some good friends and his dad along on this journey, and I've brought my grandfather, my dad, and my mum. Even if we don't see them in the ballpark, we know they're there with us.

Snap throw from the catcher to third base on a 1-1 pitch. From the woman behind me I hear, "Get dirty, Gibby!"

"He doesn't like getting dirty."

"Too bad. If you don't like getting dirty, you don't like baseball."

A walk and a hit batter load the bases with one out. Hunter Dent, the Windsor catcher, hits a ground ball back to the pitcher, who throws home for the second out of the inning. But when the first baseman drops the ball as they attempt to turn the double play, a run scores and Dent takes off towards second. He gets caught in a rundown, but gets tagged sliding back into first base before the runner—who hesitated rounding third base—can score. Nicely played by Dartmouth, perhaps aided by a bit of a baserunning error by the Selects. 3-0 Windsor going into the last of the seventh.

Three singles put Dartmouth on the board with runners on first and second and only one out. One of the singing women says, "I'm going to have a heart attack."

The other replies, "It's what you live for."

A double scores the second Dartmouth run, puts men on second and third. Still one out.

The Windsor coach signals for a pitching change.

The men sitting behind us run through the possibilities of how the tying run could score.

"Suicide squeeze?"

"Fly ball scores a run. Ground ball to the right side."

Foul pop to the catcher for the second out.

Fastball high. Fastball for a called strike at the bottom of the zone. Foul straight back. Fastball inside.

The batter calls time, steps out of the box, adjusts his gloves, looks to the coach at third base.

Wild pitch scores the run and puts the game-winning run at third. If that possibility had crossed the mind of either of the men, they didn't voice it.

Ball low. The walk puts runners on the corners.

No one in our section speaks or even breathes, their hands collectively raised to their mouths in anticipation of what's to come, of how the endless possibilities will sort themselves out.

They don't have to wait long, the next pitch in the dirt skittering past the helpless catcher. Nova Scotia win 4-3 on two wild pitches.

There's no singing as the Windsor delegation pack their things and Pook and the Dartmouth starting pitcher are announced as the game MVPs. I haven't heard anything official, but the parents seem to think they can't advance now. If true, it's a tough way for the season to end. I feel for the relief pitcher.

Final Score: 4-3 Nova Scotia

Saturday, August 18, 2018

Québec
vs
St. Thomas

Emslie Field, St. Thomas ON
Game Time Temperature: 24°C

We're just getting out of our car back at Emslie Field when a couple pull up next to us. The woman driving rolls down her window, asks, "Do you know where the pickle ball fields are?" We smile politely, tell them sorry, but we don't know.

It's a beautiful sunny afternoon and Québec, rather than St. Thomas, are the home team. The broadcast crew from Rogers are a few rows ahead of us; two camera operators are stationed on either side of home plate. I overhear one of them say that there is a sixty-pitch limit for this tournament—this weekend we'll see nothing like we saw from Tommy Parsons or Chris Horvath.

Before the game started, I spent a few minutes looking at the index of the teams we've watched all summer: Canadian, American, pro, semi-pro, historic, college, high school, men's league. Watching the crowd come in with tambourines and vuvuzelas, I realize this is the first French-speaking team we've seen play, and they immediately raise the energy level in the stadium. Even the St. Thomas bat boy gets in the act, dancing the floss in front of the home dugout as the players cheer him on. The announcer speaks in both French and English. *"Maintenant. Numéro. Huit."*

In the section to our left sit a big group of Québec fans. It's the first time I've heard more than a smattering of French at the ballpark. The introduction of the Québec players as each comes to *le rectangle des frappeurs*, the chatter from *l'abri des jouers*, the hopeful murmurings from fans as the ball is hit to *la piste d'avertissement*, the cheer that swells above the noise of the tambourines and vuvuzelas on *le coupe de circuit* that gives them a 4-0 lead in the bottom of the third. As the French baseball lexicon floods over me, I'm ten years old again, watching the Expos with Dad, the game beamed to us on the CBC from the old Jarry Park in Montreal.

While the game on the field is pretty much the same, the atmosphere in the stands is like nothing else we've experienced. These are the most sonically-organized fans we've seen all summer: they don't just cheer, they perform. They're loud, they're musical, they're organized. "Let's go kay-bec!" they chant en masse, using their instruments for the normally clapped response. If there were championships for energetic supporters, these Québecois baseball fans would have a bye to the finals, no questions asked. They make the Anglo fans look pretty tame and uninteresting. Not just today but, truth be told, in all the other games we've seen this summer. It's good to be reminded of the multiple ways one can be a fan of the game.

The Selects walk into the park, quietly slide into seats a couple of sections to our right. They've already lost to both of these teams and, at the moment, don't know where they stand in the tournament. I don't see any of the Windsor parents.

"Sweet Caroline" plays over the PA between the top and the bottom of the fifth inning. The Québec fans break off their "Let's go, Québec" cheer long enough to sing along. Unfortunately, they stick with the English words. Maybe it would sound better in French.

#20 hits *le deuxième coupe de circuit* to dead center, over the 385 sign, in the bottom of the fifth to increase Québec's lead to 5-0. Tambourines and vuvuzelas make a lot of noise.

And indeed, *ces supporteurs québécois de baseball* have a lot to cheer about. In the top of the sixth, it's 5-0. One player has two home runs. The hits are 4-6 and one error. I say to Dale, "This is one of those games that could turn on a dime" and, as if saying the magic words, St. Thomas get a grand slam and it's 5-4 and finally *les anglophones* have something to cheer about. The Québec fans also cheer for the man selling 50-50 tickets when he says, "*Dernier appel pour le moitié-moitié.*" In spite of his valiant linguistic efforts, I note, he sells no tickets.

Down only a run now, #12, the St. Thomas starter, comes back out to the mound for the bottom of the sixth, trying to keep the game close enough for his teammates to at least tie. There's no way he's thrown fewer than sixty pitches.

By the time St. Thomas do finally come to bat in the seventh, they find themselves down 8-4. The Québec starter, #17, opens the inning, despite being over sixty pitches. But when he gives up a two-out single, he's pulled from the game. The Québec fans give him a standing ovation, his only mistake that hanging curve in the sixth.

I make a note to tell John about the thing I've never seen before: the ball passively falling out of the pitcher's hand as he stares down the batter. It simply plops to the ground the split second before he starts his windup. It's a balk.

St. Thomas score a couple of two-out runs and have runners on first and second with #9, the young man who hit the grand slam, up to bat. His double scores the third run of the inning, but the third base coach stops the trailing runner at third, unwilling, it seems, to test the outfielder's arm.

The Québec coach, catcher, and entire infield converge at the mound.

"Let's go, Tomcats!"

I realize in the final inning that absolutely anything could happen. A St. Thomas pop fly could mean a Québec win. A home run means St. Thomas go ahead. It's been two outs for what seems like an excruciating amount of time. Once the pitcher's throwing arm goes up, there is total silence as this definitive pitch soars over home plate and the ump yells, "Strrrrike." Three outs. Game over. Québec move on.

The batter yells at the ump, slams his helmet into the ground, but it's over. As the MVPs are announced—#9 for St. Thomas and #20 for Québec—I wonder how the game might have played out differently if the St. Thomas coach had been willing to send the runner.

Final Score: 8-7 Québec

Sunday, August 19, 2018

Mississauga North
vs
New Brunswick

Emslie Field, St. Thomas ON
Game Time Temperature: 23°C

It's the time of year when I begin to think of Gerard Manley Hopkins' poem "Spring and Fall." I used to read the poem to myself every year; now I take the short cut and just mentally summon the first line: "Margaret, are you grieving / Over Goldengrove unleaving?" No other poem quite captures that grief of realizing another year has gone by. Today's game seems very much like "Goldengrove unleaving." We got here fairly early, 11:30 for a 12:30 game. One of the players was hitting balls to the seven- and eight-year-old batboys.

Above us are scattered clouds, some dark with possible rain. On the field, ready for the game to begin, are Mississauga North, the home team. Since it's the tournament semi-final, there are umpires at every base. A dull murmur echoes around the park, like an engine revving in anticipation, punctuated by cheers from the Mississauga North fans when the second baseman lets a soft liner drop so he can turn the 4-6-3 double play.

Two singles and a couple of walks bring in a run and load the bases for Mississauga in the bottom of the first. As the woman behind me yells at the home plate umpire to be consistent, a sacrifice fly scores the second run of the inning. Another walk—his third in less than an inning—ends the day for the New Brunswick starter.

There are probably about a hundred people here. They're quiet, but very into the game. The score is 2-0 for Mississauga and the New Brunswick pitcher is clearly struggling. While they're changing pitchers, AC/DC is played over the field. A father is teaching his little girl how to dance appropriately for each player's walk-up music. Right now, he's got her headbanging.

Dale says, "Perfect curveball to the outside corner." It's 5-0 in the second. This could be a long game—or, it could feel that way. A home run just scored three more runs, making it 8-0 in the second inning.

At this point, it feels like a waiting game, a matter of time before the ten-run mercy rule kicks in. #23, the starter for Mississauga North, is cruising, getting strikeouts and off-balance swings on a mix of fastballs and changeups. New Brunswick have had a runner in almost every inning, but the Mississauga pitcher is so dialed-in that it never feels like there's any real chance of them scoring a run. Plus, the defense behind him has been sparkling—not only the heads-up double play in the first, but the pretty first-to-short-to-first double play in the fourth. I saw them practicing it before the game, the kind of play that players in a lot of the games we've seen this year, especially at this age, wouldn't even try to turn. In a lop-sided game like this one, it's those individual performances, the beauty in those singular plays, that hold my attention.

A parent in a New Brunswick shirt shouts, "Let's start something here, kid!" With an 8-0 score, this isn't what Dale would consider a "well-played game." I sit back and watch it happen. Data saturation has occurred and I feel free to just soak in the second-last game of this adventure. There's a flubbed double play and Dale says, just as I'm thinking about this, "You can't score that an error because you can never assume the double play."

One of the New Brunswick supporters comes over to us in the bottom of the fifth, asks if we're from Nova Scotia. I'm momentarily confused, then remember that I'm wearing a Tatamagouche Brewing t-shirt. I tell him no, explain that we're from Windsor, Ontario, at the end of the 401. It's his turn to look confused, as Windsor are currently playing against Québec in the other semi-final.[1] I tell him we're just here to watch baseball and that we haven't seen these two teams play yet this weekend. He nods, though it still doesn't seem to make sense to him.

I say, "Too bad the game got out of hand so quickly."

"We weren't expecting to be playing for a medal, so we're just happy we'll at least be playing for bronze."

As the fifth inning ends and the man returns to his seat, the public-address announcer informs us that the score is 2-0 Windsor over Québec in the top of the sixth at Cardinal Field.

A three-run home run in the bottom of the inning makes it 11-0 and brings the mercy rule into effect. The teams shake hands and the announcer informs us that Windsor are now leading Québec 3-0 in the top of the seventh. I don't hear the announcement of the game MVPs, but I would bet the Mississauga North starter was one of them. I have no idea who it might have been for New Brunswick.

Final Score: 11-0 Mississauga North

Sunday, August 19, 2018

Windsor
vs
Mississauga North

Emslie Field, St. Thomas ON
Game Time Temperature: 22°C

Here we are. Game fifty. The last game. Heidi and I spend a lot of time together, but the time this summer, snatched away from the rest of our lives, has felt extra special. The conversations about the project, about baseball, about fandom, about what we notice and what we don't. I think we'll both be glad to be done, to have more than baseball in our lives. But I'm going to miss it. I already feel like I'm mourning the passing of this summer of baseball.

As the pre-game action starts to buzz around home plate, the Black Eyed Peas sing that they got a feeling that tonight's going to be a good, good night. I think they're right. There's a nice buzz in the air and everyone's excited. I realize there probably couldn't be a better night to attend and write about Game Fifty—our final game. We're happy to piggyback on this festive mood. No one in the stands knows why we're excited; they would probably just assume that we, like they, have a horse in the race.

Mississauga North are taking infield—smooth fielding, crisp throws. They run the 3-6-3 double play we saw yesterday as the catcher crouches behind home plate, tosses balls away from him to simulate pitches in the dirt. He scrambles after each ball, throws to first, repeats. When I played, I caught a bit—never very well, mind you—but now my knees will barely let me squat for the time it takes him to run the drill a couple of times.

Windsor come out for their fielding practice, the coach standing on the mound hitting fly balls to the outfield. After each catch, the ball comes in, gets whipped around the infield before being tossed back to the coach. He moves to home, hits grounders to a drawn-in infield. See the ball, react, throw to first. Watching these fielding practices makes me think again about repetition, about the muscle memory that baseball requires, about how you need to be able to make a play without thinking about it.

Behind us sits an older man, probably in his mid-sixties. He's wearing jean shorts, a blue check short-sleeved shirt, camo hat, and running shoes. Square glasses frame the moustache that hides his mouth. Next to him sits a young boy, possibly his grandchild. He says to his young companion, "Things happen fast in baseball. You can do nothing for a long time, then all of a sudden ..."

Just before the game begins, the teams huddle near their respective dugouts. Both have played a lot of baseball this weekend (Mississauga North are 5-0, while the Selects are 3-3) and again I wonder what kind of pitching they can have left so late in a tournament like this one?

The umpires emerge, a box of fresh balls tucked under the arm of the home plate umpire, as "The Imperial March" from *Star Wars* blares from the park's speakers. The stands are full—several hundred people at least are here for the final. Everyone stands as the teams line up along the baselines for the national anthem. Mississauga North will be the home team.

People in the stands are in a great mood and a lot of them are talking to Dale. Mostly people just smile at me, assuming I'm just along for the ride. Or a scout in a sundress. After a montage of music clips that seems to encapsulate every possible mood at a championship game—"Under Pressure," "We Will Rock You," and "Centerfield"—"O Canada" plays. Somewhere in the park a faint soprano sings along, everyone else just stands. At the end of the anthem, the man behind me mutters, "Pitter patter, let's get atter." And so, their championship game and our Game Fifty commences.

In other games this week, I've been unable to think about the baseball in front of me because my thoughts have been so occupied with what this project means. Tonight, though, I'm focusing on the field because it's too difficult to think about what tonight means. This is the end of the project. The end of our beautiful summer. This is Golden-

grove unleaving. I fear I'm going to lose my mum. I feel the first pangs
of grief. Focus on the field, Heidi. Focus on baseball. You got this, kid,
you got this. The rhythms of the game keep me together.

A few rows in front of us sits Bernie Soulliere, just to the first base
side of the plate. He wears a blue warmup jacket with white piping,
his red-and-black Selects cap shading his eyes. His right forearm
rests atop his cane as he leans forward, intent on every pitch, taking
it all in. I can't help but watch him as he watches the game. How
many baseball games has he seen this year? In the course of his life?

There are two quick outs for Mississauga, but then a single gets
past the pitcher and bounces out of the first baseman's hand. I see
Pook is up to bat. I look for and find his mom filming him. Pook belts it
past first and the runner gets to third. There's a runner in scoring position and two outs, but a 4-3 gets the third out.

Mississauga North score two in the bottom of the second on a
walk, single, and double, and another in the bottom of the third on a
walk, groundout, and double. Behind me, I hear the older man with
the moustache say, "Walks generally bite you, don't they?"

Umpires from across Canada are sitting in front of and beside me.
These are men who know every detail of the game and I watch them
watching the game. I listen as they compare notes about the tournament and the plays.

In the top of the third, the first batter skitters the ball along the
third base line. It's caught and the runner is out 5-3. I've seen this play
flubbed, missed, overthrown, and avoided this summer and I now
know how hard it is to achieve, all the things that could go wrong if it's
messed up.

Pook opens the top of the fourth with a long home run over the
Lions Club sign in left center. He tosses his helmet towards the dugout as he greets his teammates at home, his screams of joy echoing
around the ballpark. I can imagine the grin on his mom's face as she
stands near the fence, filming.

A few batters later, the Selects have runners on the corners with two out. The runner breaks from first base and a second later, as the ball sails from the catcher to second base, the runner takes off from third. The second baseman's catch-and-release is quick, but the catcher drops the throw back and the run scores. A perfectly executed baserunning play by the Selects.

We've been doing a lot of social media for this project and now we're tweeting to celebrate Game Fifty. I've kept a tally in my notebook of songs we've heard the most at ballgames. As the game winds down, and we hear "Sweet Caroline" for what we hope is the last time this summer, I ask our Twitter followers, "What's the only band we've heard played more than Neil Diamond in our fifty games?" Adam Kowalski, a Saginaw Sugar Beet, quickly and correctly responds: AC/DC. We've heard AC/DC twenty times. Florida Georgia Line tie Neil Diamond at eleven times each.

Mississauga North have a man on second in the bottom of the fourth and it looks like they're going to add to their lead on a line shot, but Kyle Gagnon, the Selects second baseman, steps to his left and leaps to grab the ball that looked well over his head. His flip to the shortstop covering second base completes the double play and holds the score at 3-2 for Mississauga North. It's one of the most athletic pieces of defense we've seen all year. In my head I hear Dad saying, "Nice play."

I've just correctly identified a curveball and a fastball on my own. I notice the pitchers are different in their approaches.

By the time Mississauga North come to bat in the bottom of the fifth, they trail 5-3, thanks in large part to two errors, both by the shortstop, Ryan Kula. It wasn't the precise fielding we had seen in warmups—these were the team's fourth and fifth errors of the game. Meanwhile, Windsor come up with another stellar defensive effort in the bottom of the inning, Kyle Renaud at third in full layout on a ball down the line, popping up, a strong, accurate throw to first just in time to get the hitter. Nice play, indeed.

I watch pitching so intently I forget to take notes. I see each pitch as a point on a narrative plot, not something that sets up hits.

As the game turns to the bottom of the sixth, Heidi turns to me, says, "Another inning and a half." Neither of us says anything else, but the bittersweet smile we share is enough. A run for Mississauga North makes the game 5-4 and the last out of the inning brings our summer of baseball that much closer to its end.

It starts to fully sink in that our summer is nearly over. I fill my notebook with scattershot notes to prolong it. The runner gets on base on an error and the runner on first leads off. There's a misplayed pick-off at first and the runner at first gets to third. The batter's out and the inning is over. The first batter is walked. The second batter is out 6-3. A bounced ball near the shortstop scores a run.

After a few pages of these play-by-play notes, I realize I'm essentially keeping a scorecard without a scorecard. I have, curiously, ended up where I started as a baseball fan—someone who looks around and keeps a scorecard. I see more things now and I understand so much more. But, at the end of this summer, I'm still a watcher of baseball who needs to keep a scorecard. And look around. John's right: every game has something you've never seen before on the field. But every game also has a pair of maize pants.

Kula comes to bat with one out in the bottom of the seventh for Mississauga North as a group of New Brunswick players chant "E6! E6!" from the bleachers. I feel for the kid and wish someone would tell them to shut up, but no one does. The count goes to 1-2, but Kula manages to foul off a pitch away. "E6! E6!" Kula fouls off the 2-2 pitch before singling the other way past the shortstop. The taunt fades away as the Windsor coach signals for a new pitcher.

Brett Stenger, a hard-throwing right hander, takes his warmup pitches as the infielders stand behind him, arms folded, watching. When he unleashes a pitch six feet over the catcher's head, the Mississauga North bench erupts in derision.

Stenger gets ahead in the count to Johnny Liu and induces a high chopper back to the mound, but with no one covering first base on the play, both runners are safe. It won't officially be scored an error, but it's a big mistake in an important situation, a mental error that has to sting when Tyrell Schofield-Sam singles to the opposite field on the next pitch to score Kula. As he skips across the plate, no one is chanting "E6! E6!"

In the bottom of the seventh, it's a 5-5 tie — this could be anybody's game. The fifth batter up for Mississauga, has two balls, two strikes, and he's fouling it off like a pro. The level of noise coming off the field from the dugouts is deafening, but the crowd in the stands is silent. Mississauga single and score a run. Mississauga win gold. Windsor win silver. I look at Dale. We're done our fifty games. Part of me imagines that the Mississauga fans are cheering for us, but, of course, they're not. We walk towards our car — which I've finally, instinctively, parked out of foul-ball territory.

We're quiet as we walk to the car, the sounds of the Mississauga North celebration echoing in the background. The drive home to Windsor can wait until tomorrow morning. Tonight we'll have dinner at the hotel, talk about today's game, about the season, about the writing we have ahead of us. I look back at the lights of Emslie Field, imagine every park we've seen this summer superimposed on top of it, a palimpsest of baseball, layers on top of layers on top of the layers of baseball that were already there. Dad. Kurt. Rick. Dave. Charlie. Summers at Czar Lake. The Expos on the CBC from Jarry Park. The Royals. The Tigers. Heidi. Always Heidi.

We drive back to our hotel, silent and wordless.

Even though there are still weeks left in the baseball season, our summer of baseball is ending, but its layers will stay with me, with us.

Final Score: 6-5 Mississauga

EPILOGUE

February 2020

Today, while going through box scores and game recaps of the All-Stars' out-of-town exhibition games in 1935, a small ad in the corner of a sports page from the *Windsor Daily Star* catches my eye. "Baseball. Stodgell Park. Saturday, 14th. 3:30. Chatham Coloured All-Stars vs Sandwich. Intermediate OBAA Semi-Finals." Stodgell Park? After pulling it up on Google Maps to confirm my hunch, I dash down the stairs, pull on my coat, struggle to get boots over my thick socks. I'm halfway down the block before it sinks in. In September 1935, Boomer Harding, Flat Chase, King Terrell, and the rest of the Chatham Coloured All-Stars played 450 metres away from my house.

Writing this book let me live those games and that summer again, let me drive down those back roads with Heidi, let me spend some more time with my father. Writing let me make sense of everything we saw and experienced. By the beginning of August 2019, though, we were on a short break from the book, a pause between drafts to give us some distance from what we had written. Heidi took advantage of the break to fly to Alberta for a few days, while I opted to stay in Windsor. I noticed that the Ontario Men's Senior Elimination Tournament was back in town over the long weekend and immediately knew what I would be doing for the next few days. It was time to see a third baseman edging towards home in case of a bunt, time to hear the chatter of the dugouts, time to watch a slider dip into the dirt. Time to reconnect with baseball in the present tense.

A few years ago, the City removed the two chain-link backstops that sat on opposite corners of Stodgell Park and replaced them with swing sets and playground equipment. Since then, the park has looked lopsided, like something is missing. I recall numerous occasions when I would stand in the snow beside Stodgell's hardly picturesque ball diamonds, thinking about spring and the Tigers. Back then I could easily calculate how many days there were until pitchers and catchers reported. I knew how many weeks until Opening Day. Today, I can only hazard a guess. Instead, I'm thinking about whoever lived in my house in 1935 and whether they wandered down the street to check out a baseball game that September afternoon at 3:30 pm. Maybe a woman like me walked out this front door and went to watch a few innings with her husband in the dying days of summer.

I drove to Cullen Field, walked through the gates, weekend pass in hand, and set up my lawn chair just to the third base side of home plate, in the same spot Heidi and I watched so many games in 2018. Beside me was a woman who looked vaguely familiar, someone I didn't know, but had seen many times. It wasn't until she got out her video camera that I remembered who she was. Pook's mom, setting up, as always, to record his at-bat. I didn't expect to see Pook—or his mom—since in my mind he was still with the Selects, still caught up in that final, heartbreaking loss in St. Thomas. But, of course, he was not. He was at Cullen, now a year older, aged out of the Selects, good enough to make the Stars and to pinch hit. As I watched Pook settle himself in the batter's box, foul off a couple of pitches, and finally hit a ground ball to the shortstop, I caught glimpses of his mom out of the corner of my eye, heard her cheering him on once more.

She and I chatted a bit over the next few innings, about baseball, about her son, about the book Heidi and I are writing. I thought about all the games she's watched, about how much she seems to enjoy it all, not just when Pook is playing, but the game in general. I thought about telling her that she's featured in the book, that her filming Pook at the plate is, for me, part of the fabric of that summer. But I didn't. Instead, I sat next to her, speaking occasionally, but mostly just watching the game we both love.

The wind is cold and the late afternoon darkness settles in. I should be heading home, but I can't bring myself to leave. I feel a longing well up in me. At first I think it's because I'm missing green grass, blue skies, and warmth. Maybe it is that. But my mind keeps coming back to the woman I imagine walking from her house—now my house—to this very ballpark in 1935. As the January winds pick up, I realize I don't just want the sunshine I imagine her feeling, I want to be her right now. Not just watching the actual Chatham Coloured All-Stars, but watching baseball on a Saturday afternoon in a small neighbourhood park with someone she loves. Maybe she sees a legendary Flat Chase home run or one of King Terrell's famous left-handed third-base plays. Or maybe she smiles when her husband, rapt in the game, says, "Did you see that curveball?" "Beautiful," she'd say. Maybe she really did see it. Or maybe she was distracted by the way the autumn sun warmed the hints of orange breaking into the oak leaves on the trees lining the streets. Or by Canada Geese flying overhead. Or by a fellow spectator's funny-coloured pants. Either way, she'd smile at this beautiful afternoon, with him, with baseball.

As the grey of January presses down on me, I find myself fantasizing about sunshine on my bare arms as I watch infielders take ground balls before a game. I look at flights to Arizona and wonder how many Cactus League games we could see in a week. I try to find out where the Division II regionals will be played. I plot out road trips to Cedar Rapids for the Division III World Series and to Omaha for the Division I World Series. I try to calculate how long it will be until the Green Giants are back at Lacasse Park, Heidi and I back on the worn green grandstand behind home plate.

POSTSCRIPT

August 23, 2020

In mid-February 2020, we wrote the above Epilogue and, several days later, left for two weeks in Ireland. Before we left, both of us independently looked at various team schedules, plotting our own return to the game for the 2020 season. We wondered when it would be warm and dry enough to go watch baseball again. As we packed for our trip, we talked briefly about the Coronavirus that was making the news. Both Ireland and Canada seemed safe and isolated at the time.

In the last week of our trip, however, we started seeing reports of the virus moving rapidly across Europe and the first outbreaks in Canada and the United States. Museums we had visited days earlier in Dublin were announcing closures and there was talk of cancelling St. Patrick's Day celebrations. What had seemed almost unthinkable two weeks ago was suddenly real.

On March 10, on our way back to Windsor, we spent a layover at Toronto's Pearson Airport in a restaurant where half the TVs were on news stations with Coronavirus coverage and the other half were playing a Blue Jays preseason game. "At least we'll have baseball again," one of us said.

Days after we arrived home, everything starting changing rapidly, as if the whole world were turning upside down. Things we'd not known we'd taken for granted, like being with our friends, being part of a crowd, or being anywhere but our homes, were suddenly denied to us.

Sports seemed insignificant, especially in those first months, and the prospect of baseball in 2020 felt remote. On March 12, MLB announced the remainder of spring training games would be cancelled and the start of the season delayed. Days later, they postponed the 2020 season indefinitely; by late June, a sixty-game season had been announced, with play commencing on July 23. While teams would play in their home ballparks, they would do so without fans in attendance. Meanwhile, minor and amateur leagues across North America and at all levels began to announce the suspension of play for the 2020 season.

On March 21, the Canada/United States border was closed to all but essential traffic. As of writing, the border has remained closed, and there is no indication it will reopen in the foreseeable future. The days of slipping across the river to watch baseball, something we did almost unthinkingly, were over, at least for now. Between the imposition of physical distancing measures, the cancellation of all forms of spectator baseball, and the closed border, the project we undertook in 2018 would have been impossible, if not unimaginable, this year. As we reread the preceding pages, the summer of 2018 emerges as something even more remarkable and magical than we realized.

From the outset, this project's central question was "what would happen if we went to fifty games inside a one-hundred mile radius in one summer?" This book is our answer to that question. As our epilogue suggests, another question emerged for us as we researched, wrote, and edited *100 Miles*: "Will writing this book make us want to watch baseball again? Will writing this book make us watch baseball differently?" Both of us were looking to this year's baseball season as a way to answer those questions. As it has unfolded, however, the 2020 season has been further from expected than either of us could ever have imagined.

Despite long odds against it—and perhaps unadvisedly—baseball returned in 2020, but only at the major league level and only on television. We've both been watching, holding tight to the only baseball on offer. Smiling to each other at the cut-out fans. At the unexpected sounds that echo through empty stadiums. At Casey Mize's split-fingered fastball. The empty parks are still strange, but on the field it's still baseball. And, for now, it's what we have.

There have been no trips to Lacasse or Ray Fisher Stadium or Errol Russell Park this summer. No long summer nights spent behind home plate. No parents and children sharing the game. No noticing maize pants or slow curves. It's been a year without the kind of live baseball that seeped into both our beings in the summer of 2018. Those games have only been gone for part of a summer, but they make us realize what baseball has offered, what we've taken from it over the years, and all the ways we've needed the game. Baseball is about connecting—with people we've just met, people we'll never meet again, people we know, people we love and miss. Above all, baseball, with its springtime opening, is about new beginnings, about possibility, about hope. Perhaps that's what we miss and need the most right now.

100 Miles of Baseball begins at Wayne State University's Harwell field where, along the outfield wall in left, you can see the "Detroit/ Visitors" scoreboard. Although this scoreboard is never used, it remains there as a sort of constant, its emptiness a site of possibility and new beginnings. A site of hope.

NOTES

One: Opening Innings

1. In 2019, The Social Club Grooming Co., a small barbershop, opened in one half of the 1515 space, while Paramita Sound, a record store/wine bar, opened in the other half. Andrey Douthard, the co-owner of Paramita Sound, said in an interview published in the *Detroit Free Press* on August 30, 2019, "This space, 1515 Broadway, is synonymous with so much of the underground culture of the arts scene in this city." They are attempting to maintain this tradition.

Three: Three Games in Twenty-Four Hours

1. Michigan would go on to play in the College World Series in 2019, coming second in the country to Vanderbilt.
2. Schuemann would be drafted by the Oakland Athletics in round 20 with pick 593 in the 2018 draft.
3. Seven of the nine starters for the Mud Hens in this game played at least part of the season in Detroit.
4. In the summer of 2019, new condominium construction began beyond the outfield walls. The view of downtown we saw in 2018 will soon be no more.
5. There are two particularly interesting connections between the Chatham Coloured All-Stars and MLB. The first is that the losing pitcher for the final series in the 1934 OBAA championship was Phil Marchildon, who went on to play for the Philadelphia Athletics and the Boston Red Sox. The second is that Ferguson Jenkins, Sr, the father of Fergie Jenkins, Canada's first National Baseball Hall of Fame inductee, played for the Chatham Coloured All-Stars starting in 1935.

6. In addition to leading the league in home runs and pitching victories for several years, in 1934, Chase's batting average was .488.

Six: Are You From Virginia?

1. While Tommy Parsons was not selected in the 2018 draft, he signed a contract with the St. Louis Cardinals organization, finishing the 2018 season with Johnson City of the Appalachian League (Rookie). In 2019, he began the season with the Peoria Chiefs of the Midwest League (A) and finished the season with the Memphis Redbirds of the Pacific Coast League (AAA).

Seven: Crooked Numbers

1. Any discussion of women and baseball needs to consider women as players as well as fans. Regretfully, we were not able to see any women's or girls' baseball teams for this project. While we know there are women's softball teams in the region, we were unable to find women's baseball teams in our 100-mile area in the summer of 2018.

Eight: A Study in Contrasts

1. In his second year in 2018, Palm makes $800/month, rather than the $600 he made the previous year as a rookie, and lives with a billet family. It is the same for all players in the USPBL.

2. Each year, the Fan Cost Index (FCI) attempts to calculate the cost for taking a family to an MLB game. In 2018, the average FCI in US dollars was $230.98. The two MLB teams in our hundred miles were lower than average: the Tigers' FCI was $201.60 and the Cleveland Indians' was $210.16. The Fan Cost Index is comprised of: "the prices of four average-price tickets, two small draft beers, four small soft drinks, four regular-size hot dogs, parking, two game programs and two least-expensive, adult-size adjustable caps."

3. Palm would be signed to a minor-league deal by the Minnesota Twins on June 13, 2018 and assigned to the Elizabethton Twins of the Appalachian League on June 18, 2018. In 2019 he played for both the Cedar Rapids Kernels and the Pensacola Blue Wahoos, in the Twins organization.

4. Fowles writes, "Anyone who has fallen head over heels in love with this game knows that the favourite player is a gateway drug. He's the first step in developing an all-encompassing obsession—a personality or performance that suddenly makes you take note and find the will to care about the game."

5. Indeed, it was the last time we would see Granderson play. He announced his retirement from baseball in February, 2020.

6. On July 31, 2019, moments before the trade deadline, Nick Castellanos was traded to the Cubs for two minor league pitchers.

7. The "Maddux" is named after Greg Maddux, who had thirteen shutouts of this kind during his career; the next closest pitcher on the list since 1988 has only seven.

Nine: Middle Innings

1. Located at the forks of the Thames River, Labatt Park is a designated historic site. As is the case with much early baseball history, technicalities cause a number of controversies when attempting to establish any kind of "first." Labatt Park, established in 1877, can claim to be the "oldest continuing baseball grounds in the world." However, because Labatt Park moved its home plate within the field, Fuller Field, established in 1878 in Clinton, MA, can claim to be the "oldest continuously used baseball field" because its plates are in their original 1878 locations. The controversy endures.

2. We recently discovered that the Chatham Coloured All-Stars played here at what was then Tecumseh Park on September 26, 1934 in an OBAA playoff game against Welland. The All-Stars won 11-7, advancing to the next round.

Ten: If You Build It . . .

1. In 2019, a new grandstand was constructed at Errol Morris Park.

Eleven: Ohio Swing

1. As of the 2020 season, the Frontier League will merge with the Canadian American Association of Professional Baseball. The new league will consist of fourteen teams in two divisions (Midwest and Can-Am).

2. In 2018, Cleveland finished the season with a record of 91-71, first in the American League Central. They went on to lose the American League division series to the Houston Astros.

3. Larry Doby (1923-2003) played in both the Negro Leagues and MLB. He was the first Black player in the American League and the second Black player in MLB, playing three months after Robinson's first game in 1947.

4. In 2019, Edwin Jackson was once again signed by the Tigers. As of this writing, Jackson has played for fourteen MLB franchises, more than any other player in MLB history.

5. Our friend Dave Burke says about playing baseball for Woodslee, "We talk about great plays over and over again, through the years. Like an oral history, we remember the good plays but can't remember the last time we played in Courtright and whether we won or lost."

Twelve: The Golden Rule of Baseball

1. In our attempts to find women's baseball in our one-hundred-mile area, we found a reference to a women's historic baseball team called the Detroit River Belles who, unfortunately, were not playing in 2018.

Thirteen: Beet, Beet, Sugar Beet

1. The Saginaw Sugar Beets were formed for the 2018 season, but were placed on hiatus for the 2019 season.

Seventeen: Final Innings

1. The Selects finished third in Pool A and then won their quarter-final game against Oshawa to advance to the semi-final against Québec.

APPENDIX

100 Miles of Baseball: Fifty Games, One Summer
PROJECT STATS

	Date	Game	Score	Location	League/Level	Tickets for Two	Miles (round-trip)
1	March 30, 2018	Wayne State vs Ashland U	12-4 Ashland	Detroit, MI (Harwell)	DIVII, GLIAC	0.00	14
2	March 31, 2018	Henry Ford CC vs Macomb CC	12-3 Henry Ford	Taylor, MI	JUCO, MCCAA	0.00	60
3	April 1, 2018	Detroit Tigers vs Pittsburgh Pirates	1-0 Pittsburgh	Detroit, MI (Comerica)	MLB	52.00	10
4	April 22, 2018	Albion College vs Adrian College	18-1 Adrian College	Albion, MI	DIV III, MIAA	0.00	200
5	May 1, 2018	UMich vs EMU	6-4 UMich	Ann Arbor, MI	DIV I Exhibition	2.00	100
6	May 2, 2018	Toledo Mud Hens vs Indianapolis Indians	7-5 Mud Hens	Toledo, OH	AAA, International League	26.00	140
7	May 2, 2018	UM Dearborn vs Concordia U	11-6 Concordia	Detroit, MI (PAL)	NAIA	0.00	10
8	May 6, 2018	Tecumseh Thunder U18 vs Sarnia Braves Midget Major	6-2 Tecumseh	Tecumseh, ON	Midget Major	0.00	16
9	May 8, 2018	Riverside HS vs Herman HS	4-2 Herman	Windsor, ON (Riverside)	WECSSA	0.00	8
10	May 10, 2018	Tecumseh U18 vs Amherstburg Sr	14-1 Tecumseh after 5	Tecumseh, ON	Essex County Men's Senior League	0.00	16

						▼ Event pass/combined ticket	▲ Same location/trip
	Date	Game	Score	Location	League/Level	Tickets for Two	Miles (round-trip)
11	May 13, 2018	Ashland U vs Davenport U	8-4 Davenport	Detroit, MI (PAL)	GLIAC Tournament	▼20.00	▲10
12	May 13, 2018	Davenport U vs Northwood	5-4 Northwood	Detroit, MI (PAL)	GLIAC Tournament	▼	▲
13	May 17, 2018	Wabash C vs College of Wooster	Wooster 4-2	Adrian, MI	DIV III Tournament	▼30.00	▲160
14	May 17, 2018	Ithaca College vs La Roche College	La Roche 5-1	Adrian, MI	DIV III Tournament	▼	▲
15	May 17, 2018	Adrian College vs Otterbein U	Adrian 11-5	Adrian, MI	DIV III Tournament	▼	▲
16	May 18, 2018	Wabash College vs Marietta College	4-2 Wabash	Adrian, MI	DIV III Tournament	▼	▲
17	May 18, 2018	Ithaca College vs Otterbein U	5-4 Ithaca	Adrian, MI	DIV III Tournament	▼	▲
18	May 20, 2018	Port Lambton Pirates vs Wallaceburg Warriors	9-1 Port Lambton	Port Lambton, ON	Western Counties Sr League	0.00	160
19	May 23, 2018	Brennan vs Villanova	6-5 Villanova	Windsor, ON (Cullen)	WECCSA Playoffs	0.00	8
20	May 27, 2018	Tecumseh Green Giants 35+ vs Tillsonburg Old Sox	6-5? Tecumseh	Woodslee, ON	Essex County Men's League	0.00	40

	Date	Game	Score	Location	League/Level	Tickets for Two	Miles (round-trip)
21	June 1, 2018	Harrow Sr Blues vs Woodslee Orioles 35+	8-1 Woodslee	Woodslee, ON	Essex County League	0.00	40
22	June 2, 2018	East Side Diamond Hoppers vs West Side Wooly Mammoths	8-2 Diamond Hoppers	Utica, MI	USPBL	24.00	60
23	June 3, 2018	Detroit Tigers vs Toronto Blue Jays	8-4 Blue Jays	Detroit, MI (Comerica)	MLB	34.00	10
24	June 7, 2018	Windsor Selects vs Windsor Stars	9-2 Stars	Windsor, ON (Cullen)	Can Am Senior League	0.00	10
25	June 30, 2018	St Clair Green Giants vs Lake Erie Monarchs	9-8 St Clair	Tecumseh, ON	Great Lakes Summer Collegiate League	14.00	16
26	July 1, 2018	London Majors vs Barrie Baycats	14-2 Barrie	London, ON	Intercounty League	18.00	200
27	July 4, 2018	Sarnia Braves vs Exeter Express	2-1 Sarnia	Sarnia, ON	Southwestern Senior Baseball League	0.00	200
28	July 6, 2018	Five Tool vs the Illinois A's	12-12, called for time	Lorain, OH	CABA U18 Aluminum Bat World Series	20.00	152
29	July 6, 2018	Lake Erie Crushers vs Florence Freedom	4-0 Florence	Avon, OH	Frontier League	22.00	20

	Date	Game	Score	Location	League/Level	Tickets for Two	Miles (round-trip)
30	July 7, 2018	Cleveland Indians vs Oakland A's	6-3 A's	Cleveland, OH	MLB	110.00	20
31	July 8, 2018	Lake County Captains vs West Michigan White Caps	7-1 Lake County	Eastlake, OH	A-level Midwest League	24.00	210
32	July 14, 2018	Saginaw Old Golds vs Detroit Early Risers	12-7 Detroit	Brooklyn, MI (Walker Tavern Historic Site)	Vintage Baseball Tournament	▼9.00	▲170
33	July 14, 2018	Detroit Early Risers vs Canton Union Base Ball Club	15-12 Detroit	Brooklyn, MI (Walker Tavern Historic Site)	Vintage Baseball Tournament	▼	▲
34	July 22, 2018	Saginaw Sugar Beets vs Lake Erie Monarchs	4-3 Monarchs in 11	Saginaw, MI	Great Lakes Summer Collegiate League	▼10.00	▲200
35	July 22, 2018	Saginaw Sugar Beets vs Lake Erie Monarchs	2-2, called for rain in 8th	Saginaw, MI	Great Lakes Summer Collegiate League	▼	▲
36	July 27, 2018	Windsor Selects vs London Badgers	3-2 London	Windsor, ON (Cullen)	PBLO	0.00	10
37	July 28, 2018	Oakville Royals vs Mississauga Terriers U17	8-7 Terriers U17	Windsor, ON, (Soulliere)	PBLO	0.00	10

	Date	Game	Score	Location	League/Level	Tickets for Two	Miles (round-trip)
38	July 29, 2018	Mississauga Terriers U17-London Badgers	3-2 Terriers	Windsor, ON, (Cullen)	PBLO	0.00	10
39	August 2, 2018	St Clair Green Giants vs Saginaw Sugar Beets	3-2 Saginaw	Tecumseh, ON	Great Lakes Summer Collegiate League	14.00	16
40	August 3, 2018	Sarnia Braves vs Bolton Brewers	11-1 Sarnia	Woodslee, ON	Ontario Men's Elimi-nation Tournament	▼30.00	40
41	August 3, 2018	Windsor Stars vs Tecumseh Thunder	9-4 Tecumseh	Windsor, ON (Cullen)	Ontario Men's Elimi-nation Tournament	▼	10
42	August 4, 2018	Windsor Stars vs Mississauga South-west Twins	7-5 Mississauga	Windsor, ON (Cullen)	Ontario Men's Elimi-nation Tournament	▼	10
43	August 4, 2018	St Clair Green Giants vs Saginaw Sugar Beets	10-9 Saginaw	Tecumseh, ON	Great Lakes Summer Collegiate League	14.00	16
44	August 5, 2018	Strathroy Royals vs Brampton Royals	10-8 Strathroy	Windsor, ON (Soulliere)	Ontario Men's Elimi-nation Tournament	0.00	10
45	August 6, 2018	Tecumseh Thunder vs Ilderton Red Army	3-1 Tecumseh in 10	Windsor, ON (Cullen)	Ontario Men's Elimi-nation Tournament	0.00	10
46	August 14, 2018	Lansing Lugnuts vs Bowling Green Hot Rods	7-4 Lugnuts	Lansing, MI	Midwest League	26.00	200

	Date	Game	Score	Location	League/Level	Tickets for Two	Miles (round-trip)
47	August 17, 2018	Manitoba vs Oshawa	4-1 Oshawa	St Thomas, ON	U21 Canadian Championships	▼90.00	▲200
48	August 18, 2018	Windsor vs Nova Scotia	4-3 Nova Scotia	St Thomas, ON	U21 Canadian Championships	▶	▲
49	August 18, 2018	Québec vs St Thomas	8-7 Québec	St Thomas, ON	U21 Canadian Championships	▶	▲
50	August 19, 2018	Mississauga North vs New Brunswick	11-0 Mississauga	St Thomas, ON	U21 Canadian Championships	▲	▲
51	August 19, 2018	Windsor vs Mississauga	6-5 Mississauga	St Thomas, ON	U21 Canadian Championships	▲	▲
					Total	589	2802
					Average	11.549	54.941

Acknowledgements

As we worked on this project, we were helped along the way by so many important people. First, we'd like to thank Dan Wells and Biblioasis for believing in the project even before we attended our first game. As well, we'd like to thank the University of Windsor, particularly the English Department and Leddy Library, for their support as we worked on this project. Chris Wainscott provided us with valuable information about baseball in Windsor and Essex County and alerted us to the Division III Regional tournament in Adrian. Tim Girard, John Wing, and Griff Evans acted as invaluable sounding boards as we attempted to process what we were seeing and experiencing in the summer of 2018, while Adam Kowalski, of the Saginaw Sugar Beets, offered us a player perspective throughout the season. Devon Fraser helped us tremendously with background research and in fact-checking specific details. We would also like to acknowledge Anchor Coffee, Riverside Pie, Sandwich Brewing, Frank Brewing Co., Chapter Two Brewing, and Taloola Café, sites of much writing, editing, and discussion of the manuscript.

Early readers of the full manuscript—Holly M Wendt, Dave Burke, and Peter McCullough—provided us with invaluable feedback that helped make it stronger. We are also thankful for Emily Donaldson's keen editorial eye. Biblioasis staff have been fantastic throughout the process; we'd especially like to thank Vanessa Stauffer for the clarity and organization she brought to the process of shepherding the book through production. We would also like to thank our brilliant and supportive editor, Sharon Hanna, for understanding what we were trying to do with *100 Miles* from the very beginning, and for giving us such nuanced and detailed feedback. Her work has made the book better in every way.

Finally, we would like to thank the players, coaches, families, and fans who, without knowing it, shared our summer of baseball. Here's to many more days in the sun.

Dale Jacobs is the author of *Graphic Encounters: Comics and the Sponsorship of Multimodal Literacy* (Bloomsbury Academic, 2013). He is the editor of *Sunday with the Tigers: Eleven Ways to Watch a Game* (Black Moss Press, 2015) and *The Myles Horton Reader* (University of Tennessee Press, 2003), and co-editor (with Laura Micciche) of *A Way to Move: Rhetorics of Emotion and Composition Studies* (Boynton Cook/Heinemann, 2003). His academic/creative nonfiction book, *The 1976 Project: On Comics and Grief*, is forthcoming from Wilfred Laurier University Press. He is the editor of *The Windsor Review* and teaches in the English Department at the University of Windsor.

Heidi LM Jacobs' novel *Molly of the Mall: Literary Lass and Purveyor of Fine Footwear* (NeWest Press, 2019) won the Stephen Leacock Medal for Humour in 2020. She is a librarian at the University of Windsor and one of the researchers behind the award-winning *Breaking the Colour Barrier: Wilfred "Boomer" Harding & the Chatham Coloured All-Stars* project. She is currently co-writing a book about the 1934 Chatham Coloured All-Stars, the first Black team to win the Ontario Baseball Amateur Association Championship (forthcoming from Wilfred Laurier University Press). Originally from Edmonton, she now lives in Windsor, Ontario.

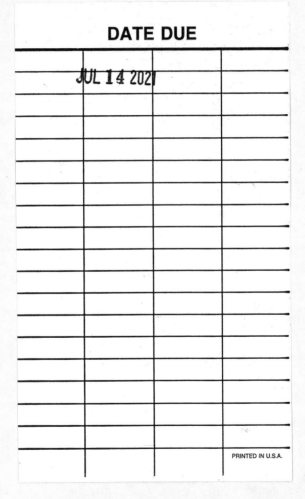

DATE DUE

	JUL 14 2021		
			PRINTED IN U.S.A.